Drum Circle Facilitation

Building Community Through Rhythm

by Arthur Hull

Edited by Angela Marie

Village Music Circles
Santa Cruz, CA

Village Music Circles
719 Swift St., Suite 65
Santa Cruz, CA 95060
USA

Phone: (831) 458-1946
Fax: (831) 459-7215

http://drumcircle.com
outreach@drumcircle.com

Printed in Hong Kong

Library of Congress Cataloging-in-Publication Data

Hull, Arthur 1947-
  Drum Circle Facilitation: Building Community Through Rhythm/Arthur Hull.
  Includes biographical references and index.
  ISBN #: 0-9724307-1-7
  1. Group facilitation–Instruction and study.   2. Community music–Instruction and study.
  3. Percussion instruments–Instruction and study.   4. Musical meter and rhythm–Instruction and study.

Dedication

I dedicate this book to Don Davidson and Cameron Tummel, and all of my students who have become my teachers and the teachers of the next generation of drum circle facilitators.

Margie Heart Facilitating an Inter-island Community Drum Circle in Hawaii

The conversation began with a single heartbeat,

The rhythmic pulsing, steady and strong.

Soon different voices echoed out, one to another,

Sharing and expressing Self, as the conversation

of the many became the Voice of One.

Giselle Felicia

Welcome to Drum Circle Facilitation!
Enjoy the journey.

Table of Contents

List of Exercises

List of Stories

Foreword

by Barry Bittman, MD

According to Arthur Hull, father of the modern facilitated drum circle movement in our nation, "You won't find the word, 'rhythmaculture' in your dictionary." This Rhythmical Evangelist refers to it as an "Arthurian" word, a term he coined to describe "a culture that has integrated ritual, dance, song and music into almost every aspect of its existence, its expression of itself, and its celebration of life."

These powerful words emanate from an outspoken yet humble ambassador who has dedicated the major part of his life to advocating for cultural musical expression as an innate human right. His dreams are to foster a deep and enduring sense of community through creative musical expression, and to reestablish group drumming as an effective tool for unity.

In the Arthurian context, drumming is a natural expression of who we are. It demonstrates our capacity to build unity and synergy when we learn to express the essence of the rhythms within us. Yet beyond self-expression, Arthur recognizes that a community is far more than just the sum of its parts. It functions best when an evolving sense of order and self-regulation are encouraged, and it becomes predictably effective when people are willing to work together.

Hull is perhaps best described as a rather unique and eccentric community architect. Beyond his fisherman's vest and beanie (the traditional Arthurian drum facilitator uniform), one immediately recognizes both musical and cultural genius. Beneath his elf-like comic demeanor is a caring and compassionate leader who is genuinely devoted to the communities he serves. Through precise timing and phenomenal rhythms, which seem to naturally emanate from the unassuming counselor within, he has elevated the art of reading a group and its individuals to an unprecedented level. His humor is exquisitely tuned, with a brilliant orchestration of laughter that creates a healing rhythm.

Speaking of orchestras, while a conductor precisely follows a musical score, Arthur nurtures the evolution of his unwritten symphony one beat at a time. He attributes his success to the trust he places within the circle. Through precise use of body language, sculpting and listening (Arthurian "tools" of facilitation), an empowering rhythmaculture seems to magically evolve through a living, breathing organism he refers to as "community."

In his quest to foster personal empowerment, Arthur strongly emphasizes listening over playing. His students learn to develop a heightened awareness of what's actually transpiring within the circle. They also study the art of carefully listening for signs of "impending train wrecks," the critical points at which the music predictably begins to dissolve into a state of cacophony. Novices soon discover that early recognition prevents such disasters while enabling new opportunities for developing successful rhythms. The inherent value of such insights immediately transcends the drumming experience, and these discoveries readily transfer into societal realms.

While Arthur's workshops cover elements such as rhythm patterns, tempo, pitch, volume dynamics and time signatures, everyone knows he really isn't teaching music.

Five minutes into the workshop the metaphor smacks you in the face. It's obvious from the start that his protocols are basic methodologies for enabling community, and his tools are the foundational implements for building societal bridges.

Arthur's formula simply works. It brings out the best in each person while creating a functional, supportive environment for self-expression and group cohesiveness. Synergy naturally results as the overall effect of an Arthurian drum circle represents far more than just the additive effects of each individual part. Strangers emerge as friends, with a heightened awareness and understanding of each other and a sense of cohesiveness that extends beyond words.

A few years ago I spent a week filming Arthur at his annual Hawaii Facilitators' Playshop which drew more than 120 participants from 11 nations, many of whom had attended previously. Roughly two thirds of the group comprised human services workers: educators, nurses, counselors, rehab specialists, corporate trainers and music therapists. Despite diverse cultural differences and professional backgrounds, they worked and drummed together as a community. Arthur and his staff served as the glue that held them together by imparting a wealth of insights and valuable lessons in a light-hearted, nurturing and enriching atmosphere.

Arthur's extraordinary team includes Don Davidson, whose depth and brilliance takes drumming deep into the realm of cultural anthropology, and Cameron Tummel, whose charisma, enthusiasm and spirit touches the heart of everyone fortunate enough to learn from him. These three "faciliteers" (sorry … the word is not Arthurian – it's mine) enabled the creation of a rather remarkable rhythmaculture within the Playshop. Bonds of friendship, camaraderie and support now extend thousands of miles across the globe as the vast drumming community continues to evolve.

While you might be wondering why I spent a week learning about group drumming, my goals were simple. As a physician, I primarily hoped to discover important insights for inspiring and bringing out the best in our patients. I was also searching for enjoyable rhythmical ways to encourage the development of supportive communities of individuals facing serious health challenges. In essence I returned with far more.

Perhaps Arthur's greatest lesson is cherishing and respecting the unique person you are, and using that sense of internal harmony to build rhythmical and cultural bridges of understanding with others. Drumming for Arthur is a joyful bliss that transcends the boundaries separating us from each other. Seeing, hearing and feeling that bliss is amazingly contagious!

Invention as the Mother of Necessity

by Don Davidson

There was a palpable charge to the culture in Santa Cruz, California, in 1980 when I arrived as a student at the University of California. It was a place that valued innocence, creativity and innovation, and sought out the practices and wisdom of human beings across disciplines and across cultures the world round. And there was a sense that anything could and just might happen. On hearing the call of drums in the distance, my new friends and I literally charged out of the redwoods and down the hill to discover a gymnasium floor filled with an ecstatic mass engaged in an African-inspired dance class. There in the corner with his ensemble was Arthur Hull, churning out this driving music and thus through that music was my first acquaintance with the man who was to become a cornerstone of my life for the next 25 years.

There were limited choices, back then, to anyone in love with hand drumming. The jam-based hippie-style thunder drumming was great fun and magical, but limited by its formlessness. Traditional African drum music presentation became artistic representation, cultural mis-representation, or a sterile specimen of ethnomusicology removed of its context. The Afri-can-American community was often and perhaps justly perturbed. Very simply, there comes a point for any serious student of traditional music, once you've mastered the parts, learned songs and served the dancers, where you yearn to fulfill the traditional goal of elevating the spirit and restoring the health, balance, wisdom and prosperity of your own family, community and culture. And perhaps a culture will smile to itself when it succeeds in focusing its own exigencies into the life of one person. Its own goal of rebirth and metamorphosis finds a carrier, an agent of change in that reflection. Arthur lived those changes.

I don't believe the birth of the drum circle movement could have arisen outside of the context of corporate America. Julian Jaynes suggests in "The Origin of Consciousness in the Breakdown of the Bicameral Mind" that consciousness began at the frontiers of culture where traders negotiated with those most different than themselves, where the task was dependent on good, harmonious relations. Over the course of a series of team-building sessions with Apple Computer in the late eighties, I watched Arthur evolve from a master teacher of drumming into a facilitator of the human spirit. Those sessions shifted from celebrating an African model of community to a true and uniquely powerful celebration of a learning organization. The result was a quality of relationship virtually unknown before to a highly motivated, very task-oriented and highly intelligent community of people. Thus was born this new, powerful musical form–the drum circle.

Because it is more often true that invention is the mother of necessity, we sought out other populations whose needs could be served in this new way by the drum. We brought drum circles to kids and school teachers, men's and women's groups, corrective institutions, cancer survivors, orchestras, corporations, departments of defense and religious groups. Drummers and musicians, as well as many, many people who never believed in their own sense of rhythm or musicality, all responded to the magic of joining together in a drum circle.

Here and now, in the new millennium, the Arthurian drum circle has touched hundreds of thousands of all types of people in all manner of situations across many cultures around the world. And yet the experience is so deep, so powerful, so difficult to describe that, true to life itself, it is as the poet Rumi said, "Those who hear not the music think the dancers mad." To truly understand the power and the humility, the clarity of the message in that wall of sound, you must put yourself into a drum circle. Within that universality, there is a great gift just for you.

Time with Arthur

by Cameron Tummel

In the beginning of my time with Arthur, in the Village Music drum classes at UCSC in 1990, I enjoyed his teachings tremendously. He made me laugh, he taught me how to drum, and I had a great time with all of my fellow classmates.

Over the ensuing weeks and months, I met most of the players in Arthur's drum classes at the University, and we all seemed to enjoy his teachings very much indeed. We found great value in what he taught, and especially in how he did it. He helped us to laugh at our mistakes and then learn from them. He showed us how group cohesiveness can be much more powerful than individual competency, and that each one of us has something uniquely special to contribute to the song. I soon realized he was also teaching a great number of people in other communities, nationwide, and that everyone enjoyed his wonderful way of sharing the joys of playing rhythmical music.

During the decade of my apprenticeship with Arthur, I became increasingly aware that wherever he went, all over the world, people loved the way he taught them to play together. They appreciated how he taught them to celebrate their uniqueness, their togetherness, the joy of alchemy, the joy of community drumming. *All* of the people whom he taught seemed to find his teaching methods to be very valuable, and they often spoke of how it made them feel good; made them glad to be alive. And, the more I learned to emulate the style, the methods and the spirit with which he taught, the more successful I became in sharing the joy and the beauty of drumming with the people I met, everywhere I went.

By the year 2001, when Arthur offered the annual Village Music Circles™ (VMC) Hawaii Facilitators' Playshop, there were over a hundred participants, from all walks of life, who had traveled from a dozen different countries, in order to spend time with Arthur. They came to learn his teachings, and to absorb the style and spirit with which he taught them. Every one of those people expressed their sincere enjoyment of his techniques, and their appreciation for the valuable methods he modeled while sharing and teaching the joy of drumming. As one of the senior facilitators for Village Music Circles, I have never been more proud, or more grateful, for the effects of his teachings than I was then, as they were so plainly manifest in the smiles and personal growth of the participants.

If all of Arthur's accomplishments were just the result of an intriguing fad, it would have died out long ago. If it were all just the effect of a magnetic personality, or his tremendous sense of humor, the novelty would have long since worn off. If the methods he has been espousing were limited in their scope, depth or relevance, we would have hit some walls by now; we would have found some flaws in the canvas; the shortcomings would have long since been revealed.

But we have not.

While the success of Arthur and his methods is partially due to his personality, his humor and his leadership, the bedrock of the success lies in the teachings themselves. His techniques, applications, intentions and spirit are the true gold of which the success has been wrought.

After many years in his study, and many years as a practitioner of his techniques, and after witnessing their effects upon many tens of thousands of participants in communities all around our world, the beauty and the joy are greater, higher, more harmonious and more potent than ever. I have watched his special method of facilitating rhythmical music grow from a small patch of grass on a university hillside to the far reaches of the world.

And y'know what? It is still growing...

Acknowledgments

I would like to acknowledge and pay homage to the wisdom of the ancient cultures that have given us the gift of drumming together. Much of the material in this book is based on my years of eclectic study of rhythmacultures around the world. The wisdom of the ancients is timeless. I offer my humble thank you to the teachers of source who have shared their knowledge, wisdom and cultures with me: Abdoulaye Diakite, Abrihame Adzinia, Allassane Kane, Benet Luchion, Candido Obajimi, Chalo Eduardo, Danjuma Adamu, Dumisani Maraire, Fred Simpson, Gordy Ryan, Hamza El Din, John Amira, John Santos, Ken Okulolo, Mabiba Baegne, Mamady Keita, Marcus Gordon, Mbimba, Michael Pluznick, Nurudafina Pili Abena, Onye Onyemaechi, Pedro De Jesus, Suru Ekeh, Titos Sompa and Yaya Diallo.

I would especially like to acknowledge Babatunde Olatunji for teaching, inspiring and guiding me. He represented the true spirit of African culture and traditions. At the same time, he encouraged his students to adapt what they learned from him to meet the needs of their own evolving rhythmacultures. As a mentor and friend, Baba allowed me to stand on his shoulders, making it possible for me to see further down my chosen path. Although he has passed away, his voice still guides my conscience and mission.

I have had the privilege of watching many of my former Village Music Circles (VMC) students develop rhythm-based careers in service to their communities. These facilitators now stand on my shoulders so they can see further down their chosen paths. After sharing their rhythmical spirits in the world, they bring their experiences back to VMC trainings, teaching both me and the next generation of rhythm-event facilitators. I wish to thank these mentors who have contributed stories and insights throughout the book.

I particularly want to acknowledge Don Davidson, one of my first-generation students, and Cameron Tummel, who in turn stands on Don's shoulders, for their many years of advocacy and support. During their apprenticeships with me, they contributed to many of the concepts I present. As recognized elders in the facilitation community, they each continue to contribute to the ongoing growth of our drum circle community.

To Jim Boneau for mentoring both me and the attendees during VMC leadership trainings, and to Mary Tolena Anderson for being the "king's counselor" during many of the VMC trainings, I say, "Thank you." These two people added an extra layer of depth and organization to our VMC facilitator trainings, helping me fine tune the curriculum, and as a result this book.

Thank you to Jonathan Murray for helping develop the facilitators' shorthand into a training and communication lexicon. This shorthand was born during the first VMC Facilitators' Playshop and has been evolving over the past ten years. Jonathan contributed the design of the shorthand card, as well as well as many of the shorthand symbols and examples in this book.

I would like to thank and acknowledge Ken Crampton, Jaqui MacMillan and Jonathan Murray for their tireless work developing the Drum Circle Facilitators' Guild. While incorporating many Arthurian facilitation concepts into the organization of the Guild, they fine tuned and enhanced those concepts, thus helping me integrate them into both my facilitator trainings and the book.

After recognizing that the nonprofessional hand-drumming movement was more than just a passing fad, Remo D. Belli provided never-ending support and far-reaching vision. Since 1991 he has been a major supporter of our recreational drumming community. Thank you, Remo, for recognizing this as a true grassroots movement and for supporting it.

Long before anyone else in the music industry, Remo's company supported community, education and wellness through drumming. Remo Inc. was the only drum company with a music therapist on their staff and a medical doctor as an adviser. They continue to provide extensive financing for literature and human resources that promote a healthy lifestyle through recreational drumming. Remo has funded research by neurologist Dr. Barry Bittman in the field of drumming and wellness. The results of Bittman's research have had a major effect on the medical industry's viewpoint related to drumming and wellness.

I would like to thank Rick Drumm, Dick Marcus and Mike Morse, who have each been Remo's marketing managers, who also drum. Over many years, each of these men, along with Christine Stevens, have edited and distributed the instructions I initially wrote for music store managers. I adapted these instructions for facilitators to create Advertising, Starting and Producing Drum Circles in Chapter 10.

Thank you to DRUM! Magazine for their permission to include my interview with Babatunde Olatunji as part of A Cross Country Conversation in Chapter 12.

Thanks to my fourteen-year writing relationship with Angela Marie, my editor, I have become a writer. Angela's insights have influenced my perspective over the years, and they are reflected in this book.

I would like to thank the Santa Cruz drum circle community. I met most of the people who helped me with the book's construction, including Angela, when they were my drumming students. As professionals artists, book designers and editors, they helped me give birth to both this book and my original drum circle facilitation book. Peter Cerny has once again translated my words into his artistic dotting spirit. Bee continues to share his computer expertise and saves us, time and time again, from computer crises. Bonno Bernard designed our book cover and is our production artist. Cliff Warner helped develop our initial design, and Staci Sambol completed the design and layout of the interior of the book. Susan Schrag proofread our final manuscript. Maraya Hull and Kim Dowling transcribed my Arthurian gibberish into readable form.

Thank you to Jerry Sitser for sharing his library of photographs from Seatle World Percussion Festivals, to Dr. Barry Bittman for contributing his Hawaii 2001 Playshop photos, and to Arturo Carrillo for sharing his photos from the Hawaii 2005 Playshop.

To my son Aryn and my daughter Maraya (yes, I miss-spelled their names correctly and deliberately) thank you for putting up with a dyslexic drumming elf for a father.

I give thanks and praise to Diana my wife, who, without laughing at my crazy dreams, has been my strong and supportive partner for twenty-five years, both in business and in life. She is a guiding light for me as I follow my dreams.

And finally I give thanks to you, for thinking that this book might be worth reading.

Arthur Hull

1 Birthing a Rhythmical Community

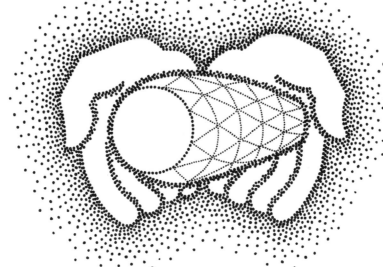

The Boy and the Box

I am at the Breitenbush Rhythm Festival outside Portland, Oregon, busing my dirty dish from the dining room to the kitchen through a transfer window. Through the window into the kitchen, I see a square hard plastic food container fly across the room to bounce and tumble across the thick industrial-strength rubber floor pad and come to rest at the back of the feet of a man scrubbing away over the sink. If the plastic container had hit the cement floor under the rubber matting, it would crash noisily and probably break. But instead the pad acts like a rubber mallet, causing the container to "sing" each time it bounces. Immediately after the food container stops bouncing, I hear a delighted squeal and giggle. Looking across the kitchen from the dishwasher, I see a happy two-year-old blond-haired boy sitting on a table with his legs hanging over the edge. The boy's whole body is wiggling with delight.

    The dishwasher dad, cleaning my dish in the sink, has his back to the boy.

After the boy's happy laughter subsides, the dad picks up the food container at his feet, brings it back to the boy, hands it to him and goes back to washing dishes.

I decide to get out of the way of the people behind me waiting to clear their plates, so I go over to the open kitchen door to watch the dance between the boy, the dad and the food container.

Rhythm Expression is Ageless

The open-ended clear plastic box is about as big as the boy's chest. He moves the container in his lap around in his hands, seriously contemplating his grip. He finally looks up with bright eyes while pushing the plastic box away from himself and into flight. It bounces on the mat with a "BOING", flipping over itself a few times in the air, creating a reverb vibrato in the sound. "BOIYOIYOING." It lands on the ground with a "KERPLUNK" and stops. The boy gives a short quiet laugh. Then the dad delivers the "song box" to the boy and returns to the sink.

To my delight, I get to watch this throw-and-return scenario repeat itself many times. With each throw, the difference in the boy's physical and vocal response is determined by the quality of the "rhythm song" created by the bouncing plastic box. The more bounces per throw, the longer the "song" created by the box, the longer the laugh from the boy. The higher the box bounces, the fuller the reverb vibrato note per box bounce, creating a fuller note in each of the boy's laughs. When the box song is a really good one the boy adds a squeal at the beginning of his laugh.

Each of the boy's giggly-wiggly laugh responses reflects the quality of a specific box song. The dad is happy to play fetch with the boy while working. The boy is happy to play the tossed-box song. Meanwhile, I am happily watching a fresh spirit play with the rhythmical world in a way that we adults would be embarrassed to do.

The dad is empowering the boy to express his rhythmical spirit. Simply by returning the box to his son and allowing and encouraging him to throw it, the father is manifesting the very essence of facilitation and rhythmical empowerment. The meaning of the word facilitate is to "help make easy." The dad is making it easy for the boy to explore his ability to create a rhythmical and musical song, and I learn a valuable lesson in how to allow rhythmical spirit to manifest.

Drum Circles

My friend and mentor Babatunde Olatunji has said to our ever-growing drum and dance community, in many different ways, that drumming is the simplest thing that groups of people can do to come together and unite in peace, harmony and love. Playing drums and dancing together put us in touch with a creative force that directly connects us to our own humanity. When people come together and drum they are a fully participating, interacting group creating and sharing a rhythmical and musical experience. This results in harmony, camaraderie and a feeling of wellness among all the participants.

> Drumming is the simplest thing that groups of people can do to come together and unite in peace, harmony and love.

Now, more than ever, we find ourselves seeking ways to build community with an intention to serve, to inspire and to reach beyond what separates us. It is my belief that facilitating rhythm-based events does exactly that.

People choose to facilitate rhythm events for many reasons. To me, the best reason to facilitate is to help a group of ordinary citizens discover the musical magic they can create. When you put percussion instruments in their hands and help them collaborate in the creation of rhythmical alchemy you empower your community in the many ways that will be explored in this book.

Drum circles are not just a passing fad. They are being integrated into many different parts of our society as tools for unity, wellness and fun. Facilitated community drumming events can now be experienced all over Europe, Asia, Australia and the Americas. A vast number of different types of drum circles are being facilitated in our communities. Each one is designed to deliver a particular type of service to a specific group.

Women, who are empowering themselves in their exclusive drumming circles, are strengthening their community as a whole. Similarly, men's gender-empowerment circles serve that function for the men in a community. Drum circles are facilitated at school assemblies and corporate team-building events, as well as with well elderly and music therapy groups. Kids-at-risk circles, mentally challenged groups and teenage pregnant mothers also drum. Each specific rhythm event does a bit of good for everybody involved, and, as a consequence, helps everyone connected to those people.

In its simplest form, a drum circle is a group of people who use drums and percussion to make "in-the-moment" music. We create a physical vibration that penetrates, excites and, at the same time, relaxes our physical, mental and emotional states of being. These vibrations massage and melt away any physiology of separateness that may exist in the bodies of the participants. When we pay attention to where we connect with each other, by the very nature of this entrainment activity, we are led into the now of each musical and rhythmical moment. For these few moments, drumming releases us from our past and gives us more room for the possibilities of the future.

Each individual's contribution to the music at a recreational drum circle is equally important, regardless of their rhythmical, musical or technical expertise. Group mind develops as the event unfolds, and community building is inherently part of the experience. Participating in the magic and excitement of an in-the-moment rhythm circle creates a much deeper connection between people than a quick introduction and a good handshake. Any time a group of people come together and cooperate to create an interactive musical event, they make connections beyond the music produced. When they do so, their community is strengthened and the world is a better place to live.

> Now, more than ever, we find ourselves seeking ways to build community with an intention to serve, to inspire and to reach beyond what separates us.
> —Diana Hull

Midwives & Pioneers

If any individual deserves credit for birthing our rhythmical community it is Baba, who spent over fifty years in the U.S. teaching dances, rhythms and songs from the African diaspora. I stand on Babatunde Olatunji's shoulders. It is from this platform prepared by Baba and with his blessings and mentorship that I developed the concept of facilitating rhythm-based events. At the end of this book, I share "A Cross-Country Conversation" with Baba.

Although I have been called the father of the modern facilitated drum circle movement, my role has been more that of a midwife, facilitating the birth of recreational drumming communities in many parts of the world. I have been a pioneer for most of my life. A pioneer is one who goes before and prepares the way for others, and a midwife assists in the delivery of new life into the world. I believe that, as a rhythmical evangelist, I have been doing both.

Today there are many more recreational drumming midwives facilitating around the world. These people are birthing rhythmacultures in many different parts of their communities by facilitating all types of rhythm-based events. These are the real heroes and heroines who are tirelessly working locally to build a grassroots recreational drumming community around them. Many of them are also using rhythm-based events as a tool to serve special populations in their community. They are doing this by sharing their rhythmical spirit and empowering others to do the same.

You will find, throughout this book, the contributions of many facilitators from our growing international drum circle facilitator community. In addition to their stories and contributions, I asked each of them to answer these two questions:
- What is a drum circle facilitator?
- What is a facilitated drum circle?

They gave me many descriptions but spoke with one voice. You will meet each of these people individually as you read this book, but with their permission I have melded their answers into that one voice.

What is a drum circle facilitator?

A drum circle facilitator guides a group of people as they play instruments together in a circle. A good facilitator is a skillful host and a creative and sensitive leader who makes the drum circle experience as easy and fun as possible for all who participate.

The facilitator need not be an expert drummer, but needs to have a reliable sense of rhythm and some playing skills. Throughout an event, they help transform the group's consciousness, taking people from an individual perspective to group awareness, using fun and engaging sequences. The facilitator's role is to serve the circle, while leading the group to its highest musical level.

A skilled facilitator creates an inclusive atmosphere for players of all musical levels, ages and ethnicities, where everyone feels safe and comfortable. They lead the group by facilitating musical successes that entrain and teach the circle to listen to itself.

A great facilitator will also highlight the unique gifts that each individual shares with the circle. They also understand and encourage participants' feelings of, "Yes, I can do this," "I like this," and "Wow! I'm making a real contribution to this rhythm."

Become one and know it in your heart.

What is a facilitated drum circle?

A drum circle is a fun drum and percussion jam, typically with players of varying musical levels, ages and ethnicities. Most commonly, a drum circle is an entry level event into the world of recreational musicmaking, as you need no previous musical experience.

Music in general and percussive music in particular brings people together in a common, celebratory mood. At once, participants are released from constraints of language, differing social or economic status, age or skill level, and any other trait which would tend to separate them. These constraints are replaced with endless possibilities for successful musical expression.

The definition of facilitate is "to make easy." Participants at a facilitated drum circle play rhythms in a group setting, with a facilitator who guides their musical direction when it is needed. The players have a spoken or unspoken agreement that the facilitator will guide them to their highest musical level. This cooperation enables both the advanced and the beginning drummers to play happily together. Participants experience tremendous freedom to play what they feel, rather than following a complex set of rules.

The same values we need for a strong community are nurtured and rewarded in a facilitated drum circle:

- good listening skills
- respect
- patience
- cooperation

Each individual is equally valuable to the whole. Everybody has a part to play, and no part is any more or any less important than any other part.

The modern facilitated drum circle is one prescription for fragmented parts of today's society. Its unifying power can be an elixir to assist us with our common goals of both personal and community-wide health and wellbeing.

While playing together in a drum circle, a group often moves through several musical transitions. These changes are challenging, and often create chaos in an unfacilitated drum circle. With help from a facilitator, a group is more likely to move smoothly through transitions. When they do this, they create both a new rhythm and a much deeper musical relationship. Their confidence in their ability increases and they play together much better

than they each would typically have been able to play alone.

Attend one and feel it in your body.

Birthing a Rhythmical Community

I published my first drum circle facilitation book in 1998: *Drum Circle Spirit—Facilitating Human Potential Through Rhythm*. It has helped create an international community of rhythm event facilitators and the modern facilitated drum circle movement that we have today. Since 1998, our rhythm-based event facilitation community has continued to grow from a handful of facilitation pioneers to a vast international grassroots recreational hand-drumming movement. This movement now has a network of rhythm-based event facilitators scattered all over the globe.

Knowledge is power. Sharing it is empowerment.

In *Drum Circle Spirit*, I presented a foundation for teaching almost anyone the basic technologies, techniques and philosophies of rhythm event facilitation. That book is peppered with many personal stories of learning experiences. These stories help share the experiences to the reader. Many facilitators who have been inspired by reading *Drum Circle Spirit* have attended my Village Music Circles™ (VMC) Facilitator Playshops.

Our initial VMC Facilitator trainings were based on *Drum Circle Spirit* for many years. As the drum circle facilitator community matured and evolved, so did the VMC trainings. Over the past several years I have continued to develop and fine tune my material, introducing and teaching my updated technologies, techniques and facilitation concepts.

My current VMC Facilitator Playshop trainings are based on the book you are now reading. Even though this is the workbook for all my facilitator trainings, you need not take the trainings for this book to help you learn to facilitate. We explore many advanced facilitation technologies, techniques and concepts, but the book is written to be accessible to beginning-beginner facilitators, so anyone will be able to glean the basic information that they will need to successfully start facilitating rhythm-based events. This book offers a variety of ways you can use drum circles to inspire your community to play together while you facilitate their human potential. The information is designed to help you build your leadership skills, using the community drum circle as a model.

In this book you will learn how to lead a successful rhythm-based event regardless of your musical background or previous rhythmical experience. This book will help you create your own unique way to guide a group to its highest musical potential. The facilitation tools, techniques and concepts presented in this book are applicable to many diverse groups and cultures. Many of these facilitation tools, techniques and concepts are also applicable to the facilitation of any group of people for reasons other than creating rhythm-based events.

After hundreds of Village Music Circle facilitation trainings there are now thousands of facilitator graduates manifesting their rhythmical evangelism all over the world. This book represents the accumulated knowledge, wisdom and maturity of those people who are the driving force of the international drum circle movement. This book represents the growth of that community of rhythm-based event facilitators. It shares some of their stories, learnings and insights as well as my own. My students have truly become my teachers, and with their help and contributions to this book, it has become a collaborative effort to impart the accumulative knowledge of our experiences to you the reader. With deep humility and respect I thank these people for contributing their spirit and wisdom to this book and to the larger mission of rhythmical evangelism and rhythmical empowerment.

My ultimate mission is to help birth a rhythmically and musically enabled and connected population. Knowledge is power. Sharing it is empowerment. By sharing our knowledge with you, we hope this book will help lead you to your own rhythmical empowerment. In turn we hope you will share your knowledge and rhythmical spirit with others.

Evolution of Chicago's Rhythmical Community

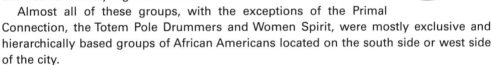

John Yost, a respected drum circle facilitator, performer and teacher from the midwest, shares his perspective of the birth of rhythmical community in Chicago.

In 1995 the Chicago drumming community consisted of several disparate factions: the 63rd Street beach circle, Muntu Dance Theater, a few semipro dance companies, the Primal Connection, the Totem Pole Drummers, Women Spirit Drummers, and Joan's Tuesday night drum circle.

Almost all of these groups, with the exceptions of the Primal Connection, the Totem Pole Drummers and Women Spirit, were mostly exclusive and hierarchically based groups of African Americans located on the south side or west side of the city.

I met Sarina Kates via an ad in the paper just after I started holding "bongo jam sessions" at a park. She explained that what I was calling a "bongo jam" was, in fact, a drum circle. Soon Sarina started offering a circle on Sundays, with her friend David Blood, under the moniker Rhythm Revolution (RR). It was advertised as "an experiment in consciousness expansion." After I attended RR for a few months, one day Sarina and David approached me and asked me to help with their drum circle, by opening, closing, leading, collecting donations to pay the rent and whatever else—just in case they couldn't make it. I didn't see David for years after that day and Sarina would be around once in a while, when she had the time. For all intensive purposes I had inherited a drum circle simply by saying "yes."

Those early days were lean and mean. Sometimes many people would come to the drum circle and sometimes there were very few participants. Some people didn't have money to donate, so I would sometimes pay to rent the space myself. I knew that the community needed direction and information, so Sarina and I sponsored a day-long drum festival featuring workshops, performances and drum circles. After this success, Sarina moved to Arizona and Michael Taylor of Holy Goat Percussion stepped up to co-sponsor workshops with people of source - teachers and musicians within the ethnic traditions. We brought in Carlos Quinto, Yaya Kabo, Michael Markus, Mbemba Bangoura, Madou Dembele and Eichi Saito. When bringing in these teachers we would gather a select few students for master classes. Those dedicated students formed a study group. Many of the members travelled to Africa to study, and later the group evolved into Dahui-Ensemble du Rhythm. Dahui initially formed as a house band to support the performances of the master rhythmatists, but later developed an identity of its own.

In 1996, Sarina had heard through a friend that Arthur Hull was coming through Chicago to do a drum circle at the Guitar Center. She and I decided to co-sponsor one of Arthur's Rhythmical Alchemy Playshops. We made music for hours with this crazy elf, without a single musical crash. That was the day I saw the light. My life changed. I wanted to do what he did.

Arthur needed a lift to the airport so I seized the opportunity to drive him so I could ask him how I could learn to do what he does. He told me to call his office to register for a facilitators' training he was planning to hold in Hawaii. The next day I called Village Music Circles and was told that this was a figment of Arthur's imagination and that nothing was definite. They kept my name, and finally I got the call that the Playshop was going to happen, so I was able to participate in Arthur's first annual Hawaii week-long Playshop.

Arthur Hull became my drum circle mentor. I took his message of community building very seriously and devised a plan to build a drum community in Chicago. The plans were simple:

- Inspire people with percussionitis.
- Connect players to people of source via workshops and classes.
- Reach out and network to the existing South Side and any other factions of the community,
- Create a newsletter and website to keep people informed and connected.

In 1998 when I hosted Arthur for a weekend facilitators' playshop, we featured six percussion ensembles in a double-stage club setting on Saturday night, and then on Sunday we held the largest cross-cultural community drum circle in the Midwest, with about 500 participants. All factions of the existing community were honored and everyone pulled together for the first time to be in community with each other. That event solidified and legitimized the concept of a drum community in the hearts and minds of players throughout Chicago.

Since that weekend in 1998, there have been major advances. More people have begun teaching. Master drummers continue to be brought to the forefront and connected with the community, to enrich the knowledge and nurture the respect of tradition. Local stores now carry a broad array of percussion equipment, and music schools have established extensive drum and dance programs. A regional drum magazine has been established, which is now an international one. Teachers and musicians move to Chicago to take advantage of the growing interest as more percussion-based groups continue to be established.

The biggest major development and the next stage in the evolution of the movement in Chicago has been the establishment of Rhythm, a night club dedicated to drums and drumming. Drum circles unfold three nights per week in a three-tiered drum pit designed to accommodate a hundred drummers. Shelves are lined with a menagerie of drums and percussion instruments, and live rhythm-based performances and percussion workshops and classes happen regularly there.

There are also several drummers in Chicago who now make drumming their profession via teaching, performing and facilitating rhythm-based events and programs. It has been a great experience helping build the Chicago drum scene. Many have made lifelong connections at my weekly Rhythm Revolution drum circle. I met my wife there. The world is truly a better place when people connect to themselves and each other through the drum.

Logistics of Reading This Book

This section describes symbols you will encounter as you read this book and explains what they mean.

The Stories

 Any time you see a single Peter Cerny dot drawing in the text you will find one of my stories. Photos of the facilitators who share their experiences typically mark the locations of their stories in the book. Skipping through the book from story to story will give you a very quick and entertaining read.

The Exercises

 The exercises that you find throughout this book are designed to be performed in a study group of ten or more people who are working on their facilitation skills. You can also adapt the exercises to be integrated into many scenarios as you facilitate drum circle events. While adapting these exercises into your rhythm event facilitation, please remember to keep them as simple as possible to ensure the musical and rhythmical success of the players in the group as well as your own. Remember, if you are practicing these exercise while you are facilitating an event, you want to ensure the facilitation and learning success that these exercises are designed to create. You do this by keeping them simple.

Teaching Without Teaching

 Teaching without teaching is a fundamental Arthurian facilitation concept that you will find addressed in many ways through this book, including specific applications and techniques to use as you facilitate drum circles. Look for the T in a circle.

Triplicity Elements

 On page 43, I explain the concept of triplicities. Each triplicity is composed of three elements. Whenever an element is introduced in the text, you will see this symbol.

Facilitators' Shorthand

Facilitator's shorthand is my way of notating drum circle facilitation activities with a minimum of pen strokes, so the scribe can pay more attention to what's happening at the event than to their writing.

The drum circle facilitation community has been developing and using facilitator's shorthand since the first Hawaii Facilitators' Playshop. We use the shorthand at every playshop, at Bumbershoot and wherever VMC and Arthurian peer reviews take place. This shorthand has evolved as the community continues to use it, and is still a work in progress.

In the back of the book, I provide the shorthand on a page you can remove from the book and laminate to use as a reference at drum circle events. The symbols are also listed on the next page for your enjoyment.

Shorthand Notation
ACTIONS

+	Start of Sequence
↻	Call to Groove
→	Group in Groove
G	Continue to Play
!	Attention Call
⊗	Stop Cut
∿	Rumble
↵	Call and Response
∅	Sculpt
⊖	1/2 Circle Sculpt
⊖	1/4 Circle Sculpt
⊘	1/3 Circle Sculpt
♡	Clap
⦦	Listening
///	Layering In
\\\	Layering Out
√	Accent Downbeats
↗	Volume Up
↘	Volume Down
↑	Speed Up Tempo
↓	Slow Down Tempo
☆	Showcase
△	Pass Out Part
↖↗	Teeter Totter
↜	Switchback
∿	Modulation
∫	Wave

Shorthand Notation
THINGS

O	Whole Circle
⊓	Platform
V	Vocal
♂	Men
♀	Women
K	Children
ROC	Rest of the Circle
P	Percussion
B	Bell
S	Shaker
W	Wood
T	Tambourine
Bw	Boomwhackers
◎	Window of Communication
D	Drums
L	Low Pitch
M	Medium Pitch
H	High Pitch
A	Ashiko
C	Conga
Dn	Dunnun
Dj	Djembe
Dk	Doumbek
F	Frame Drum
Ss	Sound Shape

Guerrilla Drum Circles

Nurnberg Brass and Percussion Days, a Bavarian musical festival held at their main concert center in Nurnberg, Germany, focuses mostly on marching music. The year I attended, their brochure referred to a Arthur Hull drum circle *demonstration* instead of presenting the event as a drumming workshop, clinic or drum circle. It was scheduled for the second floor music hall classroom, which was far away from all other activity at the festival. Because most of the drummers at the festival were either marching or trap kit drummers and had no idea what a drum circle was, only five participants came to the demonstration. I explained to the program officials that to do a demonstration of a drum circle I would need enough volunteers to constitute a circle. With their permission, we took the drums down to the entrance of the performance hall, grabbed some chairs, formed a circle and started jamming.

Because no bass or frame drums were available, I ran around the site gathering trash buckets from the hallways. I bought some mallets from a percussion sales booth, came back to the circle and handed the new instruments to the spectators who had gathered. Once the low-pitched trash cans locked the rhythm together, our groove called more spectators to the circle.

With the help of my support person, I ran back to the percussion booths and borrowed drumming equipment from people who knew me. We brought the extra drums to the eager spectators.

I had a lot of fun facilitating these music students and musicians, who were very responsive. They learned my facilitation body language quickly, and played with dynamics, engaging in an interesting rhythmical dialogue.

Throughout the day we did a series of impromptu drum circles near the entrance of the convention site, as bus loads of bands unloaded and came into the hall. At each drum circle about fifty participants played the rhythm equipment, but sometimes as many as two hundred people stood around the circle of drummers.

During each drum circle, I encouraged the people watching to clap and create rhythms with their hands. I would then stop the drummers, uncovering the clapping circle surrounding the drum circle. Then I encouraged the drummers to clap as well, until we included everybody in a clapping rhythm. At that point I would signal to the drummers to resume playing. The explosion of a drum groove into the middle of the clapping circle consistently evoked yells and cheers.

At the closing of the last circle of the day, I instigated one of these clapping to drumming transitions. At the point in the music where the drums resumed playing someone broke into a rousing song. All two hundred people joined in with full gusto. At that time my German vocabulary consisted of twelve words, so I didn't know what was being sung. I was later told that it was a popular beer drinking song.

The clapping group continued to sing along with the drumming group, until I facilitated a series of "calls and responses" to bring the musical piece to a close. Along with the usual drum response, the clappers used their voices to respond to my calls. During the final drumming rumble all the clappers joined in a climactic vocal explosion. We gave each other a standing ovation and dispersed.

A group of people came up to me with that special wide-eyed look I know so well. Using one of their English-speaking friends as a translator, they asked the usual questions that someone asks after doing a facilitated in-the-moment rhythm event for the first time.

The last question they asked me was, "What do you call what we just experienced?" My first answer was "a community drum circle." Upon hearing the translation, they all opened their mouths and "ahhhh'd" in unison, while nodding their heads. My second answer was "rhythmical bliss," and they "ahhhh'd" and nodded together even stronger. My final answer was "rhythm church." Instead of ahhhing they discussed the answer among themselves, and with big smiles and nodding heads they seemed to come to agreement with each other and with me. With hearty handshakes and danke schoens (thank you's) all around, they said goodbye. Once again I changed from master facilitator to master roady. "Now where did I grab those trash cans?"

Fun in the Sun

2 We Speak Arthurian

Arthurian terminology expresses ideas and concepts particular to my style of facilitation, for which I had previously found no adequate words. Sometimes Arthurian terminology is a single word that describes a whole sequence of actions. Once you understand Arthurian, I can describe to you in one paragraph what might otherwise be several written pages of facilitation directions, as you will see in "A Facilitation Sequence Described in Arthurian" on page 37.

A Bit of Perspective

When I first began facilitating drum circles I didn't stop to name or quantify the tools and techniques that I discovered, created and developed. In the 1960s, the circuitry of facilitation was in my body and my heart, but not yet in my mind. I simply did what came naturally. I facilitated as a service to the group's musical experience. The players simply wanted to make musical magic together with their drums and hand percussion. My responses to their rhythmical expressions were mostly impulsive, unconscious acts geared to enhancing the experience that we were all creating together.

As I became a rhythmical evangelist, the art of rhythm-based event facilitation became hard-wired in my body and my psyche as my way of sharing my musical and rhythmical spirit with other people.

By the late 1980s I started sharing my facilitation techniques with some of my advanced students at the University of California, Santa Cruz. As I traveled around the United States, I discovered other people working in the growing grass-roots drumming movement. We shared our information and experiences with each other and started networking to create what is now known as the recreational hand-drumming movement.

To help my students develop as facilitators, I created a vocabulary that describes my drum circle facilitation circuitry. I developed my terminology over years of trial and error as I facilitated drum circles with various groups. My Arthurian lexicon describes the art of facilitating rhythm-based events.

By the time I had set up a facilitators' apprenticeship program at UCSC, I had established a semantic foundation for teaching the art of facilitation. I described this Arthurian facilitators' lexicon in my first book *Drum Circle Spirit*. These semantics are a collection of words and phrases such as "sculpting," "orchestrational spot" and "in full groove" that define facilitation actions and concepts. Our community's common understanding and use of these terms makes our communication with each other clearer, easier and faster. Arthurian continues to be used today as we develop additional vocabulary to meet the needs of our evolving drum circle facilitation community.

After the fourth Village Music Circles ™ (VMC) Hawaii Facilitators' Playshop training, Bob Anzlovar set up an internet drum circle dialogue list that has become the electronic meeting place for our ever-growing international drum circle facilitator community. Here is a quote from the Yahoo groups drum circle facilitators dialogue list home page that awaits you when your subscription to the list is accepted: "WARNING! We Speak Arthurian. Most of us have trained with Arthur Hull, who wrote the book on drum circle facilitation. He helped to give us a language to describe the things that happen in all facilitated drum circles and, inevitably, we use quite a lot of what might seem like jargon when talking to each other. Reading the book will help you understand."

The vast majority of people actively engaged in the Drum Circle Facilitators' Internet Dialogue List have graduated from my Village Music Circles Facilitators' Playshops. These people are speaking to each other using the Arthurian Facilitators Lexicon.

As Bob Anzlovar says, "We Speak Arthurian." He shares a story below.

We Speak Arthurian

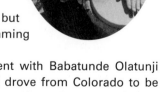

I discovered drumming by accident in 1989 when I stumbled upon people in a park playing drums. Watching, I realized that this experience was accessible. Other people were walking in, picking up instruments and playing, so I stepped up and tried it too. I don't think I played very well. My hands were hurting when I was done, but in my heart I'd found something like home.

Over the next several years, I went to many drum circles but they were mostly what we would have called "thunder drumming circles."

I met Arthur at a Drum, Dance and Pray for Peace event with Babatunde Olatunji at the Washington Monument in D.C., in the fall of 1996. I drove from Colorado to be among about 900 drummers, listening to a series of ethnic-specific performance groups. Between the acts, the drum-armed crowd would almost instantly become several distinct drumming clusters. Arthur's role at the event was to facilitate audience activities between acts. He was able to transform separate clusters of drummers into a coherent whole, using rhythmical games. As the finale for the event, Arthur arranged this huge crowd into a single drum circle and facilitated as they created rocking rhythms together, as it got dark.

I had never seen anyone actually *do* anything with a circle—my experience of drum circles was that they started, grooved and then died.

Later, I found myself at the same restaurant as Arthur and I worked up the courage to ask, "Where could I learn how to do that?" Arthur explained that he organizes Facilitator Playshops to teach how to facilitate rhythm events.

By the fourth time I attended a Hawaii Facilitators' Playshop, I realized that this growing community of drum circle facilitators needed an internet dialogue list, so I created a yahoo groups mailing list.

This "drumcircles" mailing list provides a place for discussions of drum circles and drum circle facilitation, as well as other subjects of interest to drummers and facilitators. Also, it is a place where fledgling drum circle facilitators can post successes, talk about drum circle challenges, get helpful suggestions from the online drum circle facilitation community and give and receive feedback after Playshops.

The mailing list has now grown to be the place to discuss drum circle facilitation and most other drumming topics. We have over eleven hundred members on all continents. We discuss a wide range of topics such as inexpensive instruments, special needs populations, large and small group facilitation, and networking for career development.

The drumcircles dialogue list has features that parallel those of a drum circle. We have never had heavy moderation. All voices are heard and become part of the blend. Like a drum circle, the conversation sometimes drifts, and needs an intervention to bring it back to center. This has been challenging at times, but has never required anything more than a reminder of why we participate in these dialogues. The list provides a place where everything drumming can be discussed. We speak Arthurian on this internet dialogue list, but we are here for all.

To subscribe to the drum circle email list send a BLANK email to: drumcircles-subscribe@yahoogroups.com.

Summer of Love

This is the story of my first conscious act of drum circle facilitation. Now, more than thirty-five years later, I am still experimenting and learning more about rhythm-event facilitation.

During the Summer of Love in San Francisco in the late 60s the hippies were hanging out in the Haight Ashbury district next to Golden Gate Park, where free psychedelic music concerts were being offered by the Grateful Dead, Janis Joplin and Jefferson Airplane. Also, in Golden Gate Park, drummers liked to meet on Hippy Hill. You could go there at almost any time of the day and find a freeform anarchist drum circle.

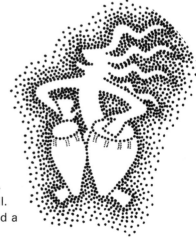

The ebb and flow of exciting freeform rhythms lured me into the Hippy Hill rhythm web. I was in my late teens, freshly drafted into the military and spending my off duty weekends at Hippy Hill. It was the drums and not the hippie drug culture that attracted me. I had taken a few Afro-Cuban drumming classes from a teacher in San Francisco who had told me to stay away from those hippie drummers. He said they would spoil my traditional hand drum training. What he did not know was that I had been a freeform rhythm expressionist from the time I could first walk.

In my earlier rhythmical explorations, I had played drum kit with musical groups, and hand drums with three or four drummers at a time. That summer, I became a Hippy Hill regular, drumming for as many as eight hours a day every weekend I could get off the military base. Ten to forty drummers sharing their rhythmical spirits at the same time in a circle was a new and exciting experience. My enthusiasm for the freeform drumming experience was tempered only by my frustration with the rhythmical train wreck that would ultimately bring any drum circle groove we created to a screeching, messy halt.

By the end of the Summer of Love, I was also studying with several drum teachers, playing established culturally specific rhythms. I enjoyed this format that defined a preset number of players with specific parts, creating a rhythm groove together. We were able to play together for long periods. But I did not enjoy being confined to playing one specific rhythm pattern without the freedom to add my spirited interpretation.

My attraction to the Hippy Hill circles was the freedom of expression that was encouraged. But I was beginning to recognize that the hippie drummers sometimes lacked an understanding of the universal principles that foster group playing consciousness. Because of this, they could only maintain a strong rhythm groove for short periods. While the culturally specific drummers offered me hours of playing deep traditional grooves while locked into a specific part, the Hippy Hill drummers offered me short flashes of freeform grace and beauty, interspersed with lots of rhythm noise and train wrecks.

I was then, and I am still now, straddling those two opposite drumming cultures.

On one of my last Summer of Love drumming weekends, before I was to be shipped out to a military base overseas, I found myself playing in a powerfully magical rhythm groove. It was only shaky around the edges, because a few drummers were paying more attention to their own rhythm instead of supporting the group's intention to play together. I could hear and feel the beginnings of a train wreck waiting for us down the rhythm track. I did not want this magic to end, simply because three out of twenty-five players were playing with themselves rather than with the whole group. I was frustrated. I understood that these few unconnected players needed only to lift their heads, look around the circle, and connect with the group pulse. The magic was too good to be rhythmically stepped on, and I wished with all my might that they would wake up and join the magic. This did not happen, though, and the groove slowly became less magical as it headed towards its inevitable demise. I saw other players in the circle noticing what was happening as we tried to keep the magical groove from turning into a regular thunder-drummer groove-ending train wreck.

> **So I did the unthinkable. I broke the most basic anarchist drum circle rule of etiquette: "No leaders allowed."**

So I did the unthinkable. I broke the most basic anarchist drum circle rule of etiquette: "No leaders allowed." After jumping into the middle of the circle and getting the attention of all the players, I marked the pulse by pounding my right fist into my left up-raised palm.

The unconnected players became more conscious of the pulse. The shaky rhythm solidified back into a magical rhythm groove and I returned to my seat and played. We continued to enjoy the renewed rhythm for a long time, until it came to its natural conclusion. Instead of a train wreck, it was as if we all decided at the same time that we were done and mutually brought the groove to completion.

After we stopped I was thanked by some of the players for "saving" the groove. Someone yelled, "Next time use a cow bell." A ding went off in my head and the next time I did.

A Facilitation Sequence
Described in Arthurian

Let's use Arthurian words to describe a facilitation sequence, and then describe it in layman's terms.

"With the group in full groove, she walked to the orchestrational spot and sculpted the low drums for showcasing. She identified them and gave them a continue-to-play signal. Then she gave an attention call and a stop cut to the remaining players for listening. She then used the low drums as a platform while facilitating a series of calls and responses with the other players in the circle. At the end of the call and response series she did a call to groove for the whole circle and then she GOOW."

Although this paragraph may sound like gibberish, it speaks volumes to facilitators. Let's break it down.

- With the group in full groove… means that the participants were playing their instruments together.
- she walked to the orchestrational spot… means that she walked to the middle of the circle where she usually delivers her facilitator body language to the whole group of players.
- …and sculpted the low drums for showcasing… means that she identified all the low pitch drums with a facilitator's body signal and told them to continue to play in preparation to showcase the low drum group to the remaining players in the circle.
- She identified them and gave them a continue-to-play signal. This means she gestured to each person playing a low drum and motioned for them to keep playing.
- Then she gave an attention call and a stop cut to the remaining players for listening. This means that she made an attention call signal, with her finger pointing up in the air, while making contact with the rest of the group in the circle. By doing this she gave a warning to everyone who was playing any instrument other than a low drum that a new body language direction was about to be given. Then she made a theatrical and see-able (readable) stop cut signal, stopping those people from playing. By doing so she gave the circle of players a chance to listen to the low drum song that she had "uncovered" (showcased).
- She then used the low drums as a platform… means that with the low drums continuing to play, she then had a low drum groove playing as a musical background from which she could facilitate different kinds of rhythmical and musical interactions with the other members of the group.
- …while facilitating a series of calls and responses with the rest of the circle. A call is when the facilitator plays a short pattern on her instrument and the response is when

the non-playing members of the circle play that pattern back to her and then wait for the next facilitation call or direction. Doing a series of calls and responses means that she did more than one call and response with the group.

- At the end of the call and response series she did a "call to groove" for the whole circle… means that when she had finished the call and response series she counted the remaining members of the group back into playing with the background groove that she had established with the low drum players. A call to groove signal usually means that a facilitator, while marking the pulse with their body and instrument, vocally calls some or all of the non-playing members of their circle to begin playing by saying a phrase, such as, "One, two, let's all play!"
- …and then she GOOW means that once the new rhythm was established she left the center of the circle and got out of their way. GOOW is an acronym for "get out of the way." When she does this, the group can play together with a clear view of the other players in the circle and without her interference.

Life is a dance! The original paragraph using the Arthurian lexicon to describe the facilitation sequence consisted of 91 words. Using lay terms, I needed more than 500 words to describe the same sequence. You can see why using Arthurian terminology when we share a dialogues on an Internet list with other facilitators helps us reduce the number of words we must type to describe our drum circle experiences. It also makes it easier for users of the list to ask and answer questions. By using the Arthurian facilitators lexicon, you ensure that your dialogue will be clearly understood by the members of our community. Without the use of Arthurian terminology, this book would be three times as long, and thick and heavy.

Below I include what I call a "facilitators' shorthand" version of the sequence described above.

$$+ \rightarrow \varnothing \ L \ G, ! \ ROC \ \otimes \ ?$$
$$= L \ \star = L \ \sqcap, \ \hookleftarrow ROC, \ O \ G \rightarrow \ GOOW$$

In the next section I describe many of my Arthurian terms. You can refer to this lexicon to help you read and digest this book with greater ease. Knowing and using these Arthurian words and phrases will help you travel along your path toward better service to your community through rhythm.

Watch out for those slippery sinceriously synergizing percussion puppies with modulated percussionitis. They could be rhythmasizing! To understand that last sentence, read further. Life is a dance!

Arthurian Words and Phrases

I list these words and phrases in order of importance. Reading the definitions of the words listed first will likely help you better understand the later listings.

Drum Circle

When I use the term *drum circle*, visualize participants facing each other across a circle and playing a balance of drums along with other percussion toys.

In-the-Moment Music

Players create *in-the-moment* music in a specific moment and then it is gone. This music is not memorized, notated or repeated. When in-the-moment music gets expressed by two or more people together, it is a sharing of musical spirit that we call *rhythmical alchemy*.

Transition Point

A *transition point* is a place and quality in the drum circle's rhythm and music that tells the facilitator that the circle needs their help.

GOOW

GOOW means **G**et **O**ut **O**f their **W**ay.

STOOW

STOOW means **S**tay **O**ut **O**f their **W**ay.

Intervention

An *intervention* is any single act of entering a circle and facilitating.

Radar

When you use your *radar* you use all of your senses to obtain all the information possible from your drum circle environment.

Reading the Circle

We read individual letters on a page. They merge into groups that become words, that in turn communicate meaning. If your facilitator radar is fully on and balanced, you can *read* subtle audio, visual and kinesthetic responses that translate into the state of your circle rhythmically, musically and emotionally. The information that you read from the group tells you what or who needs to be facilitated next.

As the facilitator, you need to be reading the circle at all times. Read the quality of the response from the group as you initiate any intervention.

Playing Consciousness

Playing consciousness is a supportive, collaborative attitude and sensitivity of players toward the group's musicmaking process.

Percussion Consciousness

Percussion consciousness happens when the group understands elements that make a drum circle sing, including timbre distinctions and creating spaces in time for each others' contributions. The players listen to each other and interact to create the developing song.

Orchestrational Consciousness

Orchestrational consciousness uses percussion consciousness as a platform. The players can focus more on the harmonic and musical aspects of their instruments and their relationship.

Sincerious

Sincerious is the combination of being playfully sincere and subtly serious at the same moment.

Synergized

When the whole is greater than the sum of the parts you have synergy. This implies that group consciousness has been achieved and they are in harmony with each other, or *synergized*. This applies to any group of people, including players in a drum circle.

Rhythm Burnout

Rhythm burnout happens when a group of people in an ongoing drum circle have explored a particular rhythm groove to its fullest but then lose interest while they are still playing that rhythm. Rhythm burnout can be easily identified by the loss of energy, dynamics and congruity in the rhythm groove. Rhythm burnout is a well-developed transition point in the music.

Facilitator Burnout

Two versions of *facilitator burnout* often happen at the same time and usually for the same reason: over facilitation. The remedy for both types of facilitator's burnout is for you to GOOW.

Percussion Toys

You are over facilitating when you are doing more facilitating than the situation demands. If you get mentally and physically fatigued and overwhelmed, you have given yourself facilitator's burnout.

Alternatively, when the players in the circle have been over facilitated, they start to feel manipulated and used rather than supported. If they are unresponsive or their response to your facilitation directions are becoming sluggish, then your circle has facilitator's burnout.

Percussion Puppies

Percussion puppies are people who love to play percussion instruments.

Modulate

When you *modulate* a group, you facilitate a change in the emotional or musical intensity.

Percussionitis

Percussionitis happens when people cannot resist playing along with the rhythms of life. This includes playing along with your windshield wipers and your turn signal blinkers.

Rhythmasizing

When you *rhythmasize* a group you are facilitating a rhythm-based activity using vocals, body percussion, movement or instruments.

In the Round

Facilitating *in the round* means to be continuously facing, addressing and facilitating different parts of your circle, much like a radar antenna that constantly turns in all directions to take in all the information that surrounds it.

Sound Bowl

In a *sound bowl*, each player either sits on the floor, sits in a chair behind those seated on the floor or stands and plays their instrument behind the chairs. For circles with more than 30 players, using these multiple layers helps players see and hear each other.

Common Denominator Tempo

A *common denominator tempo* is the speed that a particular group of players can most comfortably play a specific rhythm at a specific moment in time. As the group of players gets synergized, their common denominator tempo tends to increase.

Student Crisis Mode

Student crisis mode happens when a person tries to perform at a level of expertise far beyond their current ability, thus creating tension, frustration and poor self-esteem.

Groove

Someone creates a *groove* by playing a rhythm pattern on their instrument in a continuous fashion. Add a few more people doing the same and you have a group groove.

In Full Groove

When all the participants in the circle are playing together they are in full *groove*.

On the Run

When you facilitate the group while they are playing in full groove you are facilitating *on the run*.

Window of Communication

 A *window of communication* is the space between group rhythms when a facilitator is able to talk to the group.

Rumble

 A group of people playing very fast and non-rhythmically on their instruments will make a rumble sound. A musical term for a rumble is *tremolo*.

Pacing and Leading

Pacing and leading is a technique to lead the group from where they are currently playing to where they want to go by shifting the group's tempo, volume or dynamics.

Train Wreck

A *train wreck* happens when rhythms clash to the extent that there is no groove left and players stop.

Entrainment

Entrainment is the opposite of a train wreck. It happens when a group of players align rhythmically while drumming.

Hand Percussion

Examples of *hand percussion* are bells, shakers and wood instruments. For the examples in this book, this does not include hand drums.

Dunun

A *dunun* is a West-African-style double-headed drum, sometimes also known as a djun-djun or a doundoun. This family of drums has a small high-pitched drum called a ken keni, a middle drum called a sangban, and a bass drum called a doundounba. Some references to dunun players in this book imply the bass drummers in the circle in general.

Dununs

3 Triplicities

Throughout this book you will see various aspects of the art form of facilitation broken down into three basic functional elements. I refer to these combinations of elements as *triplicities*, and use them as a platform for teaching particular aspects of facilitation technologies, techniques and philosophies. Each of the three basic elements in a triplicity has its own strengths. Like the international kids' game "rock, scissors, paper," each element does something the other two elements do not do, while at the same time compensating for something lacking in at least one of the other triplicity elements.

Each element of a triplicity is like one leg of a tripod, holding the others up while leaning into the same point for support. Camera tripods and flip chart stands are examples of this design. As long as each leg is of equal length, the tripod is in perfect balance. When the three elements of a triplicity are in balance you both learn and facilitate from a strong platform. The elements of the triplicities are the ingredients you need to create rhythmical alchemy in your rhythm-based event.

Presentation Skills Triplicity

Vocal, Group Leadership and Body Language skills constitute the interactive and interdependent elements of the Presentation Skills Triplicity. To be a successful facilitator, you need to acquire, develop and use these three basic skills in conjunction with each other.

Let's look at the Presentation Skills Triplicity from a tripod point of view.

While developing my own personal facilitation style, I discovered how these three Presentation Skills interact cooperatively with each other. I found that I had different strengths and weaknesses within the triplicity.

Having been a mime, a dancer and involved in theater for years, I discovered that my body language skills were more developed than my vocal presentation skills. I had never given a discourse from a lectern in front of a group, been on a high school debating team, or been a member of a Toastmasters public-speaking club.

Having been a dance teacher, drum teacher, and leader of music and percussion ensembles, my group leadership skills were far more developed than my body language skills or my vocal presentation skills. One leg of my tripod was a lot more developed and longer than the other two. In other words my tripod was out of balance.

I discovered that by focusing on my weaker skills I could develop them so they would eventually equal my strongest skill. By paying attention, and with conscious effort, I have been able to balance my presentation skills. I now have a tripod whose legs are similar lengths. This gives me a strong foundation from which to present and facilitate. The tip of my triplicity tripod, where my presentation skills meet, is now centered.

Standing in the center of a balanced tripod gives me equal access to each skill available in that triplicity.

Vocal Skills

You must develop your orator's vocal skills if you want to have a speaking presence. During the "windows of communication" that happen between rhythmical pieces, your vocal presentation skills are typically your most important instrument. Your body language skills play a supporting role. You will want to develop vocal dynamics in your presentations so that you move and inspire people when you speak. It is not about talking loudly all the tine. Sometimes you must whisper to get your participants to listen.

Group Leadership Skills

To take command of a situation and instigate the people-moving logistics that are involved at any drum circle, you use group leadership skills. You direct your group to achieve specific goals. At times your group leadership skills take precedence while your other facilitator presentation skills play a supporting role.

There will also be times during an event when you will want and need to use these three facilitator presentation skills in equal amounts.

Body Language Skills

Body language skills are a major part of a facilitator's communication tool kit. From a rock-paper-scissors point of view, you need to use your body language skills to direct whenever the group's playing volume limits their ability to hear your voice. In other words, your body language skills cover the limitations of your voice.

Body language skills are at the heart of rhythm event facilitation and need to be continually developed.

Body language skills are at the heart of rhythm event facilitation and need to be continually developed and fine tuned. As facilitator, you can use body language to signal your group to start, speed up, slow down, get louder or softer, and to stop the music.

During a drum circle you will usually communicate to your participants using physical signals three times as often than you use your voice. You speak to the group with your body while the circle is loudly expressing its joy in full groove. Your body language can sometimes be as important as your vocal skills, even during windows of communication while the group is not playing.

When you encounter specific cultural groups you will want to develop body language consistent with their social mores. For example, in many cultures it is impolite or even insulting to point your finger at a person, so instead you can give them what I call the "Disneyland point" by extending your hand, with your fingers closed and your palm up, toward them.

Before participants will understand your body language, you must be comfortable in your body. I practiced my signals in front of a bunch of my children's stuffed animals and dolls before I was willing to use them in front of people.

Every time you stand on the orchestrational point, you communicate your emotional attitudes and intentions to the circle with your body, whether or not you are consciously choosing to do so. Once you understand this, you can be more aware of the kind of energy you project into your drum circle and you will be better able to make use of your opportunities to communicate your intentions, directions and spirit.

Body Language Triplicity

Body language has its own triplicity that fits within the Presentation Skills Triplicity.

Readability, ability to telegraph and congruency describe effective body language elements that I call the Body Language Skills Triplicity.

Readability ♣

Make everything you do readable. All your body movements and facial expressions need to be easily recognized and understood by your drum circle participants. They need to be able to immediately respond to your body language signals.

Some facilitators think that to be readable they need to make their body movements and facial expressions big and exaggerated. Although using big signals during the beginning of an event helps your group see and understand what your body language intends to communicate, it is unnecessary and usually detrimental to use exaggerated signals during the whole event. It would be like yelling at your group every time you speak. You want to be able to add subtlety and finesse to your body language by varying the size of your signals. Big body language done constantly can even limit your ability to establish good rapport with your circle. As the group understands and responds to your signals, you can make a specific signal more subtle and still have your motions be readable. As players respond to your finessed commands, they will likely respond with rhythms and music that have more subtlety and finesse.

Two keys to making your body language readable are to be concise and precise in your movements.

Concise

To be concise is to be clear and succinct with your body language signals.

Precise

To be precise in your body language signals is to accurately and specifically express exact movements that clearly communicate your intentions to the group.

Telegraphing

In theater and street mime, to "telegraph a punch" means that when you are called upon to pretend to hit someone with your fist, you bring your hand way back behind you before you swing your fist in a big arc toward the other actor's chin. That way you don't surprise the audience or the other actor. Telegraphing a punch lets everyone know that the punch is coming.

Telegraphing your body signals gives the participants in your circle advance warning so they can respond to the signal in a timely way. By telegraphing a signal, the group is not surprised and their response is on the beat, creating a successful musical moment for both you and them.

Not all signals need to be telegraphed to be successful, but you definitely need to telegraph any signal that requires all or part of the circle to respond at the exact time the signal is given. Some signals, such as stop cuts and accent notes, require telegraphing for immediate group response.

Stop Cut Before, as shown by Geir Hagberg

If you give a stop cut without any telegraphing, even after getting their attention to tell them that you are about to give a new signal, you will likely get a sloppy, fumbling group stop. You will have surprised some of the people in your circle. When you provide a telegraphed stop cut, your group can stop on a dime, likely accenting their last note for emphasis.

A little telegraphing also helps in call-and-response signals, as well as in speed-up and slow-down calls. By pretending to play notes in the air, you can help responders know exactly when to play their notes. For a speed up you can telegraph your signal for striking the bell to push the groove. To slow them down, you can telegraph the slower beat by exaggerating your stick's arc to the bell to retard the groove.

An important part of a telegraphed signal is your pre-signal position. For example, the pre-signal position for a stop cut is to cross your arms over your chest or over your head just before you make the stop-cut signal. The end of the stop-cut signal looks like a baseball umpire's body looks when he calls a player safe - arms down and out, fingers extended and palms down.

Stop Cut After

Most signals for actions are given on the pulse. Because you typically give these signals while players are in the groove, the timing of your pre-signal position is usually half a pulse before you give your signal for action. This prepares the players to react to the signal you will give on the next pulse.

Kathy Quain taught me to count "and one" while pre-signaling to telegraph before giving a body lan-

guage signal. The "and" is the pre-signal body position which is the beginning of the telegraph that comes before the punch. Then the "one" happens at the point in time, usually on the pulse, when the punch makes imaginary contact.

Key to telegraphing your signals successfully is to have an understanding of the use

Drum Circle Spirit

of theatrics and mime-like body movements. It is less about exaggerated movements and more about putting individual character and style into your body language signals. Without this, everybody's stop cuts would look somewhat alike. The more theater you put into your body language the easier it is to telegraph signals. Two aspects to consider when creating your unique body language signals are theatrics and the use of mime.

Theatrics

Theatrics is the art of using mannerisms and dramatic emotional behaviors calculated for effect.

Mime

Mime uses comic mimicry or pantomime to act out with gestures and body movement.

Congruency 🔗

Congruency means being consistently present with full attention to your intentions. You need to communicate to your circle what you are thinking at each moment, and avoid thinking one thought while trying to convey a different one.

Consistently using the same signals for your directions, with perhaps more exaggeration during the early part of a program, makes you predictable. Players will appreciate this congruency. You want to demonstrate the same signals for the same messages throughout a program to avoid surprising your circle.

Predictability

As a facilitator, you are predicable when you make your intentions known in advance, by showing your body language signals to your group. Then they can consistently read, and sometimes predict, your intentions.

Continuity

When your body language signals have continuity, they provide an uninterrupted sequence on which the players at your event can rely.

Facilitating Toward Self-Facilitation

Each time I facilitate the Great Northwestern Drum Circle at the Annual Seattle World Rhythm Festival, we are between eight hundred and a thousand players strong.

During the drum call, when it is time to speed up the groove, I make a big attention call, walking around the inside of the circle two times with my arm out and my finger pointed in the air to let the group know that something is going to happen. Then I walk around the orchestrational spot two more times, while keeping my arm out and my thumb sticking up in the air, to tell the group that we are going to speed up. At the same time, I use the microphone to tell the group, "Get ready to speed up. We're going to push the tempo." I then mark the pulse on my cow bell, a little ahead of the beat, as I speed the ongoing groove to its next level.

$$+ \rightarrow O\,!\,, \; O\,\uparrow \;\; \text{GOOW}$$

By the middle of the event, the players fully understand my body language for attention call and speed-up signals. Then I no longer need the mike, and I spend less time signaling and walking around the orchestrational spot before I lead the group up in tempo.

Near the end of the event, the group is fully attuned to each other and to me. When it is time to raise the tempo, I no longer make an attention call. I simply walk to the orchestrational spot, without a mike or a cow bell, and put my thumb in the air. Then I back away from the orchestrational spot while holding out my arms and hands, saying with my body, "Do the speed up yourselves." In addition to pushing the groove to the next tempo on their own, they can now read the whole group for themselves and know that if they push it further, they risk a train wreck. I rarely need to mark the pulse with my body to reinforce the new tempo.

When a thousand players manifest their one-mind drummers' consciousness by successfully settling into the next tempo, they often erupt into a massive cheer celebrating their achievement. When this eruption happens I know I have achieved my goal of guiding them to success while using more subtle body language each time we raise the tempo.

A special magic occasionally happens near the end of a community event when a circle successfully raises their tempo without a facilitator—a high achievement for all of us.

Strengthen Your Triplicities into Balance

As I explore the technologies, techniques and philosophies of facilitating rhythm-based events, I continue to experience interactive elements that can be represented in triplicities. In each triplicity I find one element to be far stronger and more developed in me, while another element is weaker and less developed. The remaining element of the triplicity is often somewhere in the middle.

Balancing your triplicities helps make you a balanced facilitator.

My weakest element can easily be some other person's strongest one. We each have unconsciously strengthened, developed and utilized specific areas of our personality, abilities and sensitivities. We discover, develop and lean on some of those while others lie dormant.

Most facilitators experience some triplicity imbalance. By identifying our strengths and weaknesses we discover which part of a particular triplicity we need to strengthen to bring our skills into balance.

Questions to ask yourself as you encounter each of the triplicities in this book:

1 Where am I the strongest and weakest in this triplicity?
2 What can I do to develop the two weaker elements in this triplicity to be as strong as the most developed element?
3 How can I maintain that balance as I continue to simultaneously strengthen and develop all the elements in this particular triplicity?

Create a plan of action that will help you balance each of the triplicities in your life. You want smooth growth in each area, thus strengthening each triplicity's foundation. Because each of us has natural strengths, it may not be possible to equally strengthen all three areas in a triplicity. Nonetheless, it is a wise goal to endeavor to strengthen each element into balance. Examples of ways to strengthen a specific element include taking a public speaking class, attending toastmaster's meetings or attending a mime workshop.

The three elements of a triplicity intersect, coexist and interact in the center. Placing your mind and your heart in this center will give you some of the most important information, personal power and wisdom you need to facilitate any group to their highest potential.

Meditating on these facilitation concepts, presented as triplicities, may give you insights relative to your personal skill level and help you decide where to focus to develop yourself to best serve your community.

Balancing your triplicities helps make you a balanced facilitator.

Sunset at Hawaii Playshop

4 Arthurian Facilitation Triplicity

You will need to use the following three foundational elements as you facilitate successful rhythm-based events:

- Tools: Ways to use body language to facilitate an ongoing drum circle event.
- Techniques: Ways to use tools to provide directions and guidance to players in a rhythm-based event.
- Intention: Your motivations for the actions you take as a drum circle facilitator.

This combination of tools, techniques and intentions is the Arthurian Facilitation Triplicity. By striving to master these elements, you will set yourself on a never-ending path of facilitation skills development and personal growth. Developing the facilitation tools and techniques will help you become a skillful facilitator. By adding a foundational understanding of your intention to those two technologies, you will mature into more than simply a good percussion ensemble conductor. As you develop this triplicity within yourself, you will bring valuable service to your community.

Tools ☙

The tools leg of the Arthurian Facilitation Triplicity represents the body language signals that a facilitator uses to provide directions and guidance to players in a rhythm-based event. Once you have a basic grasp of the body language triplicity described earlier, the mere handful of signals needed for facilitation are easy to learn and utilize.

In the next sections, I describe each of these basic body language signals used in facilitating rhythm-based events.

Call to Groove

Call to groove is a way to start a group rhythm, from no one playing to everyone in the circle or some specific subgroup starting to play at the same time. To call to groove, vocally count the group into a groove while physically marking the pulse as a model. "One, two, let's all play" is one vocal version of call to groove. When you do this it is helpful to the players if you set the pulse and pace of the upcoming groove with your voice, your body and your musical instrument before the call. You want to start each rhythm with minimum cacophony and maximum congruency among the players.

The group will almost always make rhythmical adjustments during the first few measures after you start the groove, but there are ways to minimize the adjustment they must make after each individual player starts their own independent rhythm on the same first beat.

Counting the first two pulses "one, two" and then using the last two pulses in the starting measure of "Let's all play" to verbally indicate where to start playing does not always give participants enough time to be ready to play. Prepare your group rhythmically using your voice and body language before you lead a call to groove. Otherwise, you will almost always put some, or most, of your circle into crisis mode, especially if it is the group's first drum circle experience.

A few tricks can make the call to groove less of a surprise and a lot smoother, with less adjustment needed after the first note:

- Play a pulse on a cow bell, starting at least one cycle before your count to groove. Continue playing the pulse on the bell as you count and after the group starts. Marking the pulse helps lock in the groove for the players.
- Step in time at the pace at which you want the rhythm to start.
- Prepare the group for the call to groove by speaking to them at the pace at which you want the rhythm to start.
- Use a series of calls and responses at the pace you are going to start the rhythm. Then, after the group's last response, start your count to groove.
- Have one dunun player start a groove and verbally count the remaining players into that groove.

Because call to groove does not have an internationally understood body language, it is helpful to learn how to say the phrases listed above in the native language of the country in which you are facilitating. A few examples:

- Cantonese (Hong Kong): yat, yi, yat-chai da
- German: eins, zwei, alle spielen
- Norwegian: en, to, sett i gang
- Japanese: ich knee o skinny dozo
- Portuguese: um, dois, vamos, tocar

Attention Calls

Attention calls are body signals that gain the group's attention and let them know that a new facilitation signal is about to be given. These calls are typically given by the facilitator when the group is in full groove. In some situations you can use vocal calls to help reinforce the body language attention call signal.

Full Group Attention Call

A *full group* attention call from the orchestrational spot gives notice to the whole circle that something new is about to happen. Do this by simply holding up your hand with your index finger pointing to the sky while you walk around the orchestrational spot and make contact with the circle.

The following two specific attention calls, tempo-up-or-down and call-and-response, each communicate an upcoming facilitation direction, while simultaneously calling attention to the facilitator.

Tempo Up or Down Attention Call

Body language for tempo up looks like a full group attention call but instead of pointing your finger in the air, you use a closed fist with your thumb in the air to let the circle know that you are going to raise the group tempo. Point your thumb down to let the circle know that you are going to slow down the tempo. You can also use vocal reinforcements, such as "We are going to speed up."

Lulu Leathley Gives an Attention Call

The famous French mime Marcel Marseau traveled all over the world for years and entertained audiences for hours without saying a word. Most facilitator body language signals are recognized all over the world. Regardless of the many different languages that we speak on this planet, we can communicate many things to non-native speakers using only facial expressions and body language. If body language signals are not immediately understood, it is easy to educate a group of players about a new signal by using it with its connected action a few times until participants understand.

A few body language signals mean one thing in western cultures and something entirely different in other cultures. For example the thumbs-up signal we use as a tempo-up signal in most western countries means something entirely different in Australia.

Up Yours

When I first visited Australia I noticed hitchhikers standing by the side of the road with their arms out, their hands in a fist with their thumbs sticking out like any hitchhiker, except that their thumbs were pointing down to the ground instead of up into the air. On that same trip, my American friend and I were dropping off our American business consultant friend at a steel plant south of Sidney. The headquarters sat on a hill overlooking several big rusty buildings and blast furnaces. When we arrived, the CEO and all of the executives had been told of our arrival and were waiting outside to greet her. As we got out of the car, she proceeded to introduce my friend and me to the group of thirty men. It seemed evident that these men had

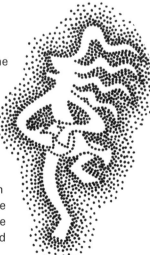

risen to their executive positions from the huge gritty plant below. They were all big, tall, burly men with faces as rough as their hands, which were enveloping and crushing mine in greeting. After the introductions and a few pleasantries, my friend and I returned to our limo and drove away, leaving our petite business consultant friend surrounded by a half-circle mountain of men. As we drove away she took two steps forward, thrust her arm high into the air and made a fist while giving us the good old American "thumbs up" as a symbol of good luck and best wishes. Without a word, my friend and I reciprocated in kind by sticking our heads and half our torsos out of the open windows on either side of the car. We each stuck an arm high in the air and gave two big thumbs up back to her. A second later, I noticed strange looks on the executives faces as the car disappeared around a corner and started jerking its way along the twisty road heading down the hill. My friend and I immediately sat back in the car and put on our seat belts as the poor driver was trying to control the car while having convulsions of belly laughs. He finally got control of himself and the car enough to be able to speak. With tears in his eyes from laughing so hard, he said, "I don't know what you Yanks were saying to each other with your goodbye gestures, but down here at the steel plant in Australia thumbs up means "Up Yours" or "Go F--k yourself." Now I know why they hitchhike with their thumbs down in Australia. Needless to say, whenever I am in Australia I experiment with new gestures to give a circle a speed-up signal.

Call-and-Response Attention Call

Hold up a bell and point first to the bell and then to the circle with your drumstick. Alternatively, hold up the bell while repeatedly pointing to yourself and then to the circle. A drum can be used in place of the bell.

The Whistle

Each time I do a REMO drum circle tour in Italy, we gather volunteers who are potential facilitators. We travel together on the tour for days down the west coast of Italy south of Rome, and boat together out to the islands in the Mediterranean Sea. I facilitate drum circles for communities, personal growth programs and retreat spas on the islands. The volunteer facilitators participate in the circles and take notes, and at the end of each event we have a question-and-answer meeting. By the end of each tour, I create a situation where the volunteers get a chance to jump into a drum circle and facilitate.

One of the volunteers, Giovani, is a well-known singer and musician who performs Cuban, Salsa and World Beat music throughout Italy. Bright-eyed, with a winning smile and convincing body language skills, he shows great promise as a facilitator. At the end of the tour when it was Giovani's turn to facilitate, he accompanied each attention call he did with an ear-piercing whistle, by putting his fingers to his lips and blowing. With that whistle as a part of his attention call there was no mistaking that something was about to happen.

A year later, on the next Italy tour, Giovani demonstrated to me that he had developed a different-sounding whistle for each of the different types of attention calls. With this new development, by the sound of the whistle he makes as he enters the center of the circle, players are able to tell whether they are going to do a speed up or a call-and-response before he gives the physical version of a specific attention call. By the end of an event he is facilitating, Giovani does not need to give the body-signal attention calls. His whistles do the job just fine.

Stop Cut

A *stop cut* is a facilitation action that stops a person, a subgroup or the whole circle from playing. By giving a full group attention call and then giving a full group stop cut at the beginning of the rhythm cycle you are often able to stop the circle's music on a dime.

The stop cut is the most powerful technology in your facilitator's tool box and must be used with the utmost care, integrity and humility.

The body language for a stop cut signal is well documented in "Body Language Triplicity" on page 45.

The Sharpie Catch

At a playshop training, Stephen Sharpe was facilitating a circle populated entirely by drum circle facilitators. In the middle of a particular sequence, Stephen gave a large theatrical stop-cut signal to the whole circle. In the same stop cut, as his hands and arms were making the sweeping movement across the front of his chest, he grabbed a hand

Stephen Makes a Sharpie Catch

full of air and held it above his head in a fist as we all stopped playing. He shook it vigorously as if something was inside trying to get out of his fist. We all sat in stunned silence as we realized that Stephen had caught our rhythm and was holding it in his hand. He then teased us, asking with elfish glee, "Do you want your rhythm back?"

We all yelled yes with excited anticipation. Stephen then gave us a call-to-groove count and threw the rhythm back into the circle. We all started the rhythm on the same beat with shouts of joy and excitement. As you might guess, the Sharpie Catch began to be used internationally as soon as all the facilitator-training graduates returned home.

Exercise: Starts and Stops

This fundamental exercise provides an opportunity to work on three of the most-used facilitation moves: starting a group groove, giving an attention call to the group and creating a clean stopping point in the music. You can use each of these three moves as a full circle intervention. Alternatively you can modify the exercise and use it with specific sections of the circle.

While the group is not playing, each player takes a turn, one at a time.
- Walk into the center of the circle.
- Give a vocal call to groove, such as "one, two, let's all play" to start the rhythm.
- Let the rhythm develop and solidify for a few cycles.
- Give an attention call by raising a finger up into the air and doing a 360 degree turn on the orchestrational spot while connecting with all the players.
- Make a stop cut.
- When the circle stops, walk off the orchestrational point, and return to your place in the circle.

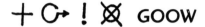 GOOW

Sculpting

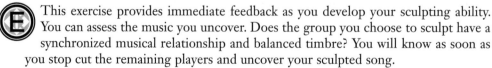

Sculpting is a basic facilitator's tool that you use throughout a rhythm-based event. It is the action of selecting and identifying a person, a group, a drum type or a timbre in order to give specific facilitation direction to that group. That action prepares whomever you have sculpted to react to the upcoming direction. You *only* give a sculpting signal when you plan to give that person or group another signal. You usually use sculpting body language while your event is in full groove. Sculpting can also be effective in the windows of communication. Depending on the different sound level scenarios that you might encounter, you may choose to use vocal sculpting directions in conjunction with body language signals.

ROC   When you sculpt you identify a specific group of your players. By definition this includes some while excluding others. You can think of the sculpted group as your platform, and the remaining players as the rest of the circle (ROC).

Described below are some examples of different ways to use sculpting, depending on your drum circle situation.

Sculpt a Song

To *sculpt a song* choose participants around the circle who are playing a variety of different instruments. Make eye contact with the person who you would like to sculpt. Give them what I call the "Disneyland point" by extending your hand, with your fingers closed and your palm up, toward them. Give the selected players a continue-to-play signal. Stop cut the remaining players to unveil your song.

Exercise: Sculpt a Song

This exercise provides immediate feedback as you develop your sculpting ability. You can assess the music you uncover. Does the group you choose to sculpt have a synchronized musical relationship and balanced timbre? You will know as soon as you stop cut the remaining players and uncover your sculpted song.
- Enter the circle while it is in full groove.
- Sculpt a song, choosing a variety of instruments.
- Stop cut the rest of the players.
- Let the song go for a few cycles.

- Signal to all the players who have stopped to resume playing with a call to groove.
- Leave the circle in full groove for the next facilitator-in-training.

$+ \rightarrow \varnothing\ L, \varnothing\ W, \varnothing\ Bw\ G, ROC\ !\ \boxtimes = LWBw\ \star$

$= $ Sculpted Song, $O\ C\!\!\rightarrow$ GOOW

Sculpt by Timbre or Drum Type

To sculpt a *full group* by timbre or drum type, identify every person in your circle who is playing a certain type of instrument and signal to them that they will be part of an upcoming facilitated action.

By *timbre* I mean all the people playing bells, or woods, or shakers or drums. By *drum type* I mean the people playing specific membrane instruments such as the djembes, ashikos, congas, dununs or bongos. Alternatively, sometimes drum type can mean small, medium or large drums.

Arthur Sculpts Bells, Shakers and Wood

If you are sculpting a small group (ten to thirty people), then it will be easy for you to individually sculpt each of the players throughout the circle who is playing a particular timbre or drum type. It is similar to sculpting a song except you are sculpting each person who is playing the same type of instrument or timbre.

If you decide to sculpt a large circle by timbral group or a drum type, then selecting that particular group by choosing and signalling each individual can be a long and daunting task. It can be long because the players you signal first may forget they were chosen by the time you get around the whole circle. It can be daunting because you as facilitator must go around the circle and signal each individual, and you may not be able to remember who you did or did not sculpt.

Instead of individually sculpting each player with a bell, to showcase all the bell players in the circle you can simply hold up a bell, point to it and make the continue-to-play sign to the whole group from the orchestrational spot. When you signal the stop cut, those playing bells will continue to play while everyone else stops. The same can be done with any other timbres and drum types.

Sculpt by Gender

To sculpt all the men or all the women in the group for showcasing, you do two things. Call from the orchestration spot "all the men" or "all the women" while making gestures that indicate which gender you are calling. Up until recently, to physically designate the men, most facilitators have taken on the position of a body builder by making a fist and flexing their arm muscles over their shoulders. To physically designate the women, most facilitators have used both their hands to draw the outline of a woman in the air in front of them—bosom, waist and hips. After years of discussing the implications of these gestures, I recognize

Yvonne Prepares to Sculpt "All Men"

that these physical signals may imply to some that all women need to be curvaceous and all men need to be strong.

While she was facilitating a circle in England, Yvonne showed me the perfect solution to this dilemma. When she was ready to sculpt all of a single gender, she simply held up the international gender sign used on restroom doors, pointed to the sign and made a continue to play signal. When Yvonne held up the sign for women they continued to play when she gave a stop cut to the men, thus uncovering the women's song.

Even if I am blindfolded, if the facilitator of a circle sculpts a gender-specific song, I find I can consistently identify which gender is playing based on the resultant song that emerges. Experiment and listen to your groups' songs. Viva la difference!

The Rainbow Women

In the sixties, the Rainbow Gathering drum circles were male dominated. They didn't call us hippy thunder drummers for nothing. With little technique and even less traditional drumming knowledge, the guys in the circle would power their way into, through and out the other side of an in-the-moment rhythm into a rhythmical train wreck. They would then start another rhythm out of the chaos. We thought that finger splits, calluses, and sometimes peeing blood were necessary trade-offs of following our rhythmical bliss. By expressing our macho energy through the drum, we were unconsciously excluding women from the circle. The women who *did* choose to play with us would have to *compete* with the rest of "the boys in the noise" for space and presence in the rhythm. Being new to group drumming at that time, I accepted that it was just the way things were.

My first lesson in drumming sensitivity came at a rainbow gathering, when I happened across a group of women drumming far away from the thunder drummer circle. I respectfully sat down outside the circle and listened. These women, like us men in those days, were ignorant of drumming styles, traditions and drumming techniques. And, like us men, they were exploring their group song through what I now call rhythmical alchemy. But the song and energy coming out of their drumming circle was totally different than any I had ever experienced. There was a sense of conscious cooperation rather than unconscious competition. There was power without loud volume. The women were using their notes to make space for each other's creativity, rather than trying to fill all the space. (At that time, playing lots of notes was standard operating procedure for the men.) The result of these combined elements was something little heard in the thunder drummer circles back then or today: subtlety, grace and beauty.

Women in Spirit

Then I heard something that I also had never before experienced in a drum circle. Without a word being spoken, the women drummers slowly faded their groove into silence. In the end, the silence was as loud as the drumming had been, and the rhythms were still moving inside. As I sat in tears and in awe of what I had just experienced, one of the women drummers looked at me sitting outside the circle and said to me, "You can join us if you promise to listen."

Sculpt by Sections

To sculpt a section of your circle you are simply cutting a piece of pie out of the circle from the center. The size of the piece of pie you cut is the size of the section that you want to sculpt.

Kenya Masala Sculpting a Section

Know what section in the circle you are going to sculpt before you start.

To sculpt a section on your left, start with your left hand. To sculpt a section on your right, start with your right hand.

Sculpt by using the Disneyland point to designate one side of the pie. Then place your other hand, palm to palm on your extended hand, and open your arms, sweeping your other hand out until you have included the complete section of the circle that you want to sculpt. The part of the circle you are now encompassing between your two outstretched hands is the piece of the drum circle pie that you have just sculpted. It looks like you are hugging all of them.

| 1/2 | 1/4 | 1/3 |

Sculpting Shorthand

Eye contact and personal contact are essential because your next facilitator's body language signal will be directed toward this particular group. Your signal to the sculpted group will typically be an active one, such as continue to play, stop cut or volume up. This contact is also essential so you will recognize which humans are part of your sculpted group when you return to them after turning away to work with others in the circle. Relationship is a key element of all facilitation.

Sculpting by Concentric Circles

> **Relationship is a key element of all facilitation.**

At a festival we co-facilitated, I saw Shakerman, aka Kerry Greene, sculpt the circle for showcasing by having different concentric rows of players continue to play while stop cutting the other rows. He showcased each row of a two hundred person drum circle. This was the first time I saw this unique way of sculpting. He tells his story:

As drum circle facilitators, we typically stand on the orchestrational spot surrounded by concentric circles of seated participants. We usually view our participants in pie-shaped sections based on the open aisles distributed throughout the circle. I had been shown over the years how to select sections of participants by pointing to and sculpting slice-of-the-pie shaped groupings.

As a facilitator who also is a musician, one of my goals is to enhance and elevate the experience of the group's hearing and perception of the ongoing music. Keeping the golden rule of "have no plan" in mind, I entered the circle with a concept I would present if it felt appropriate and would serve the circle. My concept was based on concentric circles, much like those found in a pond when you toss a rock into it. The result is a series of rings that spread out away from the center. I realized this approach would yield a result that would allow the players to hear and experience the contributions of those behind and in front of them rather than in sections far away that may not be heard at all. For example, the first row of participants would hear everyone playing behind them.

Shakerman Drumming

The technique was fairly simple to initiate. I simply waited to allow the right time and place to present itself, and while co-facilitating at a large circle in Seattle with about two hundred players, it appeared! First I indicated that the front row of drummers would continue to play. By looking into each person's eyes while turning around in the circle a couple of times until we had the necessary agreements. I then continued turning around and selecting everyone else to watch and be prepared for a shift and initiated it with a countdown from four to one with a clean stop cut. This left the inner circle playing all by themselves, and everyone seemed to like it. I next invited the second row to be ready to join in and offered a rhythm that would work hand in hand with the inner circle's ongoing rhythm. Counting from one to four this time, I invited them to play, being sure that I used multiple points in my radar to engage all the players in that second row. I repeated the process and brought in the third row, then after a minute or two, the fourth row. Finally, I released everyone to make up their own after first giving them a big thumbs up and thanking them for allowing me to interject. I was happy to have this first attempt work without a hitch, as sometimes new concepts don't work the first time.

> Like any good facilitator, as soon as I saw Shakerman's unique way of sculpting I started experimenting with different ways to sculpt concentric circles.

Like any good facilitator, as soon as I saw Shakerman's unique way of sculpting I started experimenting with different ways to sculpt concentric circles. Within a few months, the concept had spread like wildfire among the facilitator community and every facilitator I saw used sculpting by concentric circles as part of their repertoire. It is my belief that Shakerman uncovered, discovered and presented the concept.

Continue to Play

GWhen you want a selected group of players to continue playing while you give different directions to others in the circle, you can give a continue-to-play signal. The standard continue-to-play body language signal is to point your two index fingers toward each other in front of your chest and rotate them around each other.

Before sculpting and stopping a particular segment of your circle, it is good to give a continue-to-play signal to the rest of the group. Otherwise, the whole circle might stop when you give the stop-cut signal.

Because my Arthurian body language for continue to play is not automatically recognized in other countries, I also learn to speak the words "continue to play" in the native language of the country where I am facilitating. A few examples:

- German: weiterspielen
- Italy: continuata es sonata
- Mandarin (mainland China): zhi shu
- Swedish: fortsätt spela
- Vietnam: deep dop choi
- Canadian: continue to play eh?

Natural Timing

I am facilitating a team building program with two hundred corporate trainers for a medical insurance company. It is scheduled as a one-and-a-half hour program with a social hour planned afterward. Good music is emanating from a hot drum circle. The group's groove is moving through its transition points to ever higher and stronger rhythmical places. This event has elevated itself to a level equal to a very successful community drum circle. My GOOW spot is a seat in the innermost circle of chairs where I am sitting playing my drum as one of the participants. They don't need a facilitator at this point. With only five minutes left in the program, the group is deep in a great groove with no end in sight.

I am concerned about the time. If this program was a community drum circle, I would typically let this beautiful groove go on until it reaches a natural transition point where I would bring it to a close. But with an upcoming scheduled break, I am concerned that I will need to facilitate "rhythmical interruptus" to close the program on time.

One Way to GOOW

The meeting planner responsible for the program is sitting across the circle, deep in the musical trance with the rest of the circle. Reluctantly I pull her out of her trance to give her a five minute warning. I get her attention by waving my hand in the air. I then point to an imaginary wrist watch on my arm and then hold my hand up with all five fingers extended. Catching my signal she nods yes, stops playing and looks around the room and understands that the whole group is entranced. She looks back at me and with a smile she gives me the continue-to-play signal by twirling her fingers around each other and goes back into her drum trance with the rest of the group. I let the fantastic groove go on for another ten minutes until it finds its own natural closing.

Baba's Memorial

The famous folk singer Joan Baez and I are casual acquaintances. As followers and supporters of Babatunde Olatunji, we met many times at Baba's programs and at WOMAD concerts. After Baba's passing, we met again at his memorial concert, along with Mickey Hart, Santana and many of Baba's friends. Many of the audience members brought their own drums to the service. During the memorial service, Mickey asked me to facilitate a soft heartbeat rhythm with the audience while he passed around a mic to various dignitaries on the stage who spoke about their love and remembrance of Baba. I facilitated the audience of a thousand drummers to a muted heartbeat. Joan came up beside me and asked whether it would be all right if she sang low notes softly at one of the standing mics while the memorials were being given. I said I thought it would be great, but to let Mickey know what she intended to do. As Joan walked to one of the front mics she got Mickey's attention from the other side of the stage. She pointed to herself and then to the mic and gave Mickey a continue-to-play signal. He understood and gave her a nod while moving his handheld mic to the next dignitary. The combination of the audience's heartbeat and Joan's crystal clear heart-wrenching notes created a perfect emotional sound platform for the words of love being expressed for Baba.

Call and Response

In a *call-and-response sequence*, you as facilitator create a one-measure call pattern with your instrument or voice and wait for the response to come from the circle.

The call can be done with a bell, a drum, a whistle or your voice. With an attentive, responsive group of players you can extend your call to two measures. Calls longer than that may push your circle's ability to remember the pattern and respond without going into student crisis mode.

The call-and-response signal is a simple, yet powerful device that you can use to start a groove, to facilitate a musical transition or to bring a groove to a clean stop. You can use calls and responses to synergize a group's attention, especially when working with kids. You can also do call and response with a sculpted subgroup of your circle.

During a drum call at the beginning of an event you want to keep the patterns in your calls simple, while you assess the rhythmical ability of the group. Avoid playing complicated patterns that show off your playing chops, as this can create student crisis mode in your players.

You can do call-and-response signals with a drum stick on a cow bell to keep it simple. Using only the two bell notes: high and low, your signal can be easily interpreted and translated onto whatever instrument the players have in front of them. Alternatively, if you were to use a hand drum, you would be applying specific hand techniques to create any one of three basic sounds: the bass, the tone or the slap. With even a simple drum pattern you may intimidate beginning-beginner players. They may be struggling to model and reproduce the exact hand placement and sounds that you just played. But when you give a call on your bell, the drummers of the group can reproduce your pattern without worrying about the specific sounds and hand techniques. This gives the players lots of room for interpretation.

Some music teachers use the term echo for the call-and-response sequence. Music teachers expect the echo (response) to be exactly the same call that the teacher plays. As a drum teacher, it is also appropriate to expect a response to be an exact echo of the call.

As a facilitator using an Arthurian-style call and response, you may receive a response that is not exactly what you called. You want to accept your group's response without judgement. Whatever response they give to your call will be the correct one.

Arthur Plays a Cowbell

Volume Up or Down

Volume up or down means to either change the volume in your percussion orchestra as a whole, or to change the volume of some smaller group within the orchestra. This tool adds a dynamic musical quality to your group's compositions.

Volume down can be used to help the group be able to hear. With a lower volume the "hearing sphere" of each player is larger, so they can experience more of the overall orchestra's music. By lowering the group's volume, you can also create a space to vocally address the players while music is being made.

To raise the volume of a group, I extend and raise my arms with my palms turned upward, as if I am lifting the group. The higher I raise my hands, the more volume I get from the group.

To lower the volume, I extend and lower my arms starting with them above my head, with my palms turned downward. The closer my palms get to the ground the quieter the group plays.

If I want to lower the volume in a larger circle to a whisper, I first lower the overall volume as described above. But in circles with more than one row of players, the back rows of people cannot see my signal once we get quieter, because the signal is hidden by the heads of those in front. For them, I can create a visual floor by holding one hand, palm up, at a level just higher than the heads of those seated in the front row. By bringing my other hand toward that visual floor, I can bring my whole circle's volume down to a whisper.

Cameron Gives a Volume Down Signal

Tempo Up or Down

↑
↓ *Tempo up or down* means to facilitate the speed of the circle's rhythm to go faster or slower. The key element to facilitating a speed up is to lead the group, in full groove, from one tempo to the next using your body. As the facilitator you are the physical model for the tempo change.

Once you have established a relationship with your circle, you as facilitator can ascertain common denominator speeds at which your group can comfortably play. I call these speeds where the group is comfortable and plays most solidly *tempo plateaus*. Many times a transition point is created in a group groove when the players have been playing at a comfortable tempo plateau, but due to some discordant elements, the tempo has slowed below that plateau and become shaky. You can choose to lead their tempo back to the previous common group speed or past it to their next faster tempo plateau. For dynamic musicmaking, I prefer to change to the next faster tempo.

Tempo up is a great tool to use in transition points where the group's groove has slowed and become unsteady. Most facilitators point their thumb up to signal the group to speed up (but remember not to do this in Australia!)

For a group slow down, you can use one hand, palm down, to play a slightly slower tempo while giving a thumbs down signal with the other hand. Avoid moving the thumb up and down so you don't accidentally look like you are criticizing their groove.

After signalling which way you want the tempo to change, the instrument of choice to lead the change is the cow bell. By telegraphing the drum stick in a wide arc as you swing it down to the bell, you are able to show the group the basic beat of the changing tempo before your stick hits the bell.

Using the concept of pacing and leading, after you give the speed-up signal to the group, you play at the speed that the group is playing. By doing so you are pacing the group. Then you gently push the groove by playing a little ahead of the next pulse, thus leading the group toward the next tempo change.

When the group has reached the desired tempo plateau there are various ways to signal that they have arrived so they don't play even faster, toward a possible train wreck. One way to signal your players to hold their new tempo is to hold your hands out, with palms down, while moving them in an arc that stops at each pulse, thus marking the desired tempo. Another signal is to hold one hand steady, palm down, while using a drum stick in the other hand to mark the pulse in the air. A third way to signal the group is to hold a drum stick horizontal to the ground, while marking the pulse you want to solidify with the other hand.

Accent Notes

✓ As facilitator you can direct a person, a sculpted group or the whole circle to *accent* certain notes or pulses. You mark these notes or pulses by jumping into the air and giving a stop cut body signal on the way down. To prepare your circle for accent notes, teach them the difference between a stop cut and an accent note: do a group rumble and a stop cut at the end of a groove. Everybody will hit their last note at the stop cut. Then, do a simple accent note pattern. On the first accent note, perhaps only half of the participants will play, but by the end of your pattern everyone will be following your body and hitting the note each time you land. Once the accent note has been established in your relationship with your circle, you can create different accent patterns with the group.

This facilitation signal usually directs a group of players that has been sculpted. The sculpted part of the circle responds to your stop cut jump by playing a note on their instruments as your feet hit the ground. Whenever you jump they hit an accent note.

Accent notes are very popular for closing a musical piece or as a way to work with a non-playing part of a circle while another part of the circle is being showcased. You can also create accent notes within the group's music while they are playing if you are careful to give them a continue-to-play signal first. When no one in the circle is playing, accent notes can be directed to the whole circle.

Rumble

A *rumble* is an action that initiates and controls rhythm chaos. It is a very versatile facilitator's tool with many uses. You initiate a group rumble by holding your hands out in front of you and wiggling them quickly from the wrists. The group responds, creating musical chaos, a non-rhythmical noise, with their instruments. It sounds like the stampede of musical hoofs, a rumble of sound. You can direct your rumble to the whole circle or to a group that you have sculpted.

Use the rumble as its own entity or to make the transition to another groove. You can use a rumble inside an ongoing rhythm, or as a musical call for attention.

This is Parkinson's disease. This is a rumble.

My good friend Heather MacTavish has developed a technique called drum~story~song. Using this method she masterfully facilitates well elderly and special-needs groups into playing percussion instruments while singing popular songs from their formative years. Heather has Parkinson's disease, so her right hand often shakes uncontrollably. When introducing basic facilitation signals she holds up two fluttering hands and asks: "What is this?" The group members shout back "Rumble!" Then she holds up her fluttering right hand and asks: "What is this?" She pauses while others try to figure out what one hand flapping signifies. She then shouts out: "Parkinson's disease! Know the difference!"

Heather MacTavish Signalling a Rumble

There are many different varieties of rumbles. Below are some additional uses of the rumble.

Rumble Wave

 Once you initiate a group rumble, then by moving your arms up and down like an actor imitating the flight of a bird, you indicate how fast the volume and intensity of the rumble wave increases and decreases.

Stadium Rumble Wave

A stadium rumble wave passes a rumble around the circle in a way very similar to the way the audience in a football stadium does a standing wave. Instead of people taking turns standing up and sitting down, drummers are raising and lowering the volume of their rumble.

To initiate a stadium rumble wave the facilitator starts a full group rumble. Then she lowers the group's volume. Then she indicates to a section of the circle to raise their rumble volume while the people next to them keep the lower volume. Once the stadium rumble wave has been started, the facilitator can direct the volume wave at any speed and in whatever direction she prefers.

Once your circle has experienced a stadium rumble wave you may facilitate additional waves by simply pointing and turning around the circle during a rumble.

Mime Rumbling

Dirk Iwen, a mime from Germany, used a unique style to signal for rumble waves from his group when he facilitated. First, he pantomimed the shape of a ball. Then he cupped his ear and pointed to his imaginary ball. When he tossed his ball into the air, a few drummers rumbled like a snare drummer might do for a trapeze act at the circus. The drummers stopped rumbling each time he caught the ball. He tossed the ball into the air until the group caught on and everyone was rumbling to the flight of the ball. That's when he pointed across the circle to a player and tossed the ball to them. The group rumbled until the player across the circle stood up and caught the ball. That player then pointed to someone else across the circle and tossed the imaginary ball, to the accompaniment of the rumble, creating a game of toss and rumble.

Layering in a Rumble to Start a Groove

A dynamic way to start a group groove is by layering in a rumble by sections. The volume and mass of the rumble increases with each added section until the whole circle is rumbling.

Once your full circle is rumbling, you can give them a call to groove to go from full rumble to full rhythm expression with a simple count of four.

Alternatively you can sculpt your rumblers and bring in sections of players to the groove, adding sections until the whole group is in full groove.

Layering in a Rumble from Full Groove

With your group in full groove, you can layer in a rumble. When you do this you create a growing rumble crescendo. As the rumble emerges, the rhythm becomes softer in volume and disappears. Here are two ways to do it:

1 While in full groove, sculpt one quarter of the circle at a time and give them the rumble signal, Once that section is rumbling, sculpt another playing section to rumble. Continue sculpting rumble sections until the whole circle is in full rumble.

$$+ \rightarrow \text{⌀}\text{∿} , \text{⌀}\text{∿} , \text{Ⴓ}\text{∿} , \text{Ⴓ}\text{∿} = \bigcirc\text{∿}$$

2 Instead of standing in the orchestrational spot and making a rumble signal to get a full group rumble, step off of the orchestrational spot and walk up close to someone in the inner circle of players, only the people directly in front of you will rumble when you give the signal. You can then choose whether to continuously move to your right or left along the inside of the circle while giving the rumble signal. As you do this, you continuously add more rumblers to the group. The speed with which you move will be the tempo at which you create your growing rumble crescendo. You dissolve the rhythm being played by the circle into a full group rumble, facilitating a very dynamic transition from rhythm to rumble.

Layering Rumble by Instruments

Layering in a rumble by instruments is another dynamic way to either start a groove or introduce a rumble into an ongoing groove. You facilitate by sculpting specific instrument types in the circle and initiating a rumble of those instruments until the all the instruments in the circle are in full rumble.

Teeter-Totter Rumble

A teeter-totter rumble happens when the whole circle rumbles loudly. Then, with your guidance, they exchange volumes dynamically.

To facilitate this, you simply extend your arms to become a human teeter-totter. Your hands are the volume controls. The one tipped downward is lower volume and the one tipped upward is higher volume. By tipping your arms back and forth you direct the two sides of your circle.

A variation of teeter-totter rumble is to sculpt half the circle and give them a continue-to-play signal. Then start the other group rumbling. You can facilitate the volume dynamics between the rumble and the groove in the same way as you would when both halves are rumbling.

Arthur Facilitates a Teeter-Totter Rumble

Rumble Jumps to Groove

A unique way to either start a groove or change from an ongoing groove to a new one is to use a series of rumble "pulses."

First initiate a full group rumble. To end the rumble, jump up in the air and as your feet hit the floor, you make a stop cut that signals for the players to hit their last note of the rumble. There will be instant silence. Then initiate another full group rumble to a stop cut, but facilitate this rumble to be shorter in duration than the last one. Then initiate another even shorter full group rumble to a stop cut.

This process continues until you have an ongoing sequence of evenly-spaced short rumbles that set the pulse for the next group groove. While continuing to facilitate the pulse rumbles, give the continue-to-play signal to the whole group and away they go into the next groove.

Exercise: Full Group Intervention

 This exercise provides an opportunity to practice full group interventions, educating the group about your body language by teaching without teaching. Pay special attention to the clarity of your body language and to facilitating *in the round*.

While the group is not playing, each player takes a turn, one at a time:

- Walk into the center of the circle.
- Give a series of calls and responses or a rumble wave series.
- When you have completed your turn, walk off the orchestrational point, and return to your place in the circle

Techniques ⦿

The techniques leg of the Arthurian Facilitation Triplicity represents the ways we use body language signals to provide directions and guidance to players in a rhythm-based event.

Techniques are used for specific purposes. The techniques described below are utilized over a period of time using combinations of tools.

Sophistication comes into play with finesse in choosing which techniques to use and when to use them. How and why the techniques are used is based on the facilitator's intentions and philosophy.

Drum Call

Drum call is the opening groove of an event that happens as people come in, settle down and start to play together. This is your opportunity to welcome each individual, and help them feel safe and comfortable as they each make their contribution to the group's rhythmical expression.

Drum call can be thought of as a technique that will set the foundation for a successful event. These are the basic objectives while you facilitate during this time:

- Take responsibility for the physical circle.
- Teach the facilitator's body language.
- Define the roles.
- Establish trust.
- Teach without teaching.

- Orchestrate self-facilitation.
- Read the group.

Each of these objectives will be discussed fully in "Call of the Drum" on page 115.

Orchestrational Spot

The *orchestrational spot*, from which you facilitate the group, is usually in the middle of a circle of participants. You define this spot by using the same place in the circle every time you give facilitation signals to your players. By using the orchestrational spot as a group-focus technique you create a place with the power to pull the group's attention to you as you step into it. We will go into more depth about ways to use the orchestrational spot later *In the Center of the Circle* on page 139.

Marking the Pulse

Marking the pulse is a technique for solidifying the groove using your body, and bell or voice, or both, to reinforce the pulse of an ongoing groove. You can also use marking the pulse with exaggerated body language as a way to have the players accent the pulse.

Transition Point

A *transition point* is a time during which the rhythmical relationship among the players shifts. The resulting sounds tell the facilitator that the playing group is at a rhythmical or musical transition point and can use help.

Based on the musical situation at a transition point, one choice you have as facilitator is to enter the circle and facilitate one of the following actions:
- Solidify the groove by marking the pulse for the group, and possibly take the tempo to the next level.
- Guide the group through that musical transition to another groove through a sequence of facilitation directions discussed in "Tools" on page 51. As an example, you can sculpt half the circle and give them a continue to play signal, before signalling the remaining players to stop. The possibilities of what to do next are endless.
- Bring the groove to a successful close.

When you have been called by a group's transition point to help get them through a rough musical moment and have achieved your goal by guiding them through the transition point into another cohesive rhythmical expression, your job is done. If a group of attentive players is fully engaged in an ongoing groove, then by standing in the middle of the circle you are an impediment to their music process. So GOOW.

To avoid unconsciously manipulating the players during drum call, I suggest you only go into the center of the circle when the group "calls" you with a rhythmical transition point. Later in the event, when the group has developed into a fully formed orchestra who trusts you as their facilitator and wants you to manipulate their musical contribution to its fullest potential, you can bend this rule. More on that subject will be discussed in Orchestration on page 173.

Sometimes the transition point develops slowly in a drum circle situation, giving you plenty of time to choose the proper moment to go into the orchestrational spot and facilitate the group to its next solid rhythm. Other times the transition point develops so quickly that you barely have time to go in and facilitate the resulting rhythm chaos into a successful closing rumble. This type of surprise rhythmical train wreck can happen even among the most sophisticated veteran drummers.

Surprise

By the midpoint in an event I facilitated with a circle of advanced veteran players, the transition points were appearing in the music less and less often. The players were well attuned to each other as they supported the ever-changing rhythm. I was standing outside the circle relaxing and enjoying the music between transition points. The groove was so solid that it did not need a facilitator. In fact, it was enticing me to walk to my seat and pick up my drum and join the group as a player.

When all of a sudden there arose such a clatter that I raised up my head to see what was the matter. And what to my radar senses did appear, a horrible transition point is what I did hear. It was bumping and bouncing, what a terrible sound, and I couldn't run to the center before it hit the ground. Nobody knew were it came from, or why, but boy did that rhythm crash, burn and die.

By the time I made it to the center of the circle it was all over. The rhythm had come to a complete but sloppy stop. I lifted my shoulders and arms up into the air in a questioning gesture to the circle with a dumfounded look on my face. We all burst out in uproarious laughter. A clear happy voice could be heard singing, "SURPRISE, SURPRISE" above the roar. As we began to control our laughter, we each in turn chimed in to the developing song. Singing the word surprise at different pitches we created an interactive rhythm pattern that emerged as dynamic and exciting vocal "scat." Although no one had touched their drum since the rhythmical train wreck, the new surprise vocal groove was so solid that it was time for me to GOOW. I sat down in my seat and got my drum ready to play. Before long someone started playing their instrument along with the vocal groove. Soon everybody, including me, joined in and off we went into the new surprise rhythm. Sometimes a train wreck can birth beautiful music.

Platform

A *platform* is something upon which you stand, that holds and supports you.

A drum circle platform happens when some of the people in the group are playing a groove, while others are not playing. As facilitator you can choose to use the playing part of the circle as a groove platform to support your work with the non-playing members of the circle. As a simple example, you can sculpt half of the circle to continue playing and then give a stop cut to the other half of the circle. You can then use the playing half as a rhythm support group as you do call-and-response signals or rumbles with the non-playing half of the circle.

Consider your platform players as a safety net that supports you as you facilitate the other players. If your facilitation piece does not work out, your platform players will be there to catch you with their solid ongoing groove. If you facilitate the non-platform part of your drum circle for longer than a minute, be sure to turn around, encourage and thank your platform players with eye contact, a smile and supportive body language.

Platform for Taiko

I facilitated a drum circle at the Skywalker Ranch, which is part of the movie studio complex for George Lucas. A group of us came together to celebrate the retirement of a seven-time Oscar winner, for his sound design contributions to George Lucas's movie production company.

Mickey Hart's band was the headliner group on the Lucas Sound Stage and my job was to hold a drum circle to close the event, just after Mickey completed his set. Earlier during the event, performing artists had entertained throughout the party: jugglers, stilt walkers, magicians, and a mobile five-person Taiko group whose drums were on stands with wheels.

Since I was sitting in with Mickey's band, we decided to do a segue from the band to the drum circle. The band's last number was an old Bo Diddley piece that uses the clave rhythm as its musical foundation. As the band started the song, my assistants rolled boxes of equipment out onto the dance floor and started handing out drums and percussion instruments. During the song, I facilitated the audience into a half circle of players facing the band and playing with them.

As the band finished their last song, Mickey introduced me as the drum circle facilitator and I directed the players into a proper drum circle as they continued to play.

This crowd of about two hundred people, including George Lucas and Steven Spielberg, had poor visibility because they were all standing, so they were a little rhythmically unruly. I was desperately searching the crowd to find all the people who had chosen the large dununs and frame drums to play. I placed each one I found close to the center of the circle, in an attempt to solidify the rhythm–their low notes emanating out from the center.

Big Bad Bottom Taiko Drum

I was not being very successful when I began to hear what was unmistakably Taiko drums in the back of the circle. The Taiko drum performers had packed their drums away and were enjoying the band before we started passing out percussion toys and forming the drum circle. They got all excited when they realized the performance was transitioning into a drum circle. They ran out to their truck, unpacked their Taiko drums and wheeled them into the circle. Taiko drums are some of the best bass bottom drums in the world and I was glad to have them. The moment I heard them on the outside perimeter I opened a pathway through the standing crowd and invited then into the center of the circle. Their drums were on stands with wheels, so in moments the Taiko drummers were playing in the center of the circle, locking the group rhythm together with their all-encompassing bottom vibration.

I realized that I had a well-practiced professional percussion ensemble snuggled in the center of my drum circle, all playing bottom drums. While they continued to play, I told them that we were going to do some call-and-response sequences. I then stood up on one of my two-feet-tall facilitation cases so all the drummers in the room could see me and gave everyone a continue-to-play signal. This encouraged the circle of players to be a rhythm platform so I could showcase the Taiko drummers.

When I hopped off the box and stopped the Taiko players, I let the other two hundred drummers settle into a groove. Before starting a sequence of call-and-response signals with the Taiko drummers, I invited them to roll their drums to the orchestrational spot, so I could call patterns to only them and the other drummers would not be confused. Each time I did my two-measure call-and-response pattern they responded with two measures played on their drums. Then we would wait a few cycles to let the circle enjoy their groove platform before doing another call-and-response sequence.

As a musical result, every few rhythm cycles a big boomy bass pattern exploded for two measures and then the volume melted back to the drum circle groove.

To integrate the Taiko drummers back into the drum circle groove, I sang a rhythm of continuous quarter notes, which they played, slowly increasing their volume until I did a call to groove, and we all rejoined the rhythm platform: boom boom Boom Boom BOom BOom BOOm BOOm BOOM BOOM TO THE GROOVE... YEA!

Exercise: Sculpt a Platform for Rumble or Call and Response

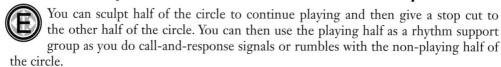 You can sculpt half of the circle to continue playing and then give a stop cut to the other half of the circle. You can then use the playing half as a rhythm support group as you do call-and-response signals or rumbles with the non-playing half of the circle.

This exercise provides an opportunity to sculpt a platform and facilitate rumbles and calls and responses. Each player takes a turn, one at a time.

→ ✛   With the circle in full groove, walk into the orchestrational spot.

⊖ G   Sculpt one half of the circle and give them a continue to play signal, making them your platform players.

ROC ↩   Sculpt the other half of the circle and give them a series of calls and responses or rumble waves.

O G   When you have finished with your call and response or rumble wave sequence, bring all your players into full rhythmical expression with a call to groove.

GOOW   Walk off the orchestrational spot, and return to your place in the circle.

Pacing and Leading

You as facilitator can use *pacing and leading* as a technique to lead the group from where they are currently playing to where they want to go—shifting the group's tempo, volume or dynamics. You will want to pace the group before you lead them to a faster or slower speed. When you give them a speed-up attention call as a warning and then pace their speed by marking the pulse of their tempo, you will more likely have a smooth speed-up as you lead them to the next faster tempo by marking the pulse just a little faster than they are playing. This will help you avoid rhythm confusion, student crisis mode, and the possibility of making all your participants wrong. If you signal for them to speed up by simply playing your cow bell at a faster speed, without pacing the group, you will likely experience a messy group speed-up as they try to catch up to your new faster pace.

Pacing and leading is to *be* where they are in order to best lead them where they want to go.

Similarly, when you want the whole circle to come to a stop, instead of running to the middle of the circle and surprising them with a stop cut, causing a train wreck, you can pace the circle. You can then even choose to lead them to go a bit faster, so that you get everyone's attention before taking them to a finish.

When you use pacing and leading in conjunction with some of the more sophisticated facilitation concepts explored later in this book, you will progress from the level of beginner facilitator technician toward the mastery of facilitation as an art form.

The essence of pacing and leading is to be where they are in order to best lead them where they want to go.

Layering In or Out

  Layering happens when you add or subtract individual players, instruments or sections of the circle in an ongoing musical piece. You can use this simple technique to create many different types of musical and emotional dynamics in your rhythm-based event.

An example of how to start a drum circle groove, by layering instrument sounds:
- Layer all your low drums into the groove first.
- Once they are "locked in," layer in the medium drums.
- Then add the high drums.
- Lastly, layer in your hand percussion instruments such as bells, wood blocks and shakers.

$$+ /// \text{L}, /// \text{ M}, /// \text{ H}, /// \text{P}$$

Alternatively, start with the wood blocks first, then the bells, then the shakers. Add one of the three drum pitches, then the next drum pitch and the next.

A dynamic way to create a sensitive ending to a group groove would be to layer out different instruments, making the groove spacier and softer until there are no instruments playing. Experiment.

Teeter-Totter

 Teeter-totter is a fun and versatile technique you can use to facilitate excitement and awareness of group cooperation in many different musical situations. To teeter-totter means to facilitate two different parts of a circle where the two groups take turns being showcased. In England, and some other places too, they call this technique the seesaw.

As an example, you can facilitate volume changes between the two sides of the circle. You signal to one side of your circle to play loudly while the other group plays softly. Then you pass the volume back and forth between the two sides like a shifting teeter-totter.

This technique can be used by a facilitator to direct players toward group consciousness, by making them more aware of the people playing across the circle from them, in addition to those beside them.

Modulated Sequences

A *modulated sequence* happens when you, as facilitator, signal for some series of musical sound bites to be repeated. The sequence modulates up when it repeats in shorter and shorter intervals. When the series repeats in longer and longer intervals we call it modulating down.

As an example, using the teeter-totter volume example above, you can modulate the volume teeter-totter up by having the first teeter-totter volume sequence between the sides of the circle happen over four measures, or rhythm cycles. Then you can pass the volume back and forth between each side of the circle in shorter intervals, such as two measures, then one measure, then a half measure for each side. The changes in volume between the two sides of your circle happen faster and faster, reaching a rhythmical climax that can transition into a new groove, a closing rumble or another musical event.

Another example of a modulated sequence uses a series of full group rumbles and stops that are modulated shorter each time until they become accents to the pulse of the next groove. Nicknamed the "bunny hop," this technique is a great way to segue from one groove to another. You as facilitator can bring the groove to a close by initiating a full group rumble, and then jumping into the air and landing to make a stop cut. Then you immediately initiate another rumble with another stop cut, and another and another, making each one shorter until you are hopping up and down, like a bunny, on the pulse of what will be the next groove. The players, following your bunny hop, will mark the pulse on their instrument each time you land on the ground. They will use the rumble pulse as a foundation for their new groove.

Modulated sequences require a group of players who are fully attuned to each other and the facilitator. As a facilitator you want to use modulated sequences after the group has reached percussion consciousness and are moving toward orchestrational consciousness.

A key to successful modulation is to listen and follow the group as they follow you, instead of using arbitrary intervals or pushing the group beyond their playing ability. Modulating up creates excitement in the circle. Modulating down creates depth in the circle's music.

Passing Out Parts

When you as facilitator offer participants one or more universal rhythm parts as the playing platform for improvisation we call it *passing out parts*.

When you pass out parts it is important to emphasize to the participants that any rhythmical part that is being shown is a guideline for rhythmical exploration, expression and improvisation. Before you start to pass out parts, you will want to explain your intention that players need not learn or reproduce any part on their instruments exactly as you show it. This will help you avoid turning your drum circle into a drum class, causing student crisis mode in your participants.

Remind your circle participants to continually improvise and experiment with any part provided to avoid locking themselves into the parts, leaving no room for their rhythmical exploration, improvisation or personal expression. You want your players to feel free to express themselves.

Using accessible universal rhythms in an event allows the music to be based on patterns other than the standard quarter-note pulse. Variety in the foundational rhythm is the spice of drum circle events.

Variety in the foundational rhythm is the spice of drum circle events.

If you are careful you can pass out parts as a teaching-without-teaching way to guide your players toward percussion consciousness. I recommend caution and KISS—Keep It Stupidly Simple.

In my earlier time as a facilitator, the only time signature I introduced at a community drum circle was 4/4, unless I knew that most of the players in the circle were experienced drummers. I had seen too many facilitators throw a 6/8 or 12/8 rhythm into a community circle without being conscious of their players' abilities. Experienced drummers were glad to explore the magical mysteries a triplet rhythm like 6/8 or 12/8 offers. Meanwhile, beginners struggled in frustration trying to play 4/4 inside the 6/8 groove, a technique only possible with extensive drumming experience. My attitude about offering a 6/8 (triplet) rhythm changed when I saw Kim Atkinson successfully initiate a beautifully simple 6/8 rhythm as a foundation for exploration at a community drum circle.

Facilitating 6/8: The Beauty of Triplet-Based Rhythms

Kim Atkinson describes a way to successfully introduce and facilitate a 6/8 rhythm in a family-friendly drum circle, by making the rhythm accessible to beginners.

As a rhythmatist and facilitator with a strong connection with African music, I am always looking for a window of opportunity to play 6- and 12-beat rhythms with people. I love the multiple layers of the African-based 12-beat cycle, which at its fundamental level is quite easy. A rhythm that has two sets of triplets is called 6/8 and rhythms with four sets are called 12/8.

As we play with this cycle, we can find many possible patterns and pathways, some of which show up randomly and without effort. These spontaneously created patterns ensure that the simplest groove can have many layers of interest and momentum that will keep the music going for a long time.

The challenge here is that the 12-beat rhythm, by its very nature, creates eddies and currents that can confuse the novice drummer. The same layers of interest that keep the circle going can also pull people away, especially if the main beat, the pulse, is not clear. A most important component then in playing these kinds of rhythms with large groups of people is that the first patterns offered to the

Kim Atkinson

group be stable, easy, reinforceable, transferable and not confusing.

What does this mean?

- A stable and easy pattern does not have many strokes. Four strokes are a good number, leaving enough space between strokes to provide moments of rest for the muscles, but not so much space that the player loses focus. The pattern needs to contain the main beat and one or two contrasting accents. Patterns with a bass note on ONE and/or leading to ONE are the easiest.

- A reinforceable and transferable pattern is one that the facilitator can play at any moment on any instrument to stabilize the groove. This is very important with the 12-beat cycle because of the many ways the group attention can be drawn through the rhythm.
- In order for a pattern to not be confusing, it needs to have a shape that is easily recognizable. For example, the pattern might have two basses at the beginning and two tones at the end. The test is whether people can play with the pattern and return to it effortlessly.

I have found a few of these patterns I like that seem easy for people to hold onto, especially once the energy starts flowing and everyone is having fun. Here is one of my favorite 6-beat patterns.

1	2	3	4	5	6	1	2	3	4	5	6
B		O	O	B		B		O	O	B	
L		R	L	R		L		R	L	R	
dm		go	do	gn		dm		go	do	gn	
1	an	uh	2	an	uh	3	an	uh	4	an	uh
1	an	2	an	3	an	1	an	2	an	3	an

B=bass, O=tone, L=left, R=right   Beat Pattern for Two-hand Drumming

Notice that the two basses in each set form a kind of heartbeat rhythm that leads back to ONE. This is very comforting and secure for all the players. The dun dun and surdo players can pick up this heartbeat and reinforce it right away.

Feeling Triplets: Practice saying and tapping on each syllable "1 triplet 2 triplet" or "1 an uh 2 an uh." This set of 6 beats is called "6/8." Another common grouping is four sets of triplets. Say and tap on each syllable "1 triplet 2 triplet 3 triplet 4 triplet." or "1 an uh 2 an uh 3 an uh 4 an uh". This set of 12 beats is called "12/8."

This pattern works best at a slow-to-medium tempo. This will keep all the layers of rhythm accessible to everyone.

When I present this groove I feel it as six-eight (two triplets), however it can also be felt as three-four, as counted in the last row of Table 1. This "feel" is easier for people unaccustomed to African cross rhythm, making it accessible to everyone. The heartbeat is still evident when you feel the pattern this way.

So, with just this one pattern, we have two possible layers of interest or ways to feel the rhythm. This will keep many people occupied for some time, however the drummers with more experience will probably want something more. I wait until the right time, then I introduce what I call "triangle triplets" over the first pattern.

Many people recognize and can copy this pattern, as it is the basis of many single stroke 6/8 patterns.

1	2	3	4	5	6	1	2	3	4	5	6
B	O	O	B	O	O	B	O	O	B	O	O
R	L	R	L	R	L	R	L	R	L	R	L
gn	do	go	dm	go	do	gn	do	go	dm	go	do
1	an	uh	2	an	uh	3	an	uh	4	an	uh
1	an	2	an	3	an	1	an	2	an	3	an

B=bass, O=tone, L=left, R=right　　　　**Triangle Triplet Pattern for Two-handed Drumming**

This beginning drum pattern is much easier to do than to read.

With the two patterns happening at the same time, there is plenty to keep up the interest level. Adding a bit of improvisation over the top of the groove using slaps and higher sounds will deepen the effect of the groove and really make it swing.

Knowing when to introduce this groove is the most important thing in making it work. I wait until I feel the unity and shared-time feeling that creates effortless entrainment. This is usually 30 to 40 minutes into the session, when several 4/4 grooves have come and gone and the individual players are warmed up and have integrated their left and right hands. The main beat or pulse must be very clear from the outset. For this kind of groove, the facilitator needs to dance and reinforce the time feeling with large energetic movements. As the rhythm cools and locks, the facilitator's movements can become smaller and more subtle.

I hope you enjoy these patterns and put them to good use building community and having fun.

Showcasing

 Any time that you sculpt a single person, or any part of your circle and give them a continue-to-play signal and then stop cut the rest of the circle, the part of the circle that is still playing is being *showcased*.

You can also showcase a player, group timbre, drum type, etc., by signaling for them to raise their volume and play on top, while signaling the remaining players to lower their volume.

Creating Musical Dialogue

Musical dialogue is an exchange of melodic and rhythmical phrases between players or groups of players in an ongoing groove. *Creating musical dialogue* is an advanced technique that encourages more listening and a deeper musical interaction. You can use the following options after your circle has jelled rhythmically into a cohesive unit ready to add musical dynamics to its interaction.

Passing out different interactive parts in your circle is an easy way to set up musical dialogue. Another way to create musical dialogue is to showcase different timbre groups, drum types or drum pitches. You can create dialogue by facilitating listening spaces in an ongoing groove where different players have an opportunity to stop and listen to a particular timbre song. When you bring the listeners back into the groove they will have a tendency to musically dialogue with the timbre song that you have just showcased.

By waiting until your group has attained percussion consciousness before facilitating musical dialogue, you facilitate them more readily toward orchestrational consciousness because they are ready to respond to this level of interaction.

Intention ✎

Your intention is your plan for facilitating rhythm-based events. Your intentions are hopefully based on your mission: the goal or task which you feel destined to accomplish in life.

Your personal philosophy and passion are the fuels that drive your mission. Your philosophy is the platform on which you stand while you use facilitation tools and techniques to meet the needs and goals of the participants in your rhythm-based event.

Your mission guides your intentions, based on your philosophy. Reflecting on your mission will reveal to you new insights about your true purpose in life and how to achieve it.

Create Your Own Mission Statement

Prior to Village Music Circle Facilitators' Playshop trainings, I give each participant reading and writing assignments to help them prepare for the program. One of these assignments is to meditate on their personal mission in relationship to the training in which they are about to immerse themselves. I ask participants to reflect on who they are, why they are taking the training and what their intended use is for the knowledge they are about to receive. I give a one-page writing assignment called the Mission Statement and request that they focus on three basic questions about their intention in relationship to facilitating rhythm-based events:

- Who are you?
- Why are you reading this book?
- What is your intended use of the knowledge you are about to receive?

At the beginning of the Facilitators' Playshop, participants share their resulting Mission Statements with each other.

Writing Assignment

After reading this section, and before completing this chapter, I suggest that you put down this book and contemplate your intended use of the information that you are receiving from it. Also think about the philosophical foundations that motivate you to read this book.

If you sit somewhere quietly and think about your mission, intention and philosophy relative to the knowledge, tools and wisdom you might glean from reading this book, I know that you will get much more out of it.

Write a simple one-page mission statement for yourself. When you finish, put your statement away and forget about it until you have completed the book. Then re-read your mission statement. Notice any changes in your mission, intention and philosophy that might have developed after you completed your mission statement, as you finished reading the book.

If you are planning on doing this assignment then do not read any further, as what comes next may influence the outcome. Do the writing assignment and then continue reading. You may be in for a surprise.

Philosophy to Mission to Intention

Even though every mission statement written by participants before the beginning of a facilitators' training program is unique and special, they all express a general intention that focuses on three basic elements. Although one of the elements might be emphasized more than the other two, all three typically appear in each individual's mission statement in different forms and levels of intensity.

The three general intentions:

- Create rhythmical empowerment.
- Create community.
- Create health and wellness.

These three elements make up the Intention Triplicity. As we investigate the Intention Triplicity below, you can read quotes from mission statements that specifically apply to each element in the triplicity. These quotes are taken from the writing assignments of some of the participants of the annual Northern California VMC Facilitators' Playshop.

The many returnees to the VMC facilitators' trainings write a mission statement each time they participate in a program. It is interesting to note that their statements change. Each time a person attends a training, then goes out into the world and facilitates rhythm-based events, and then returns for another training, their next mission statement evolves and matures much like they do. Some facilitation training graduates have written many mission statements. Yet no matter how different each new mission statement is from the last one, the three basic elements are still typically represented.

Facilitators' Playshop trainees want rhythmical empowerment, community and wellness for themselves, as well as for the population they wish to serve through facilitating rhythm-based events.

My friend and fellow facilitator Sunray has a good outlook on the difference between having plans and having intention, so I have asked him to share it with you.

Facilitating with Intention

For me, facilitation begins with developing a clear understanding of my intention for the event. It begins with answering questions like: What do I want to happen? What do I want people to experience? What do I want people to learn? I usually express the answers in writing. For example, "My intention for this rhythm circle is for people to experience connection with each other, with themselves, and with Spirit." Another example might be, "My intention is for people to become musically empowered through their success at playing rhythms together."

I will state this intention in any advance publicity and again near the beginning of the session. This becomes my contract with the people I'm facilitating and opens them to the possibility that it will happen. Why? I believe that intention is the second most powerful force in the Universe. I believe that when one holds a clear, pure intention, the unseen forces of the Universe align with us to make it happen. I'm sure we all have different beliefs about this, and the explanation of "why" it works is less important to me than my reality that "it does work."

However, it doesn't work all by itself. I always make a plan for the event based on my intention. Sometimes I make a detailed plan and sometimes my plan is as simple as knowing the first thing I'm going to do, doing it, reading the group, and making the rest up as I go. Arthur teaches us to work with what the group gives us. To me, this means continually using my three-point radar (seeing, hearing, feeling) to observe what's happening, comparing what I observe with my intention, and asking if it's working.

Someone once observed, "Our plans are for the amusement of the Gods." Frankly, I've never been smart enough to make a plan I didn't change, or maybe I've been smart enough to change every plan I ever made. I know I will never be smart enough to predict exactly where a group will want to go and what doorway will open that possibility for them. If I insisted on following my plan, it would squeeze the life out of the event. When I remain alert for the unexpected appearance of that doorway and open it, the event can become truly magical. And, yes, sometimes that doorway comes disguised as something else, so, for me, trusting my instincts is essential to good facilitation.

That is why I remind myself each time I facilitate to not be invested in my plan and to be heavily invested in my intention.

Intention Triplicity

Rhythmical empowerment, community building, and fostering health and wellness are the three elements that define the Intention Triplicity. We shall now examine each of these elements, seeing how they empower on both a personal level and at a community level.

Pay attention to your personal facilitation intentions as we take this journey. Understanding your intentions and connecting them to those of the group enables you to create the most positive and successful event possible for everyone involved.

Rhythmical Empowerment

Sharing your rhythmical spirit while making rhythm expression accessible to others is rhythmical empowerment. My personal mission, as well as the big picture mission of our growing community of drum circle facilitators, is to help create a rhythmically enabled society. In this empowered society, spontaneous expression of spirit and life through movement, rhythm and sound is encouraged regardless of age, social stature, rhythmical experience or musical expertise.

Since rhythm is the universal foundation of all language, dance, music and song, this empowerment naturally helps create a rhythmically enabled society. In a facilitated rhythm empowerment community drum circle, our intention is to offer a safe, supportive environment for exploration by giving every man, woman and child the opportunity to express their rhythmical spirit.

Everyone has rhythmical spirit and has the right to explore and express it in any form that works for them. Unfortunately not everyone believes they have this right. In fact, most Westerners believe *the big lie*. That big lie is that all people of European descent are rhythmically challenged. This belief seems to be true for most people who have grown up in societies dominated by contemporary Western culture, regardless of race.

The roots of this big lie can be uncovered by studying the systematic annihilation of many European rhythmacultures during the 1400s to the 1600s in an era of religious repression called the Inquisition.

During this era, anyone not following a very narrow social and religious viewpoint was persecuted, jailed, burned at the stake or drowned as a witch. Any rhythmical, musical or vocal expression that was deemed pagan or gypsy-like was suspect. What emerged from this cultural, musical and social genocide was a Victorian culture where drums were only used for wars and funerals.

These constraints of growing up in a Victorian-influenced social structure with oppressive Western musical teaching styles directly influence many people to feel rhythmically awkward.

As colonists conquered the new world territories, they suppressed the rhythmaculture of the heathens as devil worship. The big lie, "We are rhythmically challenged," continues from that era and is based on repression of expression in fear of judgment and embarrassment. Now the predominant cultural belief is that you must be a professional musician to express your rhythmical and musical spirit. I say that this is a big lie and that it is not true.

The recreational drum circle can be an entry level experience for someone who believes that they are rhythmically challenged and incapable of keeping a beat. If this beginning-beginner player is curious, intrigued and enticed enough to participate in an in-the-moment rhythmical expression event, then they will tend to have a fun, rhythmically empowering experience.

As a drum circle facilitator, I call the process of guiding a person toward experiencing and expressing their own natural rhythmical spirit *rhythmical evangelism*. You need not be an evangelist to facilitate rhythmical empowerment into a drum circle process, but it helps.

Rhythmical Empowerment Mission Statement Examples

Some examples of participants' mission statements, as they relate to rhythmical empowerment:

- "I am an ambassador of the eternal pulse."—Kenya Masala
- "My personal mission is to continue to share my love for rhythm and drumming with as many individuals and groups as I can, and continue to expand my own knowledge of and connection to rhythm."—Kip Hubbard
- "Through rhythm, I assist others to their own discovery of their own personal rhythm."—Barb Pitcher
- "My intention is to nurture the new rhythmaculture in my community."—Robin Cardell
- "My desire is to let out the skilled, confident, caring and highly intuitive drummer within."—Heather Pentz
- "Use both motion and thought to stimulate the growth of new neurological pathways, creating a good and ever-improving sense of rhythm."—Rex Golston
- "I want to experience, understand and share my knowledge of this form of communication with people from all over the world."—Tomoko Yokota

Community Building

During a rhythm-based event, community consciousness is built among the participants and it carries into their daily life. A facilitated drum circle event is a natural community builder. With community metaphors delivered during the windows of communication, a good facilitator can reinforce the natural community-building experience.

Comparing differences is a separation trap. Sharing differences is a community celebration. People call it "team building" in the business environment, or "synergizing" in the

Tomoko Yokota Facilitating Children

personal growth world, but the bottom line is that a rhythm-based event, in its most basic form, is a powerful tool for community building.

At the end of a facilitated drum circle, strangers seem less strange to each other. There is more camaraderie in the population as they have created a group consciousness together. The players have been in constant collaboration for one or two hours, cooperating with each other to create beautiful rhythms and music together. In the process of playing together, participants put into action the basic elements that make a community or team function successfully to achieve any goal.

As Babatunde Olatunji always said, "Drumming is the simplest thing that we can do to bring us together."

Melting the Physiology of Separation

We sometimes take on mental, emotional and physical postures that separate us from each other. It can be very subtle, but a person in a conservative business environment will relate to his or her boss differently than they would relate to their assistant or the janitor.

Where the body goes, the mind and heart soon follow.

I love to get everybody in a small company in the same room to participate in a drum circle team-building program, including the president. During the course of the event I get to watch the physiology of the business hierarchy that separates the president of the company from the janitor drumming next to him melt away and disappear. The simple act of drumming together "melts" their corporate physiology, and they begin to see and relate to each other more as people and less as job descriptions.

This melting of the "physiology of separateness" is a phenomena that happens in every drum circle event regardless of the group's age, culture or intention. Where the body goes, the mind and heart soon follow. Once this melting happens, the concept of separateness in the minds of the players also melts and dissolves. Instead of looking for and thinking about the things that separate them, they look for and think about the things that connect them. In a drum circle those connecting elements are easy to find. They are in the music and rhythm.

Community building is a very good and very important intention to have in your personal mission as a drum circle facilitator.

Community-building Mission Statement Examples

Some examples of participants' mission statements, as they relate to creating community:

Robin Cardell

- "Everything comes down to relationships. When I facilitate, teach and drum, the deep art of relating is at the core."—Kenya Masala
- "Music performance, specifically drum ensemble, is a powerful means of creating a model environment where all participants have a 'voice,' where no one person is more important than the whole, and where everyone must actively participate in order to experience the fruits of their labor."—Kip Hubbard
- "In this journey I have learned that we are all connected. I am here to share this experience of connectedness."—Linda Van Voorhis
- "My mission is to promote wellness in the community through interactive music-making."—Robin Cardell
- "I seek to weave a healing craft for bringing more peace, love and joy to the world."—Heather Pentz
- "I want to feel, share and express the collaborative vibrations and wordless communication of the drum circle."—Tomoko Yokota
- "I want to know how drum circles make some wonderful miracles happen without words."—Fumiko Hayama

Peacemaking with Drums

Northern Ireland is well known for the ongoing struggle between the Protestants and Catholics. Sha, a spirited Irish drummer, started a drum circle community in Belfast after returning from his travels in California. He had been inspired by seeing drumming used as a tool for unifying communities. He created an ongoing email dialogue with me as he started the process of birthing this drumming community, and became an active member of the drum circle facilitators Internet dialogue list.

Sha was hosting an ongoing community drum circle on neutral territory, in Belfast City Centre, so that both Catholics and Protestants could come together and play without feeling so intimidated. After only a couple of weeks of community drum circles, the Workers' Education Association, an adult education organization, hired him to teach drum classes.

Sha learned that I would be doing a REMO European tour and helped organize my visit to Belfast as part of that tour. Just before my scheduled visit, the famous annual Orange Order marches were happening. They were accompanied by the usual riots, protests and shootings. As a result of trouble in Drumcree, the main road from the airport had been blocked and barricaded more than once. We were very close to canceling that part of the tour. Everything quieted down two days before I was scheduled to facilitate, so I went.

Our first drum circle was held at the Stormont buildings, next to the Parliament, which houses the Northern Ireland Assembly. Everyone attending the drum circle passed through heavy security to arrive at the circle, which we facilitated outside the building on

government grounds. Mr. Howarth, Minister of Political Development, attended the event along with six other political executives and ministers. Both Catholic and Protestant community and youth group leaders who had been drumming with Sha also participated.

I made a short opening speech to the group of thirty players, saying that we, as the Belfast drumming community, leave our political and religious affiliations outside the circle and use the circle as a place of meeting in rhythmical spirit to create peaceful dialogue. After the first rhythm, Mr. Howarth reflected on the use of drumming as a way to bring community together and celebrate the basic elements that make us human. Staff members stood outside the circle, watching us play, until I tossed them frame drums and mallets. Given the history of Northern Ireland, a group of both Catholics and Protestants drumming together to celebrate community was a powerful message to present to a divided city.

Sha with his Djembe

That night a Belfast community drum circle was held on the streets of the city center, in downtown Belfast. Only forty players joined in the drumming due to the limited number of instruments available, but up to a hundred spectators joined us during the circle. Sha and I co-facilitated the event, including the spectators in the circle, by using vocals and hand claps.

These drum circles were a prelude to country-wide drum circle programs that Sha developed in Northern Ireland. He facilitated drum circles with the youth in Drumcree, using drumming as a metaphor for peace and understanding. Sha has brought community drum circles to some hard-core parts of Belfast, playing with both the Protestant and Catholic communities, bringing them together through rhythm.

Health & Wellness

Drumming is a lifestyle enhancement activity. Concerns about their health and wellness motivate players to drum both privately and in groups.

In some Facilitators' Playshops I ask the question "How many of you have had, or know of someone who has had a successful acupuncture treatment?" About a third of the participants raise their hands. As recently as 30 years ago, Western medical culture called acupuncture Chinese quackery. Over the years, studies have confirmed that acupuncture is a viable form of treatment in specific situations, and it is now an accepted medical practice in the U.S. and Europe.

Drumming is a lifestyle enhancement activity.

Additional ancient practices that may be effective in certain situations have yet to be tested and confirmed by modern medical science and accepted.

Music therapists know the power of music, but as members of the medical profession they are very careful about using the word healing. While I do not want to appear as a charlatan by making a broad statement that drumming heals, in my 40 years of drumming in community, I have seen some amazing positive changes in people's lives while they were drumming.

Those involved in this grass-roots rhythmical expression movement can testify to the power of drumming and its ability to relieve stress and anxiety, calm the mind and create an expressive channel to release pent-up emotions. The exercise aspects of drumming alone make it a healthy activity. Drumming is one of many disciplines that can enhance the wellness factor in your life.

Health and Wellness Mission Statement Examples

Some examples of participants' mission statements, as they relate to health and wellness:

- "It is my mission to be in reciprocity with this abundant universe; to serve the great mystery of life and share the goodness in any way that I am called to do so."—Kenya Masala
- "I am here to open myself to the possibilities of how my unique assets might influence the world for the better. I am here to continue healing myself, thereby helping to facilitate healing all around me."—Kip Hubbard
- "I am here for healing and growth in drumming with others. We create a spiritual energy that opens us up to one another, that allows us to experience the connectedness that we share."—Linda Van Voorhis
- "I facilitate to help people fill the void, left in our lives by a typically 'spiritually shallow' lifestyle"—Robin Cardell

Music Enters Where Words Cannot Pass

Barry Bittman, MD, a researcher and neurologist, is head of the Mind-Body Wellness Center, in Meadville, Pennsylvania. His research has shown that certain group drumming protocols can positively affect the immune system in your body. He has broken the AMA "sound barrier" by proving that drumming can have a measurable, reproducible, positive impact on many aspects of biology, psychology and social interaction. He shares a story about mind over matter.

Perhaps it wasn't a good idea after all. They smiled and he didn't. They played and he didn't. The group jelled through a synchronized beat that resounded their strength and commitment to living life fully, without him. The young man with cancer just sat with them, obviously detached. The group understood. They knew him well. Each was facing cancer in one way or another, either as a patient or a support person in our Cancer Program.

His stillness touched us that June afternoon with an emptiness out of sync with the rhythmical energy our leader magically imparted to us.

It wasn't an ordinary day at the Mind-Body Wellness Center, and our facilitator wasn't an ordinary drumming leader. On the surface, he was a guest presenter at a conference to be held the next day. Little did we know he was far more than that, for what we were about to learn changed each of us. Our drummer didn't appear coincidently either, nor was he scheduled. On a whim, our counselor called him at his hotel and invited him to join us. Without hesitation and within minutes, he literally bounced through the door with bubbling exuberance that immediately broke the serenity of the Center.

I suppose he was glad someone called. He claimed to have been writing an article for a national magazine all morning. Yet I had difficulty believing he could ever sit still for more than a few minutes. For after announcing his presence (does a whirlwind ever need an announcement?), he literally stormed into the meeting room—an open, airy setting where our group was arranged in a circle. A heartfelt discussion of rediscovering meaning and purpose in life was abruptly cut short by a man who couldn't contain his enthusiasm to get started. Without the slightest hesitation, he ran over to a collection of colorful REMO hand drums stacked neatly in the corner of the room. Frantically, he set to task placing then rearranging them chaotically in front of each person. He continued scurrying about without a break until all drums were in place, obviously according to some order he had in mind. We stared at each other and wondered what he would do next. After finally collapsing in a chair, he took a deep breath, sighed loudly and looked up at us. After adjusting his strange little hat and rearranging his fisherman's vest, the drummer smiled ear to ear and nonchalantly asked, "What is the problem you people have anyway?" "Cancer," our counselor responded in a subdued tone. "Have you all recovered?" he interjected. "No," I replied. "We are in the midst of a coordinated, whole-person treatment approach." While that answer didn't seem to phase him for more than a fraction of a second, there was a noticeable pause and a gasp before he began a supercharged explanation of the history of drumming. Our group didn't seem to mind. In fact, we were all wondering what would happen next.

It didn't take long to find out. Within minutes, there was an upbeat resonance emanating from a group that he might have described as rhythmically challenged individuals. We were all beginners and everyone seemed to delight in participating, except for the young man whose cancer paralyzed his painful right arm which was held close to his body in a makeshift sling. Despite a bit of lighthearted coaxing by our earnest drumming guru, a nod followed by a telltale stare at the floor revealed the young man's sentiment and it was understood and accepted by everyone in the room. While the group played on, deep inside, I wished he'd join in.

I offered him a shaker, a wooden gourd with beads inside, from an assortment of oddly-shaped tools in our arsenal of percussion instruments. He gently waved me off as his young wife continued tapping her drum and nodded thanks with a bittersweet smile—one that fully conveyed their melancholy plight without a single word.

Within minutes, our ragtag group of former pencil tappers and knee slappers actually sounded like we'd done this before. And as our leader, bigger than life, rose from his chair and signaled us for an intensive drum roll finale, our hearts, souls and enthusiasm energized each other and connected us. That crescendo boomed throughout the Center, shaking the walls and the windows. We had become one sound at one moment in time resounding past challenge, past adversity and past cancer.

Yet it didn't seem to connect with the spirit of a young man who perhaps needed it the most. More than ever, I wished he'd play with us. As our drum beats were replaced with smiles and applause for our collective accomplishment, my eyes connected with his and the pain of his suffering. I knew the seriousness of his condition and recognized the despair he felt, as well as the courage it took just to sit with us.

Before I could say a word, there was an unexpected metamorphosis in our drumming facilitator. Unpredictably and out of character, he began to speak calmly and deliberately in a soothing tone that contrasted so abruptly with the wild exhilaration we had just experienced. He seemed to know something we didn't, something hidden in a story about the first drum beat each of us had ever heard, the lub-dub of a mother's heart. He taught us to re-create it with those amazing instruments that minutes before brought us together with incredible resolve and camaraderie. As we played in unison, his gentle words took us back generations to our grand-mother's and great-grandmother's heartbeat. He guided us back through time to a place where that sound was first heard, a place where true balance and harmony existed within each one of us. It was a place where even the threat of cancer could not exist.

And as his words progressively faded and the only sounds that filled the room were the lub-dubs of our hands and hearts, something wonderful happened. As we glanced at our teacher, we sensed it, we felt it and we heard it. There was a new drum beat amongst ours, and it was perfectly attuned to the lub-dub of our hands and our hearts. Each of us nodded, sighed and welcomed back the young man whose left hand tapped in synchrony with ours, an acceptance of the healing connection each one of us extended. That June day the young man taught us something never to be forgotten: music enters where words cannot pass.

While our rhythmical alchemist, as he sometimes refers to himself, doesn't like to admit it, he is really a talented therapist simply disguised as a drummer. Arthur Hull's real magic is in the energy of the music he teaches us to express: a symphony of souls that draws us together in mind, body and spirit.

As for the young man, I'm confident he will never have to drum again with just one hand. For every time a new group of rhythmically challenged individuals seeks to synergize their souls at our Center, I sense the vibrations of both his hands leading us: Mind Over Matter!

Epilogue: Upon completing this article, I pondered placing it in my weekly newspaper column. With respect for issues of confidentiality, I called the young man's wife to present the story, and ask for permission before proceeding.

Just as each drum circle illuminates new and valuable insights, her poignant response revealed the true nature of what actually existed beneath the tip of the iceberg. She expressed gratitude for the article, yet clearly articulated that I had not been aware of what actually occurred. While we had witnessed the young man's transformation on one level, transcendence had actually evolved on another.

The couple had been married less than a year. Advanced metastatic malignant melanoma and its inevitability came with the wedding ring. And while this young woman had been able to cope with the terminal nature of her husband's illness initially, the detachment he manifested after just a few months of marriage pierced her soul.

He literally shut everyone out of his life including his young bride. His silence was unbearable. It was extraordinarily painful beyond her expectations.

The drum beat that signaled

Arthur Facilitating Doctors and Nurses at Hospice Conference

emergence from isolation to deep communication, sharing and mutual support fostered a sense of closeness between husband and wife that endured until his death three months later.

Her story reflects an expression of love that transcends even the inevitability of incurable disease. It demonstrates the true potential of active musicmaking as a powerful catalyst for human support. In the hands of a beanie-clad facilitator who instinctively knows when to get out of the way, practically anything is possible!

Chairman of the "Bored"

Heather MacTavish is considered an elder in our community, not only because of her age but because of her knowledge, maturity and wisdom. She has pioneered new ways to deliver rhythm-based events to the elderly, both those who are well and those who are physically and mentally challenged. She shares a story.

How does one support the restoration, maintenance and enhancement of health, well-being and personal dignity? How does one discover, initiate and maintain an attitude of energy, empowerment and acceptance?

At a senior day center, Peter rocks in a chair, in obvious distress. He is disruptive and demanding, constantly complaining, unaware that he has cancer. Maria slumps in her wheelchair, frowning and unresponsive. A series of strokes have shriveled and tightened her world. Eleanor sits immobile, staring, her face frozen in a Parkinsonian mask. John projects agitation and confrontation. Arms akimbo, he paces constantly, his actions and emotions shaped by schizophrenia. Stripped of personally defining roles, these individuals share the right to thrive, not merely survive.

There is a stirring—tools of change and choice appear. Nesting drums grab interest as they emerge, much like Russian dolls. Hoop drums, each with a compelling design and spirit, are placed on stands. Boomwhackers and frogs add to the mix. All are tuned to the key of C—communication and compassion.

The facilitator now sits on her rolling chair encouraging eye contact and connection. Bright shoes, outlandish socks and dancing daisies grab attention and promote involvement. Instruments of enrichment are being unleashed. Individuals join in partnership, exploring expression through rhythm, bodies moving to the beat. Using songs from the past, the facilitator summons dormant emotions. Memories emerge, wrapped in old songs and familiar melodies. Neurons are firing and brains are rewiring.

The Tip of the Iceberg

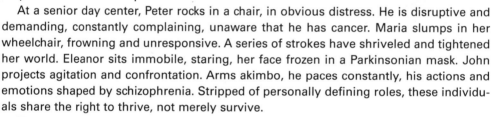

When you see an iceberg floating in the ocean you are seeing less than a quarter of its mass. Over seventy-five percent of it is submerged: an invisible platform supporting the visible tip above the water line.

I use the tip of the iceberg as a metaphor for understanding the relationship of the Intention Triplicity to the Arthurian Facilitation Triplicity. Tools and techniques are the visible parts of the Arthurian

Facilitation triplicity. Together, they are the tip of the iceberg. The tools are easy to model and learn, by watching other people facilitate. Most of the facilitation techniques are also visible, but the intentions behind them are sometimes unseen.

Your intention, powered by your mission and the philosophies that support it, is the engine that drives the tools and techniques. Your intentions steer your tools and techniques as you facilitate a cohesive and congruent drum circle event. It is your philosophy, and thereby your mission and intentions, that form the invisible platform holding up the tools and techniques.

No matter how good you are at using these basic tools and techniques, you must also have a clear intention, to avoid creating an empty, directionless drum circle that is not even entertaining. Without a well-developed philosophy of why you are standing in the middle of a circle of players and directing them, your facilitation will lack substance. Without a well developed intention, the tip of your iceberg may not be very visible.

While having experience as a professional percussionist, performer or drum teacher can give you an advantage as a drum circle facilitator, simply having that background and the tools and techniques of facilitation are not enough to make you a good facilitator. Your ability to entertain, your playing ability and body language skills are only tools. To be a successful facilitator you need to listen to the group to know when, how and why to use those tools.

Facilitating with full attention to your circle comes from an intention to serve the group. This intention both supports and directs the use of facilitation tools. When you understand your intentions, your past experience will not unconsciously steer your actions toward a manipulation that gets in the way of a successful experience.

Modeling the Tip of the Iceberg

Bill (an alias), is a well-known professional player, entertainer and performer extraordinaire. After seeing me facilitate a drum circle at a music industry show in the early 1990s, Bill rightly deduced that recreational drumming would be the next big paradigm shift in what was then mostly a professionally dominated, culturally specific drum circle movement. When he told me of his plans to facilitate rhythm-based events, I offered to help him with feedback and suggestions. His response to my offer was to let me know, in no uncertain terms, that he wanted to create his own facilitation style without my influence. Bill's attitude was that he was a veteran entertainer and professional drummer who had all the tools and experience he needed to facilitate. It looked like a simple job to him.

Respecting his wishes, I watched him facilitate at subsequent music industry events and quietly cringed at the lack of depth of his facilitation skills and the resultant lack of depth of experience he created for the drum circle players. It was obvious that he was modeling the tip of the iceberg of facilitators he had observed. He had picked up some of the standard facilitation moves, but not the invisible supporting elements that make them successful. He was using them at the wrong time, in the wrong sequence, for the wrong reason or maybe for no reason at all. I call this type of facilitation "facilitainment." I watched Bill many times give a performance as a facilitator while manifesting little real relationship with his players. In these performances, he used the tip of the facilitator's iceberg, with his only visible intention being to entertain.

Facilitate in a way so that you are not sure who is following whom.

Several years after he started facilitating, Bill asked me how he could improve his facilitation technique, due to having received critical feedback from members of the drum circle community. Due to the limited time we had together, I decided to focus on one specific facilitation technique with which he was struggling. I told him that understanding that problem and its solution would hopefully reveal the answer to his big-picture facilitation question.

We discussed Bill's bunny hop facilitation sequence, one of the techniques described in "Modulated Sequences" on page 74. From a "tip of the iceberg" viewpoint, the bunny hop looks easy enough. On the surface it appears that the facilitator need only create shorter and shorter rumble stops until the group locks onto the pulse.

So why did Bill create a train wreck rumble closing or else force his players into crisis mode as they tried to "catch up" to his hopping pulse whenever he facilitated this sequence? The reason was that Bill thought the players were supposed to listen and follow him. It was only when I described the bunny hop technique to him in detail that he realized that he needed to listen and follow the players to be successful.

Here is a secret that nearly every Arthurian rhythm event facilitator learns. Only when you work with a group of professional drummers can you create arbitrary modulated pulse rumbles successfully. If you initiate a rumble and listen for the group crescendo to tell you when to do the stop cut, then each time you initiate the next rumble in the bunny hop sequence, you will be able to gently push the group crescendo. You will be able to stop a little faster each time, until eventually you are not sure whether they are following you or you are following them.

One of the secrets to facilitation success is to do it in a way so that you are not sure who is following whom. When you listen to the group to determine how fast to do the next rumble stop, then by the time the group has turned the bunny hop into a new rhythm groove, most players won't be sure whether that last sequence was your idea or theirs.

5 Facilitation Concepts

Facilitation concepts help guide facilitators' actions. By putting the facilitators' operating principles described below into action you will make your job as facilitator, and your participants' jobs as players much easier. These concepts come into play as a direct result of a well-developed mission. They are the guidelines for nearly all the elements listed in the Intention Triplicity.

What Can I Do to Serve This Circle?

Facilitation is a service-oriented art form. "What can I do to serve this circle at this time?" is a mantra that can help keep your intentions on track as you deal with all the elements that surround you in a rhythm-based event. Drum circle facilitation is an act of service to the players in the drum circle event rather than a performance art. The true intention of a drum circle facilitator is to guide the players to perform to the highest level of their ability, instead of giving a great facilitation performance.

Although facilitation is based on fundamental leadership principles, your best possible intention is to lead the group to where they want to go, even if where they want to go is different from where you thought you were going to lead them. You want to listen to and follow the people you are leading. Ideally you will use your radar to receive the information you need to take the right action at the right moment. To turn on and maintain that kind of radar, I advise you to keep an ongoing question as a mantra in your mind as you are facilitating: "What can I do to serve this circle at this time?"

Most of the information that you need to successfully facilitate your circle is in the music and rhythm being created by the players. With a service mantra in your head and heart, you can stay open to all the musical potential in the group. This will provide many facilitation possibilities in every changing musical moment.

Facilitation is a service-oriented art form.

Using a service mantra while you facilitate can be helpful in many ways. Many times while outside the circle waiting for a transition point to develop I get a brilliant facilitation idea. I find that the more brilliant my idea, the more I am listening to the idea rather than the players. The more I am distracted by my idea, the bigger the mess I make of the group's music when I step into the circle to facilitate that idea. If, instead, a service mantra is in my head and heart while I carry this idea into the circle, then I am more likely to place my idea in proper perspective relative to my facilitation intentions. When I listen to the music coming from the players in the circle I am inspired to facilitate a fitting sequence for that moment. Sometimes, by the time I reach the center of the circle I realize that my brilliant idea is not the right thing to do in that moment. By listening to the mantra more than my idea, I avoid creating a facilitator's learning experience for myself that interrupts the group's rhythmical flow rather than enhancing it.

The mantra "What can I do to serve this circle at this time" is especially useful when you are outside the circle. Listening for the group's *one* from outside your circle is dangerous. Sometimes the real one is not a number, but the beginning of a rhythmical or musical cycle. You want to listen for the one from the center of the circle.

Your mantra of service emanates from the inside of your core and radiates out with every action you take.

When you are outside the drum circle, no matter where you are standing, you hear the players close to you more than other sections of your drum circle orchestra. What you hear is a distorted version of the drum song being created. You may hear the beginning of a particular section's musical cycle, but not in the context of the whole group. To hear the drum circle's true one you need to listen to the group from the center of the circle. The larger the circle, the further you are from the orchestrational spot, and so your sensibility of where the group's one is will be more distorted. This is why in large drum circles events I reserve a seat in the center row as my GOOW spot.

Many facilitators, including me, sometimes hear what they think is the one from outside of the circle. Then without listening to the group, they carry that perceived one into the orchestrational spot and do a full stop cut on the players' 2, 3 or 4 count. This creates a very messy rhythmical stop because many of the players are in the middle of playing a pattern. This situation can be easily avoided by remembering the service mantra as you enter the center of the circle to facilitate. This perspective puts you in the now of the musical moment, erases whatever count you were hearing outside the circle, and allows you to hear and feel the full group's melody line and rhythm cycle.

The service mantra, when used constantly in your facilitation, creates a complete gestalt that is represented in your psychology and physiology. It helps you put your mission into action. "What can I do to serve this circle?" becomes an attitude that emanates from the inside of your core and radiates out with every action you take.

Create Small Successes

Creating small successful rhythmical experiences for the players in the circle is a powerful way to educate your group and improve individual self-esteem. Small successes also inspire a stronger group consciousness. You can facilitate a combination of these small successes to guide the group toward maturing as a percussion ensemble.

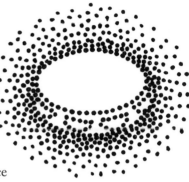

Collaboration implies that the players in the group are dependent on each other to complete a task. You can facilitate short sequences of collaborative events that produce successful positive changes in the group's music.

By creating small successes in the group's musical experience, you facilitate the following aspects of the group:

- Experiential musical transitions that teach the players about specific aspects of self-facilitation, musical dynamics and playing in a percussion ensemble.
- A positive learning environment where the players are rarely pushed into student crisis mode.
- Improvement in the group's ability to listen to each other and play together.
- A higher level of personal and group confidence and self-esteem.

These small successes also help you avoid over-facilitation, thus lessening the likelihood of developing facilitators' burnout for the players or for you.

Accessibility is the key to facilitating successful group experiences to their fullest potential. By creating simple rhythmical tasks for your circle, you generate small musical successes. In the process, you also build a foundation for group learning that encourages larger rhythmical successes.

Making a rhythmical event accessible to the beginning players, while empowering the intermediate and advanced players to express themselves, is a challenge. To meet this challenge, you can facilitate small progressive tasks throughout the event that allow intermediate and advanced players to express themselves creatively while beginners master the basic task.

Play at the edge of your facilitation experience and ability.

Make each step a small evolutionary learning experience for your group. That way each experience that you facilitate becomes a platform for the next step toward your primary goal of playing with a self-facilitating percussion orchestra.

What is good for the circle is good for the facilitator. Creating small successes can create positive personal learning situations for you as facilitator, increase your self-esteem and fine tune your skills, tools and radar.

To avoid "biting off more than you can chew" use short sequences of accessible tasks. Facilitate enough time to play the rhythm between each task to give both the players and you plenty of time to breathe into the groove.

Meanwhile, play at the edge of your facilitation experience and ability, so you can try new ideas, take chances and create learning challenges for yourself. This implies that you will not limit yourself to facilitating inside the safety of your technical comfort zone. By doing that, you would limit your opportunity to grow and mature as a facilitator, while putting your circle to sleep. However, if you are a beginning-beginner facilitator, I advise you to experiment and improvise with only one facilitation tool, technique or element at a time. Then, at the end of any facilitated sequence, it will be simple for you to figure out what part of your facilitation worked and what part might need work. "Facilitate on the Edge of Your Abilities" on page 220 explains more about exploring your edges. Hint: KISS - Keep It Stupidly Simple.

By facilitating while holding the concept of creating small successes in your heart you avoid many of the negative side effects that happen when the circle is forced to take bigger steps than it is ready to take. Some of these negative effects are student crisis mode, unsuccessful musical transitions and facilitator burnout.

Let the goals for the event guide you as you facilitate each successive task toward the desired result. Maintaining those goals will help you stay focused on the process unfolding in front of you. Take one small facilitation step at a time to achieve the goals of the group while creating a successful program.

Work with What They Give You

You, the facilitator, are only one of the many people in the circle. Together you are all collaborating together to create an in-the-moment rhythmical experience. Understanding that idea, while keeping your heart open and your radar fully on, will help you stay in the moment so you can work with the wonderful surprises and gifts that they will give you.

When someone throws a spontaneous spirited element into your event, and you are able to see it as a gift that is being offered to the circle, then you will be able to take that element and successfully facilitate it into the group's experience, as if you and the group had planned it.

If you have rigid plans and expectations as to where your program needs to go and how it is going to get there, then any spontaneous spirit that will be thrown into the musical mix by your participants may be seen by you as something that is getting in your way, instead of some new element that can pave the way to a new experience.

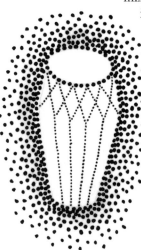

The ability to adapt and be flexible to the never-ending surprises that appear in a rhythm event is a sign of a maturing facilitator.

Dancers sometimes join your circle and you can utilize their energy. I sometimes feel I need to get out of the center of the circle, but the players need someone to mark their pulse. You can invite a dancer into the center to be the model of the pulse for your players. I also encourage spontaneous conga lines, and sometimes even lead them into the circle. If they distract players from their rhythm, I sometimes lead them out of the circle to the perimeter. Spontaneity is to be supported and enjoyed.

Jim Boneau shares a story about facilitating when a dancer appears.

Dancer

Arthur's training includes tips for ways to facilitate circles where spirit inspires participants to express themselves to the distraction of t he others in the circle. My skills with these techniques were put to the test with an enthusiastic dancer at the closing community drum circle of the 2003 Hawaii Playshop.

I was privileged to facilitate the final set of the closing circle of the Playshop. The closing circle is a graduation for the week-long training. Drummers and dancers from around the Hawaiian islands join the attendees of the Playshop to share their spirit for an afternoon. By the last set of this three-hour drum circle, the groove was rockin' and the group was a true rhythm orchestra. The beat inspired dancers of all types to move. During my facilitation of this last set, there was one dancer in particular who was sharing her spirit.

Dressed as a belly dancer, and moving like one too, she had been enjoying dancing in the middle of the circle. She drew in two others to dance with her, and the three were moving the drummers to greater heights. After a while, however, service to the circle moved me to shift the dancers out of the center so I could orchestrate the group to its close. I knew the dancers were not going to leave unless prompted, so I remembered my Arthur Hull training for situations such as this. By my recollection, there are three techniques for removing dancers from the orchestration point. The first technique I tried was to pace and lead the dancers out of the circle.

To that end, I entered the center of the circle and joined the trio of dancers. I then began encouraging them to follow my dance moves—which they did. The four of us joined hands, and I proceeded to lead our quartet of joined dancers out of the circle. Once out of the center, I planned to acknowledge the dancers and return to orchestrate. This pacing and leading worked for two of the dancers, but the belly dancer had different ideas. As I reached the edge of the circle, she pulled her hand from mine and returned to her solo dance at the center. Pacing and leading accomplished part of my goal, but now I had to return to my Arthur Hull training for another idea. I decided to speed the tempo of the rhythm to tire the dancer.

> As she and I were dancing in the center, with the drums grooving and spirit all around, she asked me a question, "Can I jump on you?"

I rejoined my belly dancer in the orchestration point, performed an attention call to the group, and increased the tempo. As the tempo of the music got faster, her dancing got faster—no "tiring out" in sight. I was clearly dealing with a pro. The music was tight, fast and in full groove. Increasing the tempo more would have unsettled the groove and I was not ready to go to such desperate measures. I once again dipped into the Arthur Hull bag of tricks for an approach. What came was this, "Be in the moment and let the moment happen." So, trusting the process, I joined her in the "dance of the belly" to see what would happen. Well, *it* happened.

As she and I were dancing in the center, with the drums grooving and spirit all around, she asked me a question, "Can I jump on you?" The amount of time it took for me to register what she asked was all the time she needed. Not waiting for my response, the belly dancer had jumped on my waist, wrapping her legs around my torso and reaching her hands high into the air, moving to the music. The only way to accurately describe the scene is that she was using me as the pole for her own personal pole dance. I once again reached into my Arthur Hull training, but I never saw the chapter on what to do if a belly dancer jumps on you, straddles your waist, and asks you to spin around in circles, all in front of a family drum circle audience of 250 participants. I decided I had only one choice—to go with it. So I held her hands and spun around in circles. She slowly leaned into a back bend, hanging upside down off my middle. I tried to keep a calm look on my face while spinning in the circle and hanging on for dear life. She rose from her back bend and with a look of complete satisfaction jumped down from my body. Completing my attempt at being in the moment, I got down on one knee, wiped my brow, and used my best showmanship to acknowledge what had just happened. Then I used Jim Boneau technique number one for handling a dancer after she jumps on you in the middle of a circle. I thanked her for her participation and told her it was time to move on to the closing. She agreed, completely happy with her performance and her opportunity to share her spirit with the group.

I returned to the orchestration point and led the finale of my most unique, exciting, challenging and fun drum circle facilitation ever. I was thankful for my training and the opportunity to answer my ultimate dancer challenge in a circle. The story lives now in the legacy of Hawaii 2003. Between the music and the sight of my face with the dancer hanging off me, no one was in the frame of mind to snap a picture. They, like me, were too drawn into the moment.

Disrupting Distractor

The closing celebration and graduation exercises for a recent Facilitator Training Playshop in Japan were held at a Buddhist temple at the foot of Mt. Fuji. One of our goals was to include at least as many local residents as graduates at our open drum circle graduation.

One of the local guests seemed more demonstrably friendly than Japanese culture predicts as likely. We soon recognized that he was rip-roaring drunk. During drum call, our first facilitator made a half-circle sculpt with her arms open wide, facing the drunk who was seated in the front row. The drunk thought the facilitator wanted a hug, so he stood up and gave her one. When the facilitator turned around to sculpt the other side of the circle, the drunk continued to stand in the center of the circle, barely, and "help" the facilitator with his loud, off-rhythm bell playing. The facilitator managed to convince the drunk to sit back down and then she finished her facilitation sequence.

It became obvious to me that this was a drum circle management situation I needed to handle, instead of leaving it to my beginning-beginner facilitator graduates. I saw that the drunk's friend was sitting just behind him in the second row. The friend reached forward regularly to remind his drunk friend to pay attention to the facilitator. Before the next graduate began to facilitate, I did a short facilitation sequence, enticing the drunk to stand up and hug me as well. If we had hugged for too long, his alcohol breath would have been enough to make me drunk. While the drunk was standing, by moving his chair, I signalled for the drummer sitting next to the drunk's friend to get up and come forward. I then placed the drunk in the vacant seat next to his friend, traded his loud bell for a drum, and signalled for the other drummer to sit in the vacant front-row seat. The drunk now sat next to his companion and two seats from any aisle.

His friend helped us keep the drunk somewhat under control for the remainder of the event. Although not belligerent, throughout the program he created all kinds of distractions that challenged the graduating facilitators. Had the drunk's behavior been more extreme, I might have waited for the right moment to ask his companion to lead him out of the circle. But this was Japan and he was not causing enough trouble for me to have him removed and cause him to lose face. Also, for me as a participant, the drunk was fun to watch. He was not causing any train wrecks, and was offering a good balance of challenging distractions and random factors for the beginning-beginner facilitators.

At the close of the circle, we thanked the guests as they left. I then critiqued the event with the graduates and we debriefed. When we discussed the presence of the drunk, I told them that he was a blessing in disguise from the gods. He represented three types of challenges that facilitators encounter in drum circles. He was an unconscious distractor, a random factor disrupter and the kid who would not behave.

Following the Group That's Following You

Our task as rhythm evangelists is to follow the players who think they are following us and use the energy and spirit they give us. When we do this, we all lead each other down the path to magical musicmaking. That happened for Christine Stevens and me at the first international music therapy conference.

Christine Stevens is a music therapist who regularly facilitates drum circles at music therapy conferences, which are traditionally sponsored by REMO Drums. She and I have an evolving facilitation relationship that has been developing since she participated in my first large public facilitator training at the music therapy conference in Saint Louis, Missouri in 1992. She

Follow the players who think they are following you.

was one of two hundred participants in that program and I did not meet her in person until a few years later at a male-dominated facilitated drum circle at the Percussion Arts Society Convention (PASIC).

All the facilitators took turns jumping into the circle to show their talents. I was surprised to see this highly charismatic female sprite facilitating a dynamic drum circle sequence as well as or better than her male counterparts. At that time I had a personal relationship with most of the community drum circle facilitators in our small but growing community, but I had never really seen or heard of Christine before this. After she completed her turn facilitating the PASIC drum circle, I walked up to her and asked, "Where did you learn to facilitate like that?" Her simple answer was "from you."

At every subsequent music therapy conference, when I facilitated rhythm circles I invited Christine to jump in and facilitate a sequence. Eventually it was time for us to truly co-facilitate a complete music therapy conference together as equal partners. This happened to be the first international music therapy conference ever held.

This program was a big step for both Christine and me for many reasons. For me, it was about sharing the responsibility of facilitating a drum circle event with other people. In this program, I trusted Christine's facilitation skills enough to let go of the safe "your turn, my turn" style of co-facilitation and embrace a truly collaborative process. For Christine, it was both an acknowledgment from me concerning her mastery of her facilitation skills, and a passing of the torch from me to her as she became a major rhythm event facilitator for the music therapy community from that time forward.

Christine and I spent about an hour carefully planning and walking through the progressive steps of the drum circle program that we would facilitate that night. We had each developed a relationship with this music therapy community over many years. They had become a group that embraced rhythm-based events as a part of their professional practice and as a part of their lifestyle.

Many of the excited participants came so early to the venue that they helped us set up the chairs and place the REMO instruments for the program. The ballroom filled quickly with eight hundred excited drum circle music therapists from all over the world, mostly women. They immediately sat down, started playing and were in full groove within min-

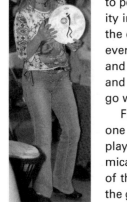

utes. The drum call went as planned but soon the experience developed beyond any program that Christine and I had envisioned.

These players evolved from playing as individuals to group consciousness to percussion ensemble in the first half hour of the event. Spirit and spontaneity infused the whole program. Every few minutes some one or some part of the circle threw a new rhythmical, vocal or body movement into the mix and everyone in the group would respond. At a point early in the event, Christine and I looked at each other and acknowledged that we had a tiger by the tail and that we would throw all our careful facilitation plans out the window and go with the flow.

Flow it did. Every once in a while we were flying like a flock of seagulls in one musical direction and a new element would be introduced by one of the players. Within a heartbeat, the whole flock would respond by taking a rhythmical dip and then flying off in another musical direction. For the remainder of the program, we facilitators were following the spontaneous impulses of the group and were helping facilitate the group's responses into their evolving

Christine Stevens musical sequences.

Instead of Christine and me giving this group a roller-coaster rhythm ride, the "one heart, one mind" drum circle gave us the roller-coaster ride. It was a truly remarkable and magical evening for everyone involved.

Respect and Use the Transition Points

An essential concept of Arthurian-style facilitation is recognizing, respecting and using the rhythmical transition points of your drum circle. This section describes when and why you will want to enter an ongoing circle to facilitate.

By listening to the group's music, you can understand their playing consciousness and their level of rhythmical connection at any point in their musical relationship. The transition point reflects the quality of the group's rhythm and music as it changes from a cohesive group connection to become more fragmented.

A transition point is an invitation by the players to you, as facilitator, to step into the orchestrational spot to help guide the group's music to a successful conclusion or through that transitional point to the next rhythm. You can use many of the facilitation tools and concepts to guide them.

If it ain't broke, don't fix it.

When you respect the transition point you avoid entering the circle when their groove is fully engaged, connected and steady. There is an old saying, "If it ain't broke, don't fix it." In Arthurian facilitation, this saying tells you that if the group's music and rhythm is good and there is no transition point, then the participants don't need your facilitation skill. What should you do? Sit down and play or step out of the circle (GOOW).

Get Out Of Their Way (GOOW)

This section describes when and why you will want to leave the center of the circle. Your role as facilitator is no more and no less important than each player in your drum circle. The better you are at facilitating the group toward playing their own music, the less you need to stand in the middle of the circle.

When you do your facilitation job right, you get called into the center of the circle when you hear, feel and see that the rhythm is a little shaky. With a few short facilitation sequences, you adjust or redirect the group's music to more solid ground. Once the group is playing a steady groove and the music is good, why would you still be standing in the middle of their drum circle? Get out of their way!

If we were being precise, GOOW would be GOOTW, but when you read or say GOOW aloud it sounds like "go." Go is exactly what you need to do when you have no real reason to be in the orchestrational spot. "You GOOW girl!" Imagine trying to use GOOTW. It would be almost impossible to pronounce and would not sound right. "You GOOTW girl!" See what I mean?

Your role as facilitator is no more and no less important than each player.

If you stand in the middle of the circle when the circle's groove is solid and the music sounds and feels good, you are standing in everybody's way. You block both the players' view and their ability to hear those who are across from them in the circle, and by doing so you take the group's focus away from their music. You want the players to focus their attention on the people around them to create the best relationship for playing together. When the music is good and they don't need your guidance, then GOOW.

Jonathan Murray, a community builder and facilitator who helped create the Drum Circle Facilitators Guild (DCFG), shares his thoughts about GOOW.

Why Do We GOOW?

"Why do we GOOW? We get out of the way because as much as we hate to admit it, it's not about us; it's about them. We are not in the drum circle to perform or showcase our-

selves. As a facilitator I work to empower the group with their own organically derived successes. I slip in some tricks occasionally to keep things moving, or to slow them down to give people a little break. I want them to enjoy the experience they are having and the music they are making."

"How much do we GOOW? As much as the circle allows. Playing with a drumming-community drum circle potentially allows you to GOOW more than at a family community (small kids with their parents) or at a transient circle, where players are continually coming and going. In the latter case, you will probably have transition points appear more frequently."

Keep GOOWing

by Cameron Tummel

"Getting Out Of the Way" also enables the facilitator to gather new information. Whenever you are facilitating within the circle, you are likely to be busy, and only able to receive a certain amount of feedback and information from the group. If you GOOW—aaaaall the way outside the circle—you have an opportunity to listen with a new perspective. Not only does it give you a moment to rest, but there is always new information to be heard, seen or felt.

Another very important aspect of good GOOWing is the message it sends to the group. As the leader, if you are comfortable leaving the orchestration spot, the message to the group is: "You can do it!" The participants realize they are not dependent upon you, and that you trust them to make their own music. By Getting Out of their Way, you are empowering their process.

Constantly Use Your Radar

To properly read the circle you want to develop and use your peripheral sensibilities. The three peripheral reading tools—vision, hearing and feeling—function together as your radar. You want to constantly develop and fine tune the use of your radar to read your rhythm circle. A well-balanced radar gives you all the information you need to best serve the group you are facilitating.

The more information you have available, the more choices you will have.

You want to gather as much information as possible about the musical, psychological and physiological environment of the drum circle that surrounds you. When you use your radar to quantify the group and their music, you want to be a sponge absorbing even the most insignificant pieces of information available. The more information you have available, the more choices you will have and the more effective your facilitation will be.

You can calibrate your radar using the constant flow of information you receive from your circle. This information tells you when, where, how and why to use your technical skills. All of your knowledge of facilitation tools and techniques is useless unless you know when, where, how and why to use them. This wisdom comes from the circle itself.

If you are not consciously reading your circle at all times using your radar, then your facilitation may be blind manipulation rather than a mutual collaboration with the group.

Because most of the information that you use to facilitate comes to you while you are in the center of the circle, some of it will always be coming to you from behind or from either side. While standing on the orchestrational spot you want to facilitate in the round. Using all your peripheral sensibilities while facilitating in the round gives you the ability read the whole circle at any one time.

In the fields of martial arts and shamanism, as well as in some other spiritual practices, students develop these three peripheral sensibilities to become more aware, sensitive and responsive to the environment that surrounds them. When you facilitate, the environment that surrounds you is a living, breathing, interactive entity called a drum circle. Developing your radar with this kind of responsive sensitivity will help you react to emerging situations with maximum speed and clarity of purpose.

Radar Triplicity

With a fully functioning radar, you calmly use your peripheral sensibilities to receive all the information you need to be a dynamic facilitator. The three elements that make up the Radar Triplicity are described below. They are the natural survival sensibilities that both humans and other animals possess, but as humans we generally have not developed them as far as we might. The more you become aware of your peripheral senses, the more you can develop them as automatic information receivers. This frees your mind to evaluate and use the incoming information.

You can then use these three peripheral sensibilities as tools to consciously attain and maintain a calm meditative state while facilitating a dynamic, interactive rhythmical relationship among a group of interdependent players. Be the calm eye in the center of the drum circle tornado that is spinning around you and the tornado's song will become rhythmical music.

Visual

With regular vision, every time you look directly at something in your circle, you see it to the exclusion of almost everything else. This regular vision takes you outside yourself to access a specific piece of visual information that is important to your facilitation of a drum circle event. You are *looking out* when you look for the person whom you can hear playing off beat or too loudly, or who is offering a particular rhythmical contribution that you would like to showcase. Sometimes this type of direct vision can be a distraction and peripheral vision could be more effective.

Using peripheral vision, every object in your field of vision has equal importance. With peripheral vision, instead of looking outside yourself to access a specific piece of information, you let all the visual information in front of you come through your eyes. Developing the attitude that you are a visual sponge will help you enhance your peripheral vision.

From the orchestrational spot, you are much better able to read the whole group with peripheral vision than with direct vision. With peripheral vision you need only *three looks in the round* to get a visual fix of your whole circle. As you fine tune your peripheral vision and mature in your role as facilitator, you will be able to prioritize the information you receive and choose what needs your specific visual attention.

Even if you could turn off your hearing and feeling senses, you could still know when the circle reaches a musical transition point by using your peripheral vision. Players provide visual cues in their body language as they start looking around with concerned faces for a better rhythmical connection or for your facilitation help. You can also tell what percentage of the group is at the transition point because with peripheral vision you can read all the bodies in front of you equally at the same time.

When you have mastered peripheral vision, not only do you see every object that is in your field of vision equally, but you see the space between those objects equally as well. This "three looks" concept also works well with the two other peripheral sensibilities.

The Hair on the Back of Their Necks

I am sitting in the back of the room monitoring a meeting of fifty partners of a large financial firm at a very exclusive five-star corporate retreat. As part of their job description, each participant daily handles financial transactions that range into the tens of millions of dollars. I am scheduled to facilitate a rhythm event using activities and metaphors that reinforce the presentation now being given by the president and founder of the company. While taking notes as the president talks, I am also making mental notes on the demographics of the partners—all male, middle 50s to 60 years of age, comfortably seated and attentive. As the president finishes his presentation with a question-and-answer session, the group sits up a little straighter in their seats. This is an opportunity to talk directly to the boss, and the partners bring up specific issues and concerns.

As the question-and-answer session winds to a close, the president takes one more question. That person asks a question I don't fully understand, but it concerns the partners' revenue percentages in certain types of transactions. As the question is being asked, I watch with my peripheral vision. All fifty heads straighten and rise in attention. The movement is very slight, but because it is compounded by the whole group moving as one body, it makes me consider its implications. In subtle corporate body language, this group movement is the equivalent of everyone in the group sitting on the edge of their seats or having all the hairs on the back of their necks sticking out in anticipation. The president looks at his watch and responds that the answer to that question would be too complicated to answer at this time. I watch fifty heads slump back down in disappointment.

As the meeting closes and the partners head into the next room for my presentation, I quickly walk up to the president and tell him that, as a part of my facilitation job, I read the body language of any group that I facilitate. I then proceed to describe to him what I observed concerning the group's reaction to that particular question. He asks, "Did you really 'see' that?" When I say yes, he says, "Thank you. We have a change of plan."

As we walk in to the next room together, I see all the partners seated in the standard concentric circles of chairs ready for my presentation. All the drums and percussion equipment are hidden from view under the side tables draped with tablecloths. The president walks briskly in front of me to the center of the circle and instead of introducing me, he says to the group that, on second thought, he will make the time to address the partners' percentage question. I didn't need a well-developed sense of peripheral vision to see every man in the circle of partners sit up in their seats and pay close attention.

Auditory 🗨

The sounds that a group of people make when they are playing drums and percussion instruments together carries a lot of information about how well they are playing together. To get a good read of the group's technical and playing ability you want to listen to the group as a whole, instead of merely listening to individual players.

With peripheral hearing you listen to all the sounds entering your ears at once. Listen for the softest sound in your circle. Then listen for the loudest sound. When you listen for specific sounds you are using direct hearing: listening only to the prominent notes played on individual instruments played in the circle. When you use peripheral hearing, you are hearing the loudest sound, the softest sound and all the other sounds between at the same time with equal clarity. Peripheral hearing is the best way to hear the whole circle.

Sometimes it is the space between the notes that holds the magic.

To activate your peripheral hearing, be an audio sponge. Soak up the group song with your ears, rather than listening for it. With peripheral hearing you are better able to hear the group's total song. Their song tells you how your group is doing on many levels: technical, rhythmical, musical and emotional. This is the kind of information that you need at any given time to facilitate the group's rhythm, music and energy successfully.

Once you master the use of peripheral hearing, you are also able to hear the empty space between the notes in the music. Sometimes it is this space between the notes that holds the magic.

Exercise: Finding the Whole

I designed this fun exercise to help you develop your peripheral hearing in a very clear and specific way that also gives you immediate feedback.

Twenty is the ideal number for this exercise, as you want a full groove and each player will take a turn for two to three minutes. As facilitator, explain the steps first and show how to do the exercise by walking through them.

Then, start a nice mellow groove using all drums, to help solidify the groove into a gentle melody line. To avoid playing a fast syncopated rhythm, facilitate the group to play a relaxed groove. The heartbeat rhythm works very well for this. Once the group is in their groove, no further facilitation is needed.

The steps for your participants are described next:

- It is your turn once the person to your right finishes their turn, sits down, starts playing and fully integrates their rhythm into the groove. Wait to start until you hear that

their drumming is a part of the group rhythm.
- Stop playing and listen to the drum song from your seat.
- Stand up in front of your seat and listen to the group drum song.
- Step slowly toward the center of the circle. With each step notice the changes in the drum song that you hear as you near the orchestrational spot.
- When you reach the orchestrational spot, turn around and face your empty seat in the circle. Notice the difference between what you heard while standing in the orchestrational spot with your back to your seat and what you now hear while facing your seat from the middle of the circle.
- Still facing your seat, close your eyes. Quantify what you are hearing.
- With your eyes still closed, begin turning to your right while still standing on the orchestrational spot. With every step that you turn, notice how the sound changes.
- Stop turning when you think that you are once again facing your seat in the drum circle. You will recognize that you are facing your seat if you can identify the particular version of the drum song that you quantified when you first closed your eyes before you began to turn.
- With your eyes still closed, point to your seat.
- Open your eyes and see how well you did. You may be pointing at your empty seat. If so, congratulations! Or you may find yourself pointing at one of your drumming friends a few seats away from yours.
- Quickly walk back to your seat, sit down and begin to play with the group so the person on your left can take their turn.

Yes! In this exercise you are quantifying where the hole is in the circle. Your seat is the only place from which sound is not emanating. To find the hole in the circle, you must listen to the *whole circle*.

Kinesthetic

Your kinesthetic sensibility is the use of your physical body to feel the music. Peripheral feeling is more than what you feel with your hands. It includes what you feel with your whole body. Strong kinesthetic vibrations permeate the general proximity of any active rhythm circle. Your body is immersed in these vibrations like a fish in water. You can receive a massive amount of information from that vibrational aura using your peripheral feeling radar.

Ability to peripherally feel surroundings is the doorway to personal intuition.

Kinesthetic learners learn best by moving their bodies, activating their large and small muscles as they learn. These are the "hands-on learners" and the "doers" who concentrate better and learn more easily when movement is involved.

The first time I facilitated a group of totally deaf children, I embarrassed myself by telling them through my interpreter to "use your body as your ears." They all laughed. Peripheral feeling is what they have been using all of their life in order to compensate for their lack of hearing. Peripheral feeling is second nature to a totally deaf person. With the many hearing-impaired groups that I have had the privilege to facilitate, I have observed that they are using their eyes to "see" the rhythm being played and their bodies to "feel" the music.

Some people think as well with their bodies as they do with their minds. If you are the type of person who has gut feelings that are right most of the time, then you most likely have already developed a very receptive peripheral sensibility. My ability to peripherally feel my surroundings is the doorway to my personal intuition. Many times my body feels some piece of information coming from the circle's musical vibration. I then find myself reacting to that feeling by facilitating an appropriate transition before my mind can get in the way.

With a fully functioning radar, you can use your three peripheral sensibilities to receive the information you need to be a dynamic facilitator. Use your sensibilities to consciously generate and maintain a calm meditative state while facilitating an exciting interactive rhythmical relationship among your players.

Kinesthetic Bath Exercise

 Take turns walking into the orchestrational point of your circle while it is in full groove. Closing your eyes, plug your ears with your fingers and turn on your peripheral feeling. Let your body be immersed in the kinesthetic vibration that permeates the air around you. What do you read? Can you feel the song?

For us seeing people, our peripheral feeling is not as well developed as it is for a person who is totally deaf or blind. A good way to start your peripheral feeling training is by having your body "listen" for the kinesthetic vibration that comes from the low drums in the circle. Once you are able to separate what you hear from what you feel, then let your body "listen" for the overall sonic compression created by all the players in the group. Once you are able to feel that continuously fluctuating physical sound wave, recognize that your body is listening to the kinesthetic drum circle song. Your body is experiencing that physical song through peripheral feeling. That kinesthetic drum circle song is packed with important facilitation information that is not readily accessible through your vision or hearing.

Auditory and Kinesthetic Exercise

 Do the "Exercise: Finding the Whole" on page 103, but cheat this time. Add the use of your kinesthetic peripheral sensibilities and see how much easier the exercise is.

Seeing Without Sight

When I met an acquaintance in my local grocery store she introduced me to her blind friend Pam. As we were being introduced I reached out and took Pam's hand and held it. As we talked, Pam reached out her other hand and held my arm at the elbow. As the conversation continued, I reciprocated the gesture by putting my other hand on her elbow. When we said goodbye Pam said, "Thanks for the touch." I did not see Pam again until a month later as I was driving out of the same grocery store parking lot onto the main street. In front of me, a woman with a white cane was gingerly walking parallel to the sidewalk in the middle of the street. Cars were slowing down and driving around her, as she was walking in their lane. I immediately stopped my car, flicked on my emergency blinker lights and ran out to the woman walking in the street. While putting one hand on her shoulder from behind and the other hand on her elbow I said to her, "You are walking in the middle of the street. May I help you get to the sidewalk?" As I guided her to safety she said, "Thank you, Arthur. Some kids in a car confused me by yelling and throwing something at me while I was in the crosswalk." It wasn't until she spoke that I recognized that it was Pam. In my concern for the situation, it wasn't until we got out of the street that I realized that she had recognized who I was and called me by my name. I said to her, "I am amazed that you could remember who I was after hearing my voice only once, a month ago." Pam's response to me was, "It wasn't your voice that I recognized, Arthur. It was your touch."

Points on your Radar

If you are a beginner facilitator, start developing your radar by being equally aware of three specific equidistant points in the circle at the same time. These might be three people or the instruments they are playing. Consciously deliver your attention and presentation to these three areas as you facilitate. Throughout your event you can constantly move these three attention points around to different players in the circle. Remember to keep the three points equidistant. In your windows of communication you will want to address the general area around each point equally. As you develop your radar, you can add more focal points until all the people and their instruments became equal references. You goal is to be able to read not only every player and what they play, but all the spaces between the people and between their notes. When you accomplish this, your radar will be functioning at a high level of mastery. No matter where you start, developing and fine tuning your radar is a never-ending process. You will continue to hear, see and especially feel more as you learn.

Three-Point Radar Sculpting Exercise

Use this exercise to help you develop your radar. Choose three players to continue to play their song after you stop cut the other players in your circle. Choose players who are spaced equidistantly around the circle, like the three points of a triangle.

The locations of the second and third players are determined by the location of the first player you choose. While the circle is in full groove, listen to your first choice while you select the second player. Then, listen to those two players while choosing the third person who will continue to play. This activity encourages you to listen to specific players in an ongoing groove, even when they may be located behind you.

1 Enter the circle while it is in full groove.
2 Select three players located in a triangular relationship to each other.
3 Choose three additional players randomly (to avoid crisis mode, in case some player(s) falter).
4 Give these six players the continue-to-play signal.
5 Stop cut the rest of the players.
6 Listen to the song for a few cycles.
7 Signal to all the players who have stopped to resume playing with a call to groove.

8 Leave the circle in full groove for the next facilitator-in-training.

You will gain immediate feedback as you develop your radar. Assess the music you uncover. Does the group you chose to sculpt have a synchronized musical relationship? You will know as soon as you stop cut the remaining players and uncover your sculpted song.

If you are facilitating a group of advanced players and facilitators, you can challenge yourself by signalling a stop cut after choosing only the first three players.

Balancing the Three Peripherals

As a dancer, contact improvisationalist and an elf who has danced with the earth since birth, my peripheral feeling was the most developed part of my radar. As a drummer and musician, I found my peripheral hearing was the next most developed and my peripheral vision was the least developed. It took awhile to find ways to develop my peripheral vision because that was the area in which I was most blind. As I began to develop my peripheral vision and hearing to the level of my peripheral feeling, my radar came into balance and became more effective, efficient and functional. I was able to develop the three peripheral reading tools of the Radar Triplicity equally. The result is that I have put that triplicity in balance as I strengthened and lengthened each leg of the triplicity tripod. By doing so I widened its foundation as well as its effectiveness.

Your radar is your eye into the soul of your circle.

Consider your three reading tools. Which of your sensibilities is strongest? Which is weakest? How can you develop your two weaker elements so they are as strong as your most developed sensibility? How can you maintain that balance as you strengthen and develop the foundation of your Radar Triplicity to be even stronger?

Your radar is your eye into the soul of your circle.

There Are No Mistakes

There are no mistakes, only opportunities for learning. You can apply this concept both to your circle participants and to yourself as facilitator.

If you see and respond to some action taken by a participant in your circle as a mistake, you will reinforce their embarrassment and self-judgment. This sends a signal to the remaining circle participants that mistakes will be noticed and frowned upon, thus generating performance anxiety in your circle. As facilitator, you want to avoid creating this situation.

If you interpret some action of yours as a mistake you will limit your ability to learn from it.

By giving verbal cues to your players during a window of communication, you encourage them to explore and improvise as they contribute to the group song. Let them know that it is fine if they try some things that may not work. For example, you could say, "If you don't like the rhythm you are playing, simply stop and try something else." Then you can add, "If you play something that you think is a mistake, but it sounds good, then keep repeating it, because you have just created a new rhythm."

As a facilitator, if you interpret some action of yours as a mistake, you will limit your ability to learn from it. Try to avoid beating yourself over the head or judging yourself harshly because of some perceived mistake. See those situations as learning opportunities for you as a facilitator-in-training. You can learn the lessons buried inside your mistakes by applying the Critique Technique Triplicity. Be gentle with yourself.

Critique Technique Triplicity

The Arthurian Critique Technique Triplicity offers an way for you to pay attention to three distinct viewpoints of any learning situation. Each of these points of view gives a specific perspective on the available information. You can improve your body language skills, facilitation techniques and leadership skills by using the Critique Technique to review any completed rhythm-based event.

By critiquing your facilitation from three sequential perspectives, each described below, you can transform each experience into a stepping stone toward facilitation mastery.

Objective Witness: What Happened

Having an objective point of view means that you are clearly seeing things unencumbered by judgments, emotional responses, or your facilitation intentions. Gaining a clear understanding of any actions taken and responses given during a facilitated sequence will give you a solid foundation for learning from that experience.

Create in yourself an objective witness who can review, without judgment, the actions and reactions of both you as facilitator and your participants. To do this, review your just-completed event as if you were someone standing outside the circle watching both the facilitator and the drum circle act and react to each other. Suspend your judgements.

Circle Witness: What Worked & What Needs Work

The people in your drum circle are your Circle Witnesses. Their actions and reactions to your facilitation provide the most direct and honest in-the-moment feedback you can possibly receive. It is important for your learning journey that you pay attention to what works as well as what needs work.

> **The quality of your communication is directly reflected in the quality of the response of your players.**

How well you are facilitating at any moment is reflected in the resulting music that you are helping create. The players in your circle best answer your question, "How am I doing?" by how they respond to you. Pay close attention to the group's responses to answer the questions, "What is working?" and "What needs work?"

The quality of your communication is directly reflected in the quality of the response of your players. The circle you are facilitating reflects the quality of your facilitation. If you direct them to do something and they do not get it right, it is your responsibility, not theirs. If they do not "get it," then you are not communicating clearly. If they cannot go rhythmically or musically where you are taking them, then you are not reading the group's rhythmical ability accurately. For example, if the group's response to your stop cut signal is musically sloppy, it is a direct result of the quality of your facilitation. Perhaps your stop cut signal is sloppy, or you are not getting their full attention before you make the signal.

Maintain an attitude that these situations are opportunities for learning. If you react to the group's feedback in an upset manner, either with yourself or with them, your judgment will get in the way of learning. Instead of thinking that you have just made a mistake and failed your objective, think of these as "learning moments." With this attitude, you can focus on what needs more work instead of what did not work. This subtle change in your thinking represents a powerful shift in your ability to learn from your facilitating experiences. Some of your best teachers are the players in your circle.

Personal Witness: Self Improvement

Finally it is all about you. You are the personal witness to your facilitation of the event. First, you review the drum circle experience as an objective witness and, second, as a circle witness. Then when you consider it from your perspective as the facilitator it will be clear where to apply your new observations toward self-improvement.

Every moment spent in a drum circle is a potential learning experience.

If you had a chance to do it again, what did you observe in your facilitation that you would do differently to make the experience more successful?

There is room for improvement in even your best facilitation actions and techniques. Sometimes fine tuning your more subtle facilitation techniques can have a profound effect on your mastery of the art of facilitating.

Every moment spent in a drum circle is a potential learning experience for everyone.

Facilitating Two Hundred Music Teachers

Jaqui MacMillan is a wise and wonderful woman of power, an early pioneer in the drum circle facilitation community. She is a recognized teacher and performer who shares a story of a facilitation experience, and then critiques herself.

I was asked to facilitate a drum circle at a conference for two hundred music teachers. The circle was planned as the grand finale after a full day of lectures. I was happy to find, on arrival, that the organizer had scheduled the event in the cafeteria rather than in the fixed-seating auditorium they had originally planned to use. They had arranged chairs in a sound bowl with four concentric circles, with four pathways leading to the center of the circle as I had requested, and provided a cordless microphone. I placed a variety of instruments on the chairs, with a mix of timbres in each section. This preparation helped to put me at ease.

The organizer introduced me to the four percussion teachers before the event started, and I asked each of them to play a djembe or dunun.

When the organizer introduced me, the group applauded, so I jumped into the circle and signalled for them to keep clapping. Then I stop cut one fourth of the group and signaled for them to clap in a simple 4/4 rhythm. Next, I cut the group directly across from the 4/4 group and signalled for them to clap another simple beat in four. Finally, I stop cut the other two groups and told them to make up their own patterns. After a couple of minutes of this groove, I went from group to group, layering in the shakers so we heard both clapping and shakers. Then I asked the dunun player to start a simple beat to provide a bottom. I layered in the wood instruments while the others kept clapping. Then I started the bells and metal, and, finally, all of the drums. Now we were in full groove. I had started with a plan, but let go of it as the program progressed.

During the groove I facilitated the following interventions:
- sculpt of songs and timbres
- had everyone sing the sounds of their instruments and stop playing them
- did a teeter-totter with women's voices and men's voices
- brought the groove back
- signalled the volume down
- showcased a teacher playing bongos

I GOOW between each intervention, so that we could groove a little. Then I sculpted half the group and had the other half do rumble waves—long ones, then shorter and shorter, then back to groove. Then I sculpted the half who were still playing the groove and did a call and response with them using a cow bell. When I made this sculpt, I noticed that half of the group had a very distinct Middle Eastern flavor to its sound and the other half sounded more West African. It was a nice combination when they played together, but it was so cool how different each side sounded. I did a teeter-totter with these two sides of the circle, until we went faster and faster before slamming back into the full groove. Very fun! I ended with a call-and-response sequence with the whole group. After the last response, I kept playing the pulse, faster and faster, with everyone playing with me until it turned into a rumble. We did rumble waves, volume down and then rumble waved the different timbres, before I stop cut the whole group with a jump.

The event went very well. I was so pumped up by the energy afterward that I was exploding with joy!

My critique model:
1 What action was taken
2 What worked
3 What needs work
4 What did I learn from this experience
5 Next time

What Worked All the sequences worked, especially the clapping to layering in the instruments to the full groove, and also the Middle Eastern / West African teeter-totter. Sculpting the different timbres was very powerful. I brought a wide variety of percussion instruments to share, and had placed the instruments on the chairs ahead of time, with a good mix of timbres in each section.

What Needs Work This was like a dream circle, I think because I was dealing with musicians. Everyone knew how to follow the signals, so the group response was tight. There are many times in the past when I have said, "one, two, let's all play," and the result would be a total train wreck. This never happened here. The only problem I had was that because it was so hot sweat kept going into my eyes. Maybe I can wear an athletic headband next time. I'm very grateful that this was my worst problem of the day.

What Did I Learn I learned that going into a circle with confidence is the only way to go. I learned that no matter how much you plan and think about it, every situation is going to be totally different and will present its gifts to you as you go along. Just go with the flow and be confident. Create the song together, and all will be fine, and everyone will be ecstatic!

Next Time I will do the same thing: go with the flow and it will only keep getting better!

Video Review

The best witness in the world is a video camera. It records everything that happens in front of its lens without judgments. When using a video camera, follow these guidelines:

- Set the video camera on a tripod outside of your drum circle and away from foot traffic.
- Set your camera to record a wide angle, so that you can view the actions of the drum circle participants as well as the facilitator.
- Cover the LED On light with a small piece of masking tape so that it will not distract you or the players.
- Turn on the camera and then forget about it until the end of the program.
- Review the video as soon as possible after your event. When you review it, do so three times in a row with the three specific points of view described in the Critique Technique Triplicity.

Objective Witness Review

The first time you review the video of your event, be the objective witness, suspending any self-judgment of your actions. Notice and notate the actions of the event. Pay close attention to your facilitation sequences and the group's responses. You can learn a lot by objectively watching this interaction. This is also a great opportunity to write down your actions using facilitator's shorthand.

Circle Witness Review

Review the video of your rhythm event the second time as if you were a player in that drum circle. Be the circle witness. Put yourself in their shoes, playing their instruments. Try to get a sense of their experience as players who are being facilitated by you. Then, from that point of view, ask yourself what worked and what needs work.

Personal Witness Review

When you review the video of your rhythm event the third time, go ahead and take it all personally. Look for the moments in the event that can help you improve your facilitation and leadership skills. Sometimes it the littlest improvements that make the biggest differences.

Rhythmical Evangelism at Its Best

In 1995, organizers hired me to bring three hundred drums to Seattle and facilitate three family-friendly interactive rhythm-based events each day as part of the four-day Bumbershoot Festival. I facilitated a drum circle each morning, one in the afternoon and one in the evening. We called the drum circle site the Rhythm Equator. By the last day of the festival, word had gotten out to the public about the accessibility of this fun family event and a long line of people waited for each drum circle to start.

When I returned the next year I asked the organizers, "Why leave all those beautiful drums idle between the scheduled circles, when I can invite volunteer facilitators to run drum circles between my official programs?" They liked the idea and a tradition was born that continued for many years. I invited the graduates of my Seattle-based facilitator training programs, as well as other drumming elders in the Seattle community, to fill the time slots between my scheduled circles at Bumbershoot. My long-term connections with the Seattle community made it possible for me to easily connect with the local rhythm community.

The Rhythm Equator program at Bumbershoot and the Seattle recreational drumming community developed in parallel. More and more of the volunteer facilitators were also members of the Seattle World Percussion Society, SWPS, a local non-profit organization. Each year I hosted the Rhythm Equator site from noon to 10 p.m., facilitating three ninety-minute drum circles. Volunteers facilitated one-hour events between my circles. As host, I introduced each volunteer facilitator and monitored the event. We created four full days of interactive family-based rhythmical expression that featured sixteen or more facilitators. It was a ten-hour work day for me and I loved it. This was an example of rhythmical alchemy at its best.

So that I would no longer need to ship drums and percussion instruments to Seattle, in 1999 I helped broker a deal between the Seattle World Percussion Society and REMO. REMO gave SWPS a great deal on a drum circle kit to use in the Seattle community. One of the conditions of the deal was that I would be able to use the SWPS drums for the Bumbershoot Festival.

The Bumbershoot Festival Rhythm Equator circles became the closest thing to a drum circle facilitators' convention that we had at the time. People flew into Seattle from all parts of the U.S. to be volunteer facilitators and to network with each other. There were as many as ten facilitators hanging out at the Rhythm Equator at any one time during the festival. With this many facilitators, it was natural for us to practice the peer review critique technique process that I had developed during VMC Facilitator Training Playshops.

The peer review critique technique process, as it worked at the Bumbershoot Rhythm Equator: while someone facilitated the circle, another person acted as scribe. The scribe was an objective witness for the facilitator, writing out each action taken, tracking and notating the timing of the facilitation sequences from when the facilitator entered the orchestrational spot to the time they left the circle. The scribe also noted the actions and reactions of the players in the event, without judgement, taking notes in facilitators' shorthand.

Meanwhile, up to three other Playshop graduates would critique the active facilitator. At the end of that particular facilitator's drum circle, the scribe and the peer review group would take the volunteer facilitator to a quiet place and give him or her feedback.

The drum circles facilitated at the Rhythm Equator were transient circles: people came and played for a while and were immediately replaced by someone else when they left. With over four hundred participants per hour and eight circles a day, close to 15,000 people benefited from the rhythmical evangelistic experience provided. During the eight-year span of this event, the drum circle facilitation community at the Rhythm Equator helped 100,000 people play together.

For me, Bumbershoot was never just a drum circle gig. I had the pleasure of being a part of one of my favorite examples of community building. The Rhythm Equator was less an act of entertainment than it was a mission of rhythmical evangelism and community building. Both the Seattle community and the national drum circle facilitator community benefitted from the fun experiences.

John Hayden Facilitates at Bumbershoot

Spirited Playing

6 Call of the Drum

There is a certain excitement in the air when you hear someone playing their drum in the park. The call of the drum attracts most of us, sometimes without our knowing why.

When one drummer is drumming by herself, it is a solo. It is an in-the-moment process of expressing her emotional, psychological and musical spirit through rhythmical exploration. With only one person drumming, it is her own personal journey. Whether she is aware of it or not, she is sharing her rhythmical spirit with those around her.

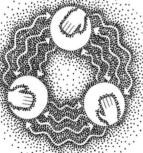

When she is drumming with someone else, they are two drummers expressing their emotional, psychological and musical spirits by talking to each other using rhythm. They are sharing their spirits with each other as well as with anyone nearby. With two drummers it is a dialogue and there is even more excitement. The attraction of the drum call is even stronger.

When there are three or more drummers playing together you have a drum circle, and their connections, the rhythms and the shared rhythmical spirit deepen. Each added player in the drum circle is another point of reference and expression that is connecting to every other person in the circle. That group connection creates and interlocks the web of rhythm and music being woven in the circle.

Even though the drummers' intent is mostly to entrain themselves and share their rhythmical spirits with each other, the public entertainment factor of a drum circle in a park always draws a crowd. It's not just the sound they hear that attracts and entices the passersby. Part of the attraction is the subsonic sound wave caused by the air being pushed out of the drum every time the drummers play their instruments. These sound waves massage the bodies nearby. The closer someone gets to an ongoing drum circle, the stronger this sensation is. When they get into close proximity to the drums they can feel it deep in their bodies.

This drum massage touches both the players and spectators. In a healthy drum circle, it is ever present. The vibrations of a drum massage not only permeate into all the fibers of our bodies, but they massage our emotions, our thoughts and our souls as well. This is one of the deeper attractions for people who participate in rhythm-based events.

The subsonic wave of a drum can carry for long distances. The original talking drums of Africa were very big, with heads the size of orchestral kettledrums (timpani). The drummer hit them with sticks and their sound could be heard a long way away. Their subsonic vibrations could be felt even further. The villagers used these drums to send messages to nearby villages.

Different people have different reactions to the kinesthetic massage that comes from a drum circle. Although most people are attracted to a drum circle and like to stay and bask in its rhythm aura, others are highly irritated by it. That drum vibration may be massaging the "wrong" parts of their bodies.

Touched by the Drum

It was a beautiful Sunday in the park by the river. What a good day to drum with my friends. We had been drumming only 20 minutes when I could see trouble coming toward us in the form of an obviously upset man.

After years of playing in drum circles in public places, I can tell by watching their body language whether an officer walking toward us to stop our musicmaking will likely be an authoritative jerk or an apologetic advocate.

I could see by the body language of the man who was walking in forced-march determination that he wanted us to stop very badly. He wasn't a policeman. He was in his late 60s and had likely walked from a well elderly apartment complex that was on the other side of the trees, across the road from the park, about a football-field length away from us. As he got closer I could see that anger was fueling his determined stride.

As a facilitator, when I am confronted with this kind of situation I choose between two approaches. One possibility is to leave the circle playing and greet the person at a distance from the players. I politely deal with the person's concerns and negotiate some mutually agreeable solution. The other option is to bring the groove to a close and speak to the person from the circle.

This man had appeared suddenly and had walked up to the circle so fast that my only choice was to stop the circle as he stood leering over us. "Hello," I said to him. "Isn't it a beautiful day for drumming?" I asked with a smile. He held our gaze in thick silence for the length of the three deep breaths that he took while standing there with his hands on his hips. "No, it is not," he said, his body visibly shaking in his angry state. Pointing back at the trees through which he had come, he said, "I could feel you all the way from across the street."

My chin dropped. He spoke the truth. Whenever someone comes to complain about the drum "noise," I know that at least one third of them are more disturbed by what they feel than what they hear. Many aren't aware enough of the feeling to articulate that idea.

Then he said, "You're touching my belly and I didn't give you permission to do that. Why don't you go home and do your drumming where you won't disturb innocent people." My jaw dropped even further as I heard him speak the ultimate truth. The lower notes on the drums vibrate the lower chakras in the body. This area, in the abdomen and lower, is where the dance comes from and where the drum's vibrations go to initiate that dance.

I profusely apologized to the man for disturbing him and told him we would move to the other side of the park. As he stormed away, and we packed up our gear to move, one of the grumbling drummers in our circle said, "That man was crazy!" "No," I said, "that man was honest."

Drum Called

Nestled in a circus tent by the river in Kassel, Germany, three hundred of us were well past drum call and enjoying a solid percussion groove that was "smokin'."

After finishing a facilitation sequence, I turned around to see standing in the middle of one of the drum circle aisles, a little (as in short) old (as in around 80 years) gray-haired lady. She was hugging a REMO dumbek with both arms, and had an excited yet confused look on her face. I walked up to her, smiling, and offered her a seat near the center of the circle.

The drum groove around us was too loud for me to speak, so I took the dumbek from her and showed her of a couple of different ways she could play it. She nodded her head yes, took back the dumbek and with a smile began to play with the circle. She picked up my body language signals easily and was soon responding to my calls with the rest of the group.

Seeing that she was settled, I put my attention elsewhere as the event progressed. Toward the end of the program, I noticed that although other people around her had come and gone, she was still participating as her bright eyes expressed her spirit. But on second look, I saw that her face was wet with tears. I took a step toward her. She saw the concern in my face, smiled at me while making a go-away motion with her hands, and then continued to play.

After the close of the drum circle, I stood outside the entrance, like a minister saying farewell to his congregation after the service. I noticed her standing off to the side of the thank-you line. I correctly deduced that she was waiting until I was alone so she could talk to me privately. The only thing that didn't quite fit was that she was clutching the hand of a young man.

It all became clear as I finished talking to the last person in line. With the little old lady still clutching his hand, the young man came up to me and explained that she had commandeered him as a translator for her.

Her eyes burned deep into mine as she looked up at me and started speaking to me in German. She spoke with the same intensity that she played in the circle. The tears were coming out of her eyes as the words were pouring out of her mouth. She realized that she had to stop talking so the young man could translate and catch up. When he began to speak, I looked at him and realized the he too was crying as well. Here is what he translated.

Her name was Maria. She was 84 years old. She lived in her apartment half a mile from the park across the river where the community drum circle was being held. She heard us playing and followed the sound of the drums through the city to the circus tent in the park by the river. When she got to the entrance, she was handed a drum and was led inside. She felt overwhelmed by the sound pressure, and didn't know what to do until I greeted her, offered her a seat and showed her how to play.

Not only had she never played a drum before, she had never wanted or expected to play one. Although she enjoyed the experience, something very profound and important happened while she was playing that she had to share with me.

Her husband had died over 55 years ago in the war. It felt to her like the drums were massaging the place inside that couldn't let go of him. As she drummed, she got in touch with that place and she was able to let go and say goodbye to him. She had been a grieving widow for half a century and I could see in her eyes that she was about to start a new life. "She can't thank you enough," the young man said. She released the young man's hand to bear hug me, and then wouldn't let go, saying over and over "Vielen Dank, Vielen Dank."

I hugged her back. Now all three of us were crying. "Vielen Dank, Vielen-Dank," she continued to say while hugging me. I looked over at the young man for a translation. He said "It means thank you, as very much as possible."

Drum Circle Etiquette

Dynamic interactive musical and personal relationships are an integral part of all drum circle events. These relationships are based on a simple set of unwritten guidelines. When players adhere to them, it is easier for them to attain their highest musical potential. In culturally specific circles, the unwritten guidelines have evolved through centuries of playing, through the wisdom of our ancestors. These guidelines apply to contemporary drum circles as well, from freeform drum jams to facilitated rhythm events. These unwritten musical and personal relationship guidelines are expressed within what I call Drum Circle Etiquette.

Good volume dynamics create good relationship dynamics.

To most drum circle regulars, these guidelines are nonverbal agreements that everyone adheres to in order to create a fun and exciting musical experience together. Below are my Drum Circle Etiquette suggestions for playing in most community drumming environments. Using these Arthurian suggestions will help you comfortably merge into an ongoing drumming circle without being obtrusive. When you adhere to these guidelines, both you and those around playing around you will enjoy the drum circle experience more. You will be a fully participating and contributing member of an in-the-moment, rhythmical alchemy orchestra, sometimes called a drum circle.

Do not wear rings, watches or bracelets while playing hand drums.

This protects the head on the drum, as well as the drum itself from the metal. It also protects your hands. Rings can be flattened if they hit the wooden rim of the drum.

Ask permission before playing someone else's drum.

For some drummers, their instrument is a very personal possession. If someone leaves the circle to get a drink or go to the bathroom do not immediately jump in and take their seat or play their drum. In some drumming communities, drummers will put something on their seat, cover their drum with something or lay their drum on its side to signify that they will be back.

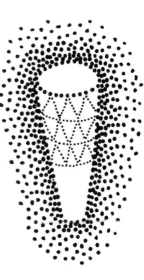

Listen as much as you play.

By listening to what is happening in the circle as you play, you will have a better sense of how you might fit into the groove that is being created.

Support the fundamental groove.

There is a fundamental rhythm groove that you hear in the drum song being created in the circle. By supporting that groove with your rhythm you connect yourself to the group experience. You need not be a rhythm robot and hold down the same part all night long. There is plenty of freedom within the fundamental groove to experiment, while expressing your rhythmical spirit.

Leave rhythmical space.

By leaving rhythmical space for other players in the circle to express themselves, you create space in your own rhythm to hear and enjoy the group's music. Do not fill the space with your own notes so much that there is little creative space left for the other players.

Play at the volume of the group.

Good volume dynamics create good relationship dynamics. Play softly enough so that you can hear everyone around you. While you are drumming, be sure to follow and support the dynamic changes in volume and tempo that the group will go through during a drum circle event. If you can only hear yourself, you are unlikely to be having a constructive musical relationship with the other players in the circle.

Share the solo space.

If you are at the advanced level of rhythmical expertise where soloing with your drum is available to you, then you know the excitement and pleasure of being able to play over, around and through the drum circle groove. Soloing through a drum circle groove is very much like a bird flying through the forest. But the "solo air" above can accommodate only a few solos at the same time. If there is more than one soloist available in a circle be sure to share the solo space. An excellent way for two or three drum soloists to play through the groove together is to have a drum dialogue with each other. In a facilitated drum circle, a facilitator will hopefully find the advanced drummers in the circle and showcase them individually or encourage them to share a dialogue or trade solos.

Do not smoke in the circle.

Drumming is a high-energy aerobic exercise. Respect everyone's need to breathe in the closely packed environment.

Advice for Beginning Beginners

Along with the standard Arthurian Drum Circle Etiquette suggestions, I have some advice for beginning-beginners who are joining a drum circle event for the first time.

Enjoy the journey.

In all the excitement, remember to have fun. Although it will help you to follow the simple Drum Circle Etiquette guidelines, you need not be an experienced drummer to fully participate and have a good time.

Do not worry.

Even if you might think that you are rhythmically challenged, do not worry. Just get started and you will find rhythms inside of you that you did not know you had. Simply participate actively in the drum circle and the excitement and rhythms surrounding you will motivate you to express exactly what fully contributes to the group song. You need not even play a drum. You can bring a simple percussion instrument such as a shaker, a bell or a wood block. They can be a lot easier to play than a hand drum.

Support the drum community experience.

If you are participating in a drum circle for the first time, have an attitude of humility and support. Be very observant of the actions and reactions of the more advanced drummers who are playing in the circle and you will learn a lot quickly.

Keep it simple.

The pulse will always be somewhere in the music. Listen for it, then play along with it or around it. It is like keeping the side of the pool within reach as you learn to swim. The pulse will always be there for you to grab onto, as is the side of the pool, if you get rhythmically lost while playing. Once you are comfortable with what you are playing, you can explore deeper rhythmical waters, while keeping the pulse in sight.

Just ask.

Every rhythm event is different, and has its own particular variations of Drum Circle Etiquette. If you are unsure about what is appropriate, ask somebody. They will likely respond with supportive suggestions.

As a basic agreement of community drumming events, each person in the circle comes to share their rhythmical spirit and personal energy with their community. This group consciousness is the catalyst for a very powerful, yet intimate experience for everybody as they create unity in their community by drumming together. The musical part of any drum circle will take care of itself when every player is there to share their spirit and have fun.

From Beginning to Begun

I love participating in the personal interactions created among participants during a drum circle. By putting my facilitator persona away when I am a guest at some other facilitator's event and becoming a participant, I become as inconspicuous as possible, given that I wear a vest and beanie. Being able to put away your facilitator persona helps when facilitating a drum circle. By hiding your facilitator body language, you can become a participant when it is time to GOOW by sitting down and playing with the group.

I was a playing participant at Mikael Khei's drum circle in Oslo, Norway when an obviously nervous uncomfortable person walked into the room. Her body and facial language were as readable as a book. She was being dragged into this event by her friend. After being given a small drum, she tried to sit on a seat outside the circle during drum call, but her friend forced her to choose a seat in the center of the circle, directly across from me.

She held the drum awkwardly in her lap with one hand while tentatively tapping the drum head with one finger of the other hand. She was obviously intimidated by the drumming that was going on all around her. I decided to get her attention, create some empathy with her and help her. Just like her, I took my ashiko drum and held it in my lap with one hand and started tapping on it with one finger from the other hand while contorting my face into a look of trepidation. I then waited for her to look up and see me. Seeing my ridiculous body language, she gave a little laugh. It is amazing how a little laughter can completely change one's physiology and psychology. When she realized that I was mirroring her she laughed so hard that she nearly dropped her drum from her lap. I now had her attention.

When I facilitate a drum circle, my mission is to lock into the magic that makes people shine.
—Mikael Khei

With the drum circle continuing around us and me still sitting in my seat across from her, I used miming body language to show her how to put the drum between her legs and use both hands to play it. While mouthing the words "thank you" she tentatively began to experiment with the sound of her drum and how to make her rhythm fit into the rest of the drum circle song.

She became progressively more confidant in her ability to share her rhythmical spirit with the other players and more experimental with other instruments. Like a kid with a free pass in a candy shop, by the end of the program she had put her hands on nearly every loose instrument in the room and tried them. At the very end of the event, we found ourselves once again sitting opposite each other, this time playing the big bottom drums as the foundation of the closing rhythm. Playing as equals, we used our drums in a dialogue with each other, responding with drum phrases between each other's patterns. The call-and-response dialogue between us pushed the excitement level of the closing rhythm to a crescendo, ending in a powerful drum circle climax, facilitated by Mikael.

By the end of the circle my playful drumming partner was no longer a timid beginning-beginner drummer. She was able to direct her rhythmical passion into the group's energy. She had become a fully empowered and shining rhythmatist. She had begun.

Drum Call

"Drum Call" is what we Arthurian-style facilitators call the first groove of a community drum circle. It is the very first piece being created as the participants enter the venue and get settled into the rhythmical groove.

A drum call does just what its title implies. As the group gathers, some of the people begin to drum. This entices others nearby who might be socializing to finish their conversations, bring their instruments to the growing circle and join in the rhythm. As more people join the circle, the drum call's loud joy may become strong enough that other people in the area, who had no plans to join the event, come over to see what's happenin'. Even if they are not aware of it, and before the sound of the drum circle piqued their interest, it was the vibrations of the drums that called them.

When you first see an opening drum call facilitated at an event, it appears to be a casual, haphazard way to bring a group together to play. But as many facilitators know, it is anything but that. Drum call is the foundation of the whole event. It sets the tone for everything that comes after it, becoming the basic facilitator's platform for creating the group-learning experience. These facilitated learning experiences create real knowledge in the participants about how to play successfully together.

Drum call initiates the relationship and builds rapport between the facilitator and the group being facilitated. As facilitator, you want to be constantly developing and nurturing that relationship throughout the event until the last note has been played.

Below I describe some of the more important aspects that you, as facilitator, will want to instigate during drum call. To ensure a successful event, continue to develop each of these elements as the circle progresses, and you will gain insights into the group's emerging capacity. As the drum call evolves, so do the players.

Take Responsibility for the Physical Circle

The seating arrangement for a drum circle is as important as the instrument arrangement. For groups of twenty to thirty, the best seating scenario is with everybody seated shoulder to shoulder for full-circle eye contact, with all the instrument timbres and pitches distributed evenly around the circle. When you have more than thirty people, concentric circles of chairs help you avoid the problem of the single row circle, where participants are too far away from each other to hear across the circle properly.

In this photo, over forty players are shoulder to shoulder in a single circle. We were able to hear with more than thirty players because we were playing in an acoustically designed symphony

Single-row Circle of Drummers

Concentric Circles of Drummers

Floor-to-Standing Sound Bowl with Two Hundred Players

practice room in Tokyo.

In this photo you see the same players, but rearranged into concentric circles, so they can see and hear each other more easily.

To put the maximum number of players and equipment in the minimum amount of space you will want to create a floor-to-standing sound bowl arrangement.

A floor-to-standing sound bowl consists of three concentric circles. On the first level, the floor circle, participants playing hand percussion and small drums can be seated on the floor in the center of the circle, leaving space in the middle for the facilitator. On the second level, the chair circle, place chairs and sit-down drums such as congas, ashikos and djembes in rings around the center of floor-seated participants. Leave at least three openings in the circle of chairs as aisles to give access to the players who are seated on the floor. On the third level, the standing circle, place your congas, timbales and bongos behind the chairs, using stands. This circle will also accommodate the frame drummers and those who prefer to stand and wear their drums, such as djembes, using straps.

In a controlled environment with a closed population, such as kids in a school, where you know the number of participants, you would typically supply all the instruments and seats. You can take responsibility for the physical circle by setting it up before they arrive, placing the instruments where you want them. When you set up this orchestrational percussion pit you facilitate the highest possibility for listening and playing success for you as well as for the group.

For open community circles, it is also important to be responsible for the physical setup of the circle and instrument arrangement. The difference is that in a community drum circle the participants bring their own instruments and choose where they want to sit. Many of your participants may not realize at the beginning that the drum circle is an orchestra pit, and the group may not be very orchestra-like. However, with any luck, and with your facilitation, they will become a percussion orchestra. It is your job to arrange the instruments in the best physical setup to create a well-balanced sound and successful playing relationship.

Just remember that the instruments that you are arranging are attached to people. If you want to move a specific person playing a certain instrument from one part of the circle to another, to balance out the sound:

- Ask them if they would help you by moving. Do not tell them to move.
- Let them know why. As examples, "We could sure use your dunun closer to the middle of the circle to help us hold the group together," or "There are a lot of bell

players sitting together in this section. Could one of you help me by mixing up your percussion sounds, or if you all really want to play bells, may I ask you to spread out around the circle?"

Sound Bowl

Orff is a professional group of music and dance teachers, dedicated to the teaching approach of Carl Orff and Gunild Keetman. I originally expected 2000 attendees when I was hired for an opening drum ceremony at the Orff National Conference in Seattle. The organizers had planned for the drum circle to occur off to the side of the stage, just after the opening keynote address. During the week before the conference 500 additional people registered, so the organizers added 500 more chairs. These chairs filled the entire space that had originally been designated for all 2,000 players to stand during my drum circle. The organizers now asked me to facilitate 2,500 seated people from the stage instead, and said simply, "Good luck."

The room was a huge rectangle with auditorium seating on a flat floor, and a tall stage lining most of one wall. Additional rows of chairs had been placed so they faced the stage from both sides. The organizers were now planning for all 2,500 participants to be seated around the stage while playing their instruments.

I came up with a secret plan to rise to the challenge they presented. I placed John Avinger, from John's Music Center, in the center of the seats with my biggest REMO surdo, and asked him to hold an empty seat for me. I placed most of the bells, woods and shakers in the middle two seating sections, surrounding John. I then placed the congas, djembes and other large drums at the aisle seats closest to the middle sections, and all the REMO frame drums and dumbeks along the outer edges of the auditorium. When the attendees walked into the auditorium for the keynote address, they found these toys waiting for them on their seats.

Each time they applauded the keynote speaker, the participants created a huge percussion rumble. By the time it was my turn, the group had tuned themselves and were raring to go. We needed no warm-up. I was unsure whether it was really possible to facilitate 2,500 seated drummers arranged in a rectangle, from the stage. It definitely helped that the players were music teachers.

As soon as I facilitated the players into a groove, I jumped off the stage and ran to stand on the empty seat John had been saving for me. After the first piece, while standing on the seat next to John and his big drum, I signalled for the players of percussion and large drums in the center section to rotate their chairs to face the center of the drum donut that we were creating. Then, I asked the dumbek and frame drummers who were sitting on the outer edges of the auditorium to stand up, push their chairs aside, and surround the seated players.

I succeeded in fulfilling my secret plan by placing the instruments on the seats in a very specific way. Together we created a sound bowl. The Orff teachers went from sounding good spread across the auditorium, to sounding great in a circle. Imagine that many sensitive drummers playing softly. AHHHHHHhhhhhh.

The L-Shaped Circle

Jonathan Murray shares a story about interesting challenges of physical space and time limits.

I was lucky enough to help Arthur with a corporate event in Philadelphia for an international conglomerate. Four hundred of their executives attended, from all different subsidiaries around the world. When we arrived at the hotel ballroom we found that several rooms were being used for this production. The room that Arthur was given for his four-hundred-person drum circle was, to say the least, not ideal. It was an elaborate L-shaped ballroom with huge crystal chandeliers and enormous mirrors with gilt frames. It reminded me of palace ballrooms I have seen whilst traveling through Europe. (Think Versailles.)

The four hundred chairs Arthur had requested lined the walls in a massive L-shaped "circle." The chairs also fit the design of the room, being high-backed carved wood and weighing at least twenty pounds each. It was immediately clear that the arrangement was not going to work as set up by the event organizers. We started the set-up process by identifying an appropriate center of the circle and then began moving the heavy chairs to create the center row. Working back from the center, we placed the chairs in twelve concentric circles, within the contours of the strangely-shaped room.

Everyone in the village has a role to play to make the village healthy, wealthy and wise. No role is any more or less important than any other.

Another part of our challenge was that Arthur's hour-long program had been trimmed to 30 minutes. With this in mind, we arranged aisles in the pattern of chairs, for quicker and easier access. Once the chairs were arranged, then we placed drums and percussion instruments on each chair.

This opening rhythm event was designed to be a surprise for the participants, so the next morning we quietly snuck into the room where we had set up the circle. The participants were all on the other side of a partitioned wall, enjoying their morning "meet and greet" over breakfast. Arthur asked each of the seven company presidents to come into the room a few minutes before our program was to begin. He gave them each a large frame drum and mallet and placed them in the center row of the circle, facing the partition doors, through which attendees would be entering. A few moments before the doors were to open, Arthur facilitated the presidents into a rhythm. Then the partition was pulled back to reveal both a set up of drums and percussion and their own presidents playing a rhythm for them.

The playing presidents motivated the group to move quickly into the room, with each participant wanting to get as close to their leaders as possible. Having everything preset encouraged each of them to sit down and pick up their instruments. Within three minutes, almost all of the participants were in the circle and playing. The group was rockin' and it was only 9 o'clock in the morning. I supported their groove by playing a cowbell. Arthur delivered a fantastic program incorporating his village metaphor into their exuberant playing. He helped them understand that everyone in the village has a role to play to make the village healthy, wealthy and wise. No role is any more or less important than any other.

He ended the program with a big climax and the group was off into another ballroom to continue with their conference.

Teach your Facilitator's Body Language

The time to show your body language signals for basic facilitation directions–such as speed up, volume down and stop–to your group is during drum call.

At the beginning of a rhythm-based event, you want to keep the interventions simple and stay away from complicated sequences of directions. Full group interventions are great for teaching your body language. Hopefully you will find opportunities to give the same basic body language directions more than once during the drum call to solidify the learning taking place. When you do this successfully, the players gain confidence in their ability to read and follow your directions.

By using consistent body language, you generate a trusting relationship with your circle. Being totally congruent when you repeat your facilitation language means that each time you make a stop cut, you do it in the exact same way, with the exact same intention for the group. When you do this, you establish basic facilitation body language signals on which the group can rely.

As the group gets more attuned to you, you can make your facilitation language more subtle and sophisticated. As a result, the group's responses to you and their musical interactions as a group also get subtle and sophisticated.

Define the Roles

One of your jobs as facilitator is to define the role of each person in the circle and your role as facilitator. You can find many different ways to do this during the windows of communication and while facilitating the ongoing grooves.

In the window of communication, the messages about different roles being played can be delivered verbally in a very direct way: "We are here to enjoy ourselves and cooperatively create a great musical experience together." Alternatively, the messages can be delivered through subtle metaphors.

A Showcasing Example

From full groove, you give the bass and dunun players the continue-to-play signal, and stop cut the other players in the circle. By doing so you expose and showcase the bottom drum melody line and groove. Then you ask all the non-playing participants, "Can you hear the grandmother drums? This is the foundation of our community drum song. It supports us as we play on top. If you ever get lost in the rhythm, stop and listen for your grandmothers and you will find your way back to the groove." Then you count the group back into the rhythm. This educates the group about the low-pitched drums and their role in the music-making.

$$+ \rightarrow \emptyset \, L \, G, \; ROC \; \boxtimes = L \, \star, \; ROC \; ?, \; ROC \; \circlearrowright \; GOOW$$

Notice by using this facilitation scenario you both teach without teaching by creating an experiential learning event and you use an appropriate metaphor.

By showcasing the pitch or timbre of a subgroup of participants, you help them identify their relationship both with each other and with the other instruments in the circle. But, most important, you give them a sense of their role in the overall ensemble.

If you get lost in the rhythm, stop and listen for your grandmother.

Your actions as you facilitate can help define different roles being played in the circle. For example, after you count the group back into the rhythm, get out of the way. Walking away from the orchestration point and out of the center of the circle after making an adjustment in the ongoing rhythm makes a statement about your role as a facilitator in the musical event. Your action says, "Now that I have helped adjust your rhythm into a solid groove I am getting out of your way, and handing the responsibility for the music back to you. Enjoy!"

Your role as facilitator changes along with the roles of the drum circle participants as the event evolves toward its conclusion.

Establish Trust

Trust is a seed that you plant in the beginning of the event and nurture throughout the program. You plant it as people enter the circle during drum call. As group consciousness develops, the trust you nurture becomes a tree. The "trust tree" blossoms into flowers as the participants develop into ensemble consciousness and the flowers become fruit as the percussion ensemble achieves musical satisfaction. The fruit can be harvested using the orchestrational process later in the event. The trust you develop as you establish rapport with your group must go both ways. You want to trust them on as many levels as you want them to trust you. That equal trust must be in place and well-balanced when you reach the orchestrational level of your program or any orchestration you attempt may not work.

Trust is a seed that you plant in the beginning of the event and nurture throughout the program.

When trust has not been developed with a group, even a facilitator with fantastic technique, 500-watt charisma and loads of style can fall flat on their performance face while participants get up and leave during the middle of the event. Trust is a foundation that can be built using the three basic elements of honesty, rapport and congruency—the elements that form the Arthurian Trust Triplicity.

Trust Triplicity

Honesty

Honesty is being devoid of all hypocrisy.

Honesty is a hard enough goal in our personal lives, and even more challenging when we are called upon to put all our facilitation, presentation and musical skills on the line in the center of a circle. To be honest with the group, you must be true to who you really are. It doesn't work to put on airs or pretend to be

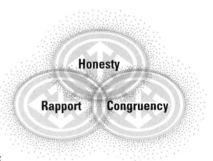

some way that you think you should be. You must be yourself to create trust.

You can fool some of the people some of the time, but you can't fool all of the people all of the time. Pretending, on any level, will separate the real you from their real potential as a group. Pretense makes you a hypocrite. Honesty is the best policy.

Honesty is being devoid of all hypocrisy.

On the other side of the coin, players in a drum circle can only be honest in their playing. Drums don't lie. A drummer's real self comes out in their playing regardless of their rhythmical expertise. It is a natural phenomena that a drummer expresses their true personality when playing in-the-moment rhythms. The beauty of recreational rhythm circles is that the music produced is the most honest representation of a group's rhythmical spirit in that moment. You want to meet that Zen honesty with the purest form of your real self that you can muster.

Rapport

To build rapport means to facilitate harmonious, mutual understanding among the participants of the circle and with you. You, as facilitator, need to consciously create rapport during drum call and then continue to strengthen it throughout the event. Rapport with your circle is a delicate flower that needs constant nurturing and attention. It can easily be stepped on unconsciously by a facilitator.

You build rapport with the group of players because you care about them. You may know where you would like to take them but do you know where they would like to be led? Even if you are being honest, without good rapport between you and the circle, there is no foundation for trust. People don't care how much you know until they know how much you care. As a facilitator in the circle's orchestrational spot, you are standing inside the heart of a group of individual players who will, by the end of the program, become a musical entity. That entity will have a group mind and personality very different from any other drum circle you have ever facilitated. To serve it the best way you know how, you want to stay in touch with that living, breathing entity at every stage of its short one-to-two hour life.

People don't care how much you know until they know how much you care.

In the beginning, a drum circle starts out as individuals, so you relate with each of those people. During drum call, your first role as a facilitator is to greet them, including making eye contact. As the drum circle develops toward its ultimate goal of making music together, you continue to develop rapport with the group, continuing to use welcoming body language. By the end of the program you will be addressing yourself to a single-minded entity that is manifesting its relationship with itself through music.

The rapport you establish in drum call sets the tone of your relationship with the circle for the whole program. That relationship changes and evolves as the event unfolds. For this reason, maintaining rapport is a full-time job for a facilitator throughout an event.

Congruency

Congruency means consistency within yourself as facilitator, over the course of an event, and consistency between your vision and the group's intentions.

Congruency is the logical agreement among all parts of your self. On the surface it refers to facilitating body language signals to the group consistently and decisively. A stop cut from your head with just your arms is not a congruent facilitation signal. When you make a stop cut from your deepest intention to stop the group, with every muscle in your body, from the tips of your toes to the gleam in your eye, you can stop a thousand drummers on a dime. On the deeper level, it is about being everything you say, rather that saying what you think you should say.

Congruency is about walking your talk during your every moment standing on the orchestrational spot, while dancing on the edge of chaos in the middle of the ever-evolving loud joy of a rhythm-based event.

Congruency implies a conscious agreement among all the participants about where the circle is going, both rhythmically and musically. This agreement includes how we are all going to get there. In terms of drum circle gestalt, congruency is the group vision manifest in sound. That group vision is what makes the magic of in-the-moment music.

Trust is a two-way street. You need to trust the people in the circle as much as they trust you. When you balance honesty, rapport and congruency in your facilitation, you have that two-way trust with the people you are facilitating. Pay as much attention to them as you want them to pay attention to you.

> **Congruency is about walking your talk during your every moment.**

By creating an honest, trusting relationship with the circle, you help participants overcome apprehension and they become comfortable to express themselves without fear of being embarrassed, over-challenged or manipulated. Some of the messages you want to convey to the group though your words and actions:

- You are there for their benefit.
- You want to discover where they want to go with their rhythmical spirit, and help them get there.
- You want to help guide them to their next highest level of musical expression.
- You will consistently show up at the orchestrational spot when they call you with a transition point.
- You won't abuse their trust by over facilitating.
- You want to play with them as much as facilitate them.
- You want to help them to progressively take on responsibility for their music and self-facilitate.
- You bring the gifts of endrumingment.

Trust is an integral part of a successfully facilitated rhythm event. Creating two-way trust will help you remember that the authority you have as a group facilitator is based on the trust you receive from the participants in your circle. Without their trust, you will not have an authoritative leg to stand on, or from which to facilitate.

Teach Without Teaching

As a facilitator, you need to transfer specific information to the group without appearing to be their teacher. I call this "teaching without teaching." This covert teaching helps create the small group successes that translate into a successful event.

When facilitating a rhythm-based event, it is important to make your teaching tools subservient to your facilitation tools and goals. This is especially true for drum teachers and school teachers. Wearing the physiology of a teacher when you are facilitating a circle can destroy the kind of rapport that you want to achieve and maintain with the participants in your event. When you as facilitator use teacher physiology, you give the message "I know and you don't" through your body language. This body language is easily perceived by the people whom you are serving and creates separation and hierarchy between you and the circle. That, in turn, hampers the empowerment process that is an important aspect of a community-based rhythm event.

While all this is true, the process of empowering the group to its highest musical and spiritual potential is also about providing the technical information to help them play together successfully. Teaching is valuable. Do it. Teaching without teaching requires you to use your awareness of how you impart information to the group.

Transfer information to the group without appearing to be their teacher.

Implanting Metaphors

Metaphors are stories or statements that reflect back and relate to the participants' own personal experience. As examples, "We are here to create a space for each others' rhythmical creativity," or "Can you hear the dialogue going on between the instruments?" Another dialogue metaphor example: "When we are in rhythmical dialogue with each other, we are listening to each other as much as we are playing with each other." By using these metaphors with a group, you can create images in the players' minds that educate them about how they can play well together.

We listen to each other as much as we play with each other.

The musical and group consciousness at the beginning of a drum circle is entirely different before they learn how to listen and play with each other through dialogue. You can guide them to a place of group consciousness much quicker if you teach them to listen rather than tell them to listen.

The windows of communication between the facilitated pieces during your event are a great place for you to guide the group towards its own learning through the use of metaphors.

To establish and maintain a positive relationship as a respectful and equal partner in the process, it is a good idea to teach without teaching throughout the rhythm-based event—in all your words and deeds. A supportive mentor helps guide the group's learning process. Staying away from words and physical gestures that make you seem superior will help you avoid appearing to be a person who knows everything. If you attempt to educate your circle by telling or lecturing them, you will damage the empowerment process and turn a drum circle into a drum circle class. By teaching without teaching you become a partner in the learning experience you are guiding them through.

Experiential Training

By creating experiential examples, you can teach a group how to listen and musically dialogue with each other. You can educate your circle, without the appearance of teaching, about the basic elements of how to play together. You can unveil to them, through sculpting and showcasing during a piece, the many different sounds, tones, pitches, timbres and instrument groupings that make up a drum circle orchestra. All of this can be done in a way that lets them see that you are facilitating their learning as a service to their in-the-moment rhythmical and musical alchemy.

Showcase the Timbres

Showcasing the different timbres in your circle is a teaching-without-teaching method that will help you direct the players toward percussion ensemble consciousness. You can facilitate an experience to teach the group about the different timbres that exist among the hand percussion players.

For example, from full groove, sculpt all the bell players and give them the continue-to-play signal. Give an attention call to the other players in the circle (ROC) and signal a stop cut. This uncovers the "bell song" that had been embedded in the musical dialogue. At the moment you showcase their song, you introduce and connect all the bell players in the circle to each other.

A facilitated experience is much more powerful for your players than telling them to listen to each others' timbres. People learn more through their own experiences than when someone is overtly teaching them. When they are having fun during that experience, they learn even more.

Orchestrate Self-Facilitation

One of the goals of teaching without teaching is to orchestrate the group's ability to facilitate itself. This is the process of showing them how a drum circle works and what each participant must do to help make it work.

Once you educate the group about how a circle works, they can eventually facilitate their own music. By orchestrating the group's self facilitation, you can hand to the circle more of the responsibility for the music being created. By doing so, you relieve yourself of some of your old facilitator duties, giving you time and space to pursue even more challenging and creative activities, like facilitating the group's spirit.

Helping the players discover how their particular instrument fits into the balance of pitch and timbre in the drum circle will empower them to be more able to self-facilitate their musical contributions.

Next, we will explore how to let the group experience and recognize the transition point. This teaching-without-teaching will help them learn to facilitate themselves.

Let the Group Experience the Transition Point

A transition point is a place where the music and people are becoming dis-connected or bored—a time for a change. Typically, in a drum call, many of the players do not yet know what a transition point is. Different people become aware of that disconnect at different times in its process. As facilitator, you need to be aware of it very early, but you would typically wait until at least half the people become aware that they are in rhythmical trouble before going into the orchestrational spot. A few people in the group won't notice, even as the transition point develops to its full disconnect and heads toward the ultimate rhythmical train wreck. They may still have their heads down, totally engaged in their own playing and unaware that the music is about to derail.

Many beginning-beginner facilitators can hardly wait for a transition point to appear in the music so they can jump into the circle and facilitate. As they mature, they learn that two-thirds of facilitation is about staying out of the players' way and letting the transition develop into something that the players can recognize and to which they can respond. When the players can recognize and respond to the transition point, then when it is time for you to step in and help them through it, you will be a collaborative member of the group, not just in an arbitrary leadership role.

In drum call it is important to give a transition point time to develop, so the players in the circle will get a chance to experience and understand exactly what it is. The participants who do not have experiential knowledge of transition points may feel that you are over-manipulating their music if you regularly jump in to facilitate before the transition point has been recognized by them. Avoid jumping into the circle as soon as you hear, feel

A transition point is a time for a change.

or see a transition point developing. If you step into the orchestrational spot too soon, many of the beginning players will not yet be aware of the coming transition point. For example, in a circle of a hundred players, if you facilitate when only ten of your players are conscious of a transition, then the other ninety players may think you are jumping in only because you feel like it. By stepping in early, you as facilitator decide the group's next rhythmical direction. If you wait to facilitate until at least half of your players are aware of a developing transition point, then, with your help and guidance, they are ready to make a change. By waiting, you create an awareness that the group of players gets to decide their own next rhythmical direction, with your help. By establishing this respectful relationship with the group, you also deliver a very important message to the players, "I am listening to you."

If you wait even longer, until the transition point fully develops and heads toward its inevitable rhythmical train wreck, then you will find many players are already doing something to help avoid the wreck, such as simplifying their rhythm or accenting the pulse. Now by stepping in to facilitate, you support the circle's rhythmical decisions as you and they smoothly transition from one piece to another.

The Groove Line

The *groove line* at the bottom of the Transition Point Illustration represents the group's groove. It starts when some players first recognize that the rhythm is getting shaky and continues as the groove deteriorates until it collapses and players no longer have a group rhythm.

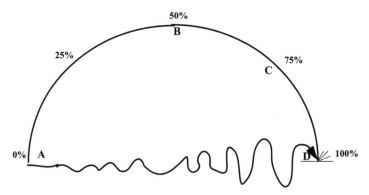

Transition Point Illustration

The steadiness of the line at the beginning represents the steadiness of the group's rhythm. As the groove becomes more unsteady the line becomes more jagged until, like the groove it represents, it comes to a complete stop.

Point A

At point A you recognize that the rhythm has begun to get unstable. You may not be the first to recognize it, thus encouraging the death of your facilitator's ego.

Point B

By the time you reach Point B, at least half of the drum circle participants are aware of an upcoming transition point. They may be looking around, wanting help. From Point B, it gets increasing difficult to successfully facilitate a transition, as the group's rhythm deteriorates.

Point C

 By Point C, three out of four players in the circle know that they are in rhythmical trouble and they look for your guidance. This provides an opportunity for experiential teaching without teaching. By stepping into the circle at this juncture you educate the group about transition points as you guide them through the transition to another rhythm.

Point D

If the group gets to Point D, no groove is recognizable and it is time to facilitate a rumble or a call-and-response sequence to avoid a train wreck.

Show a Group How to Identify Their Transition Points

Next I describe one way I might show a group how to recognize their transition points, while I teach without teaching.

 At least three times during any drum call, when I recognize a transition point forming in the groups music, (Point A in the Transition Point Illustration), I deliberately let it develop until I can see that at least three of every four players in the drum circle are fully aware that there is a problem with the rhythm and that they need help. (Point C). Then I hop into the middle of the circle and save the players from their dreaded impending rhythmical train wreck.

I do this with all the theatrics of a Dudley Doright Mountie, who runs onto the scene to untie Miss Penelope from the railroad tracks and save her, just moments before the train (wreck) arrives. "Here I come to save the day! Mighty Facilitator is on the way!"

By doing so, I save and redirect the rhythm, entertain the circle, and educate them about what a transition point sounds like, feels like and looks like. I enter the center of the circle to help guide them through those rough and sometimes scary rhythmical transitions.

When you stay out of the circle until there is a strong need for the group to be facilitated, you create a positive statement about your intention and purpose as their rhythm-event facilitator. "I am here to help you, not manipulate you." Use this experiential learning technique sparsely so your group will not feel manipulated. Three times during drum call will likely accomplish your teaching-without-teaching goals. Then when a transition point appears later in the event, let it develop until at least half the players notice (Point B). This gives the players time to recognize the transition point and take action to rectify the situation.

The correlation between the percentage of players in your circle who recognize that the groove is in trouble is directly proportional to how close the groove is to complete disintegration. The more shaky the rhythm gets, the higher the proportion of players who become aware of the situation. Also, the shakier the rhythm, the harder it will be for you to facilitate a smooth transition.

From a player's point of view, once they recognize that the group rhythm is in trouble, their ability to do something about it is limited. Without a facilitator, the conscious cooperative effort of the whole group is needed for them to make a transition to a successful closing or a new groove. Although rare, a successful group-facilitated transition does happen occasionally at in-the-moment circles. When it does happen, it is a magical moment for the group and a powerful affirmation of the players' ability to interact together as one musical entity.

If we do our jobs well as facilitators, drum circles will need fewer facilitators and more orchestra conductors.

A self-facilitated group transition can happen more often when the facilitator has helped the players identify transition points. Later in the event when the group is rhythmically synergized, you can allow a transition point to develop and the group can respond to it as one body. While monitoring the group's ability to self-facilitate, you are prepared to enter the orchestrational spot and help them if they lose control of the transition. Each time you give the group a chance to play with the transition point, you offer them a musical teambuilding experience that challenges their ability to work through a rough rhythmical situation. As your group develops a stronger rhythmical relationship, and you continue to allow them to play with the transition point, you help them develop self-facilitation muscles. By leading the players to lead themselves your intention to empower them guides the group far beyond rhythmical empowerment toward self-facilitation.

From the Arthurian point of view, if we do our jobs well as facilitators, as the drum circle movement continues to develop and mature, drum circles will need fewer facilitators and more orchestra conductors.

Late Night

With a single exception, it is my experience that many more magical self-facilitated transitional moments occur in an empowered facilitated drum circle than in a non-facilitated freeform circle. An exception is the legendary late-night drum circle at each VMC Hawaii Playshop.

When the circle of drummers is a group of drum circle facilitators who know how to self-facilitate, "we don't need no stinkin' facilitators." The transition points introduce themselves to the group and they respond like a flock of seagulls following wind currents. The group smoothly moves through many magical musical changes for hours without crashing or stopping. When it's time to stop, the flock usually lands as one body.

Late Night Drumming by the Fire

At one late night circle during a moment of silence after the group brought itself to a smooth completion of a music piece, Don Davidson said, "It doesn't happen like this anywhere else on the planet."

Read the Group

A facilitator needs to learn how to "read" the group that they are facilitating, to answer three important questions:
- What kind of instruments are available?
- What is the level of rhythmical and playing expertise of this group?
- What is their group consciousness potential?

Reading the group is an act of quantifying, or measuring, these three basic elements in the drum circle dynamic throughout the event. You want to attune your focus to the group's sound, rhythmical and playing expertise, and group consciousness. These three elements are always evolving and constitute what we call the Drum Circle Potential Triplicity.

Drum Circle Potential Triplicity

This triplicity is a map to help you assess the group's progress at each step in its musical journey. This will help you ascertain what the group needs to advance to the next level in the relationship with itself and its music.

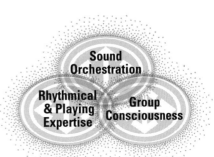

Sound Orchestration

The instruments played in a circle determine the sound of the orchestra.

You can always cheat with a closed population program because you are usually providing the drums and percussion for that group, but with a community drum circle it is a blind date. Depending on where you are on the planet and with which group you are working, anything can happen. When you open your doors you see who comes to your community drum circle and what they bring to play. Hopefully they will bring a good mix of instruments. A way of "cheating" at an open circle is to bring an extra bass drum and a bag of hand percussion to share, as needed. Whenever you can, also bring extra drums to share.

When you guide them by teaching without teaching, the group's musical consciousness evolves.

What constitutes the perfect mix of drum pitches and percussion timbres to create a good sound orchestra is up for debate.

If you ask me, and I guess you have since you're reading this book, I say that a good percussion ensemble consists of one half drums, with a mix of low, medium and high pitches, and one-half hand percussion with a timbre mix of bells, shakers and woody sounds.

As you assess your circle, these are elements to quantify in the group's instrumentation:
- Drum type: bass drum, cow skin, goat skin, bongo, dumbek, talking drum (low, medium and high pitches)
- Percussion timbre mix: bells, wood instruments, shakers
- Other sounds: gongs, Tibetan bells, cymbals, and non-percussion instruments such as flutes and didjeridoos

As the players become aware of what is needed to create a successful musical balance, with your guidance they mature in the process of making conscious musical choices about which instruments to play and when to play them. As this happens, a person who is drumming might determine that there are too many drums being played in the group and choose to switch to a bell, shaker or woodblock.

When you guide them by teaching without teaching, the group's musical consciousness continues to evolve throughout the event.

Rhythmical & Playing Expertise

The rhythmical and playing expertise of your circle will differ according to the type of group with whom you are working. Well elderly, corporate groups, kids in school, and community drum circles each have their own levels of expertise. In most community drum circles, you will get a large number of beginning-beginners, some intermediate players and hopefully a few advanced drummers.

It is a natural phenomena that the rhythmical ability of individual players and the group as a whole constantly changes for the better as the event progresses. The rhythmical expertise of a beginning-beginner, who has never drummed before, can improve dramatically over the course of a two-hour drum circle. It is less about the person improving their technique, and more about improving their self-confidence. Being immersed in a two-hour rhythm bath allows people to rediscover and express the rhythmical spirit they still have naturally from their childhood. It's a beautiful thing to see people make this discovery.

In addition to a measurable improvement in rhythmical ability individually and in the group over the course of the event, the group's ability to play together improves exponentially. How well they play together in the first thirty minutes of an event will be entirely different from how well they are able to play after an hour of having you facilitate using the elements that make a drum circle successful.

The best way to measure this amazing phenomena is to facilitate a closed population such as a corporate group. You can watch them transform from a group of individuals, who believe that they are rhythmically challenged, to a fully functioning, self-organized in-the-moment jazz percussion ensemble.

I once facilitated a group of three hundred percussion students in a college drum camp. The ones who thought of themselves as intermediate players in that group would have easily been considered advanced players in any community drum circle. Their rhythmical ability as individuals was phenomenal, but because they had come from many different backgrounds, such as rock and roll, classical and ethnic music, their ability to play with each other was horrible. It wasn't just that they were too busy showing off their chops to listen to the other players, though a few were showy. They were also unfamiliar with each other's instruments and playing styles. I quickly solved this problem by identifying the different types of instruments in the group and showcasing them. After listening to each other, the playing expertise of the group rose to the level of the rhythmical expertise and a fun time was had by all, including me.

Group Consciousness

How well a group recognizes their connection with each other and their relationship to the circle defines group consciousness. To read the spirit potential of a group, you can assess these elements:

- body language
- eye contact among group members
- musical content once they start playing
- how well they are listening and playing with each other

Group social dynamics affect the way a group listens and plays with each other. A group of high school students listens and interacts with each other differently than a personal growth group.

Having said this, no one particular category of demographics would always interact the same way. For example, each corporate group reacts differently in a rhythm-based program, depending partly on the business culture they foster, and partly on the job hierarchy of the people in the meeting. Middle managers, factory workers and mixed groups of workers each have different group dynamics.

I once facilitated a number of rhythm-based events in a middle school with four separate classes of sixth graders. Even though I ran the same program in each class, each group of kids responded entirely differently. One class of sixth graders were well behaved and obedient but emotionally dead with little spirit. The kids in that group responded to me well enough, but seemed to be afraid to take chances. The result was a muted rhythm event. Another group was just the opposite. The kids were spunky and rambunctious with lots of spirit. Although these kids challenged me to keep their attention, the musical result was always on the edge of chaos, but with wonderful surprises and great results. Each sixth grade group consciousness that I met during that day was entirely different from the next.

> **Social dynamics affect the way a group listens and plays with each other.**

At the end of the day, I sat down and tried to find the factors that had made the differences between the groups' experiences. The number of kids in each class and their ages were about the same. Although I did each program at a different time of the day—early morning, after recess, after lunch, and late afternoon—the time of day was not enough to cause such major differences. Then I realized it was the teachers' social conditioning of the kids that created a different group consciousness in each of the classes.

Now whenever I walk into a classroom, I pay close attention to read the ways a teacher maintains control of their students. This information helps me understand the consciousness of the group that will be making music

A group's identity is part of the development of their group consciousness. You can use specific metaphors to help individuals in a group connect with each other to form this group consciousness. Once this connection is made, it manifests itself in the music.

When you read this potential during your event it can empower you to empower them to manifest their highest rhythmical, musical and spiritual consciousness.

In Closing

Facilitators use the elements initiated during drum call to develop and nourish the circle throughout the life of a rhythm-based event.

By doing simple facilitation interventions, and using metaphors in the windows of communication, you teach the players the ABCs of your facilitation body language. At the same time, by creating interactive experiences, you introduce them to each other as players and educate them about the instrumentation of the percussion ensemble they are becoming. You establish to the group your role as a facilitator who is there to serve and to guide the group process. As part of this process, you unveil some of the musical and rhythmical possibilities that already exist in the group.

The group has a lot more rhythmical ability than they realize.

All of this can done without lecturing or overt teaching. Remember that creating a situation where you appear to be their superior and their teacher defeats the purpose of holding an empowering community event.

Everything you do in drum call sets up the foundation for progressive musical and emotional successes. The group has a lot more rhythmical ability than they realize. Trust, acknowledge and work with the group's potential and you will be able to guide your drum circle to cooperative successes far beyond what they perceived possible.

Wet Drum Circle at East Coast Playshop with REMO Drums

7 In the Center of the Circle

In the days when you could count the number of drum circle facilitators on your fingers, we called the center of the drum circle the power spot—the place where all the energy, spirit, passion and music converge.

A drum circle is a container for the in-the-moment rhythmical alchemy that takes place among the participants. Its center is the natural focal point for all the players in the circle, the place where the rhythmical contributions combine to create the excitement for which drum circles are famous. This center truly is a power spot.

Here, the power of individual players combines to create the group mind. That group mind, in turn, transforms the group's musical contributions into rhythmical alchemy and magical spirit. This spot is the one most facilitators choose to use as they facilitate their events.

Although the center of the circle is the power spot for the group, its name has confused some facilitators into thinking that it is their power spot. The phrase power spot sometimes creates a mind-set that feeds a facilitator's ego so they think they are somehow more important than the circle's participants.

By changing some of our earlier drum circle facilitation nomenclature into Arthurian, I hope to induce a certain amount of respect for the circle and its participants. This will hopefully shift the perspective for facilitators of their cosmic position in the whole gestalt of an ongoing rhythm-based event.

I now call the center of the circle the orchestrational spot. By referring to it as the orchestrational spot, I hope to encourage an attitude in facilitators that helps them remember to empower the group process, rather than control it.

The main priority of facilitation is not to perform, in spite of the fact that some of the skills required of an artful facilitator are a sense of theater, performance abilities and charisma.

A drum circle is a container for in-the-moment rhythmical alchemy.

The basic definition of the word facilitate means to make easy, not to entertain. With this in mind, you want to use the skills of listening, pacing and leading, and then following the people who are following you. These skills define an art form more dedicated to serving the community than to entertaining it. Meanwhile, as facilitator part of your role does include being entertaining, but it does not mean that entertaining participants takes precedence over facilitating the circle's magic.

Create the Orchestrational Spot and then Respect It

If you facilitate the whole group from the same place inside the circle throughout the entire event, then you create and mark that spot. The orchestrational spot is usually, but not always, in the center of the circle. It becomes the major focal point for the group, especially if you are standing in it. Once you establish the orchestrational spot, by walking onto it you get the group's immediate and undivided attention, whether or not they are playing.

In a smaller more intimate circle, with fifteen or fewer participants, you may want to define the orchestrational spot as your place in the circle *among* the players—the edge. This is sometimes a better way to facilitate than standing in the middle of the circle, as it helps you avoid intimidating players by being too close to them or looking down at them because they are seated. You will need to know how to activate your edge position when you are called to facilitate, and when and how to become invisible, by deactivating your spot when it is time to GOOW. You want to be able to shift the attention of the players from you back to their musicmaking. You can readily get the players' attention using any of your attention calls. When you want to become invisible you can call the group to groove and then join in as one of the players.

All full-group facilitation takes place from the orchestrational spot. In most cases this is also the spot from which the facilitator speaks to the participants. In some types of programs, I create a separate *talking spot* to deliver verbal metaphors and messages, so that I keep the orchestrational spot "clean." When I want to facilitate an individual, or a smaller group within the circle, I move away from the orchestrational spot and closer to those people.

If created properly, your use of the orchestrational spot becomes one of your more powerful facilitation techniques and needs to be used with great humility and respect. The less you use it, the more power it has. Overuse takes power away from both the orchestrational spot and you as facilitator.

The center of the circle is the best place to stand to hear and feel all of the power, beauty and grace in the music that your drum circle is offering. It is also the best place to receive the information you need to successfully facilitate the circle's contributions to their next higher potential. However, if you stand in the orchestrational spot without facilitating you get in the way of the music. Taking a *rhythm* bath without being in active service to the purpose of the event sucks the group's attention like a sponge. If you do this, you will reduce the effectiveness of the orchestrational spot and you will appear to be self-aggrandizing.

The two activities that most facilitators, including me, need to recognize, monitor and avoid relative to being in the middle of the circle, are over-facilitating during the rhythms and talking too much in the windows of communication between those rhythms.

Over-Facilitating

Over-facilitation happens when you stay in the orchestrational spot longer than is necessary to facilitate one of your three prime objectives:

- Strengthening and reinforcing an ongoing groove,
- Creating a segue between a rhythm coming to completion and a new groove,
- Bringing a rhythm to a successful ending.

The participants are not there to serve the facilitator. You as facilitator are there to serve them.

You are over-facilitating when you go into the middle of the circle and facilitate without regard for the group's transition points. You are also over-facilitating when you overstay your welcome in the center, manipulating them and their rhythm beyond your prime objectives.

Over-facilitation is a misuse of the orchestrational spot and an abuse of the position and responsibility given to you by the players in the circle. When you over-facilitate, it is usually because you are either consciously or unconsciously serving your own needs rather than serving the needs of the circle. The participants are not there to serve the facilitator. You as facilitator are there to serve them.

Talking Too Much

The windows of communication between rhythms are opportunities for short bursts of metaphor delivery and setup for the next piece to be facilitated. In the beginning of the event, you might introduce yourself and your helpers. At the end you might take time for announcements, such as those for future drum circle events. But during the other windows of communication keep your messages short.

Talking too much during these windows disconnects you from the circle. If you use too many words to get a point across, even if they are all correct words, then you are in danger of changing your relationship from "I am here to help you make beautiful music," to "I am here to give you a lecture." In most situations, people come to a rhythm-based event to play with each other, rather than to receive a lecture or drum class. But do not worry. If you talk too much during the event, someone is sure to let you know. If you stretch your window of communication too far you may hear someone in the circle shout, **"Let's drum!"**

Intervention, Sequence and Orchestration

Most teaching without teaching happens when you are standing on the orchestrational spot. Before stepping into the center of that circle to help guide the players toward their highest musical potential as a group, you need to develop a positive intention and a good understanding of your role as facilitator.

Three basic concepts help define what you do. Advanced facilitators Don Davidson, Cameron Tummel and I had a long discussion about these concepts and how to name them. We came up with metaphors that mirror these three main activities:

- Linguistic Metaphor

    A *word* is represented by a single body language direction given from the orchestrational spot, with messages such as "stop," "go," "volume up," or "speed up."

    A series of these directions connected to each other constitutes a *sentence* such as "lock in the pulse," so that we can "bring the volume down," and "speed up the rhythm."

    A combination of directed sentences becomes a *paragraph*.

- Musical Metaphor

    A *musical note* represents a single body language direction given from the orchestrational spot.

    A series of these directions connected to each other constitutes a *musical phrase*.

    A combination of directions becomes a *musical composition*.

We use the words intervention, sequence and orchestration to describe the ideas represented by these linguistic and musical metaphors. A single act of facilitation is an intervention. A small combination of facilitation directions is a *sequence*. A combination of sequences is an *orchestration*.

Intervention

To intervene means to come between to modify. This term has often been used in medical and counseling professions. We use it to represent a single body language direction during a rhythm-based event.

As a facilitator, whenever you step into the orchestrational spot, you are intervening. Whether or not you are actively facilitating, your presence in the center of the circle is enough to influence and affect the group's process. When you step into the middle of the circle and give a direction to the players, you intervene in their musical process. If the group is not playing and you walk into the circle to start a rhythm, then you are intervening in the group's "non-playing."

The orchestrational spot can be seductive and draw you into it for reasons other than service to the music and to the community.

Questions to ask yourself:

- Are you intervening on their behalf or your own?
- What moves you to go into the circle and facilitate at this particular time? Is it because you have a great idea you want to try, or are you being called by the group as it enters a musical transition point in the rhythm and needs some help or direction?
- Why are you telling them what to do? Hopefully it is to help the group make their musical experience more successful.

If you need to step into the orchestrational spot because there is a transition point, you are intervening on behalf of the group and their music, whether the process is heading for a rhythmical train wreck or is simply in transition. We call this a positive intervention.

Standing in the middle of an ongoing event, and having the full attention of the players as they respond to your slightest whim can easily feed your facilitator's ego and cause you, and your circle, problems.

If your facilitator's ego gets seduced by the power of the orchestrational spot, you may find yourself going to the center of the circle for self-aggrandizement rather than selfless

Are you intervening on their behalf or your own?

service. If you step into the orchestrational spot and intervene just because you have a great idea that you want to try, then you are not serving the good of the circle. Instead you are manipulating the situation. This is why it is important to remember that every time you step into the middle of an event and give even the smallest facilitation direction to the group, it is an intervention in their process. Hopefully, knowing this will help generate the humility needed to make good choices.

In the beginning of a drum circle, you want to use simple interventions to teach the participants the facilitator body language that you will use throughout the event. Each intervention is one simple facilitation direction given to the group. This is done through vocal directions, body language directions, or both at the same time.

When a facilitator is using a single intervention with the circle, it is usually to make a simple adjustment and then GOOW. Sometimes simply walking to the orchestrational point while marking the pulse with your body will create enough group focus to solidify an unstable groove.

Here are some examples of single facilitation interventions:

- Counting out the pulse from a window of communication to get a group groove started. With this type of intervention you dictate to the group the speed of the rhythm and you also tell them when to start, such as "one, two, lets all play." This is an example of a full group intervention.
- Walking into the circle as they play and giving them a volume down signal is an intervention because you are asking them to do something different than what they were doing: "Play softer."

Sometimes the most simple intervention can have the most profound effect.

If the rhythm is a little shaky all you need to do is solidify the pulse of the group. To do this you have many choices of simple interventions. Here are two examples:

1 Walk into the orchestration spot, and while looking at one side of the circle, pull on your ear and point to the other side of the circle and then GOOW. With your body you are saying, "Listen and play with the other side of your circle."

2 Walk into the orchestrational spot and mark the pulse with your body until the group groove is locked and then smile encouragingly and GOOW. This is another full-group intervention example.

Sometimes the most simple intervention can have the most profound effect.

Sequence

When you facilitate a single intervention with a group, you are directing the circle with simple body language. When you create a sequence of interventions you are usually facilitating a circle through a musical transition point using a combination of different body language signals.

A number of interventions used one after another creates a facilitated *sequence* of rhythmical events in the group's music.

Sequences are usually designed by the facilitator to take the group through a transition point to a new rhythmical and musical environment. Musicians call it a musical segue. A musical segue smoothly connects one song to another without stopping between them. A well-facilitated sequence can do a similar thing in a rhythm-based event. You can create a smooth musical transition from one groove to another with a sequence of interventions.

When a transition point in the groove calls you to the orchestrational point, listen deeply to the group as you go—to hear what you need to know to choose a good sequence. It is helpful to have an Arthurian-style service mantra, "How can I serve this group at this time?" going through your mind.

Hopefully, with deep listening and a service mantra, by the time you arrive at the orchestrational spot, you will have determined what intervention or sequence of interventions are appropriate to help take the group successfully through the transition point to another musical dynamic, another rhythm or rhythmical completion.

Here are some examples of simple facilitation sequences:

1 Lock in the pulse, then bring down the volume, speed up the rhythm, and bring the volume back up. Then GOOW.

 2 Sculpt one half of the circle for showcasing with a continue-to-play signal. Stop cut the other half. Encourage applause from the stopped players for the group being showcased. Count the observers back in with a call to groove signal and GOOW.

$$+ \rightarrow \ominus \, G, \, \boxtimes \, ROC = \ominus \, \text{✩}, \, ROC \, \mathcal{D}, \, ROC \, \circlearrowright \text{GOOW}$$

To bring a drum circle groove to a successful conclusion, sequences of interventions are usually more desirable than a simple stop cut. With a sequence of interventions you can bring the groove to musical and emotional closure. Walking onto the orchestrational spot and giving an abrupt stop cut can sometimes feel like rhythmical interuptus.

With each added level of facilitation interaction, from simple interventions to sequences to orchestrations, there is more intervention, and so more manipulation. This implies that you need to be even more aware of the delicate dance between the players and you, to insure that you maintain good rapport with the circle. Be careful to not over-manipulate the group's musical experience.

Orchestration

Although a simple Arthurian definition for orchestration would be a combination of facilitated sequences, orchestration is a lot more than that. To be orchestrated successfully, a group must have found their rhythmical alchemy. This alchemy gives you the permission you need to orchestrate.

Orchestration is the act of creating an in-the-moment musical composition with a fully connected and engaged drum circle.

After the group has evolved, with the facilitator's help, from each person having an individual sensibility toward having a group sensibility, they become a percussion ensemble that hears timbre distinctions and how to put rhythms together. Orchestration is usually most successful later in this process when the group gains an orchestrational consciousness, which includes hearing and being sensitive to volume dynamics and musical harmonics. This is why I recommend waiting until later in a program to orchestrate. At the beginning of an event, during drum call, your circle is just beginning to form their group consciousness as a musical ensemble.

A facilitator needs the group's permission before orchestrating a drum circle. Only after a strong rapport and trust have been established between you and the group can you orchestrate without them feeling over-manipulated.

You are the orchestra conductor, and the composition you create is based on the musical contributions of the individual players in the group. These musical elements already exist in your drum circle, and are offered to you by the participants. You must have their willingness to cooperate in your manipulation of them.

As the group gels into an orchestra, the transition points come less often, because the players are more connected and self-facilitating. You can orchestrate by composing more musical content into the transition point. Later in the program, once you have a fully-rounded relationship with the group, they will want you to come into the circle and compose with the musical elements they are contributing, even when there is not a transition point.

> **A facilitator needs the group's permission before orchestrating.**

It is my belief that any intervention in a drum circle, regardless of the intention, is a manipulation and needs to be seen as that. With that point of view, hopefully, we facilitators will use and not abuse the power given to us by the participants. With that kind of attitude, we will be able to enter the drum circle with enough humility to serve to the best of our ability.

Being conscious of and using these intervention, sequence and orchestration concepts will help you facilitate with humility.

In contrast, over-facilitating creates what I call facilitator burnout in the group. When facilitator burnout happens, people are less attentive and less responsive to the facilitator and more likely to feel manipulated.

The intelligence and rhythmical ability inherent in the group's consciousness is always a lot more than they realize. By trusting, acknowledging and working with that group's intelligence and potential, you will be able to guide your drum circle to cooperative musical and emotional successes far beyond what they perceived possible.

It is the circle's spirited contribution and collaboration, with you as their conductor, that will manifest the highest musical creation available in that moment. When that collaboration is done well, the magic and spirit in the music will be the epitome of rhythmical alchemy.

Connecting

The most important thing you do as a facilitator is to make honest and sincere connections with the people who are participating in your event. I provide techniques and exercises in this book to support you as you create this relationship with your group. The fancy tools and techniques that you might use will be for naught unless you have a sincere relationship with the people whom you are facilitating.

A rhythm-based event is not about you the facilitator. It is about everybody's relationship with each other, and with you. It is more about their music than your facilitation of it. So, to be a successful facilitator, you need to make and maintain contact with the people in the circle and with their music.

The quality of the rhythm, music and energy you create is more about the group's relationship with itself and less about their rhythmical and musical expertise.

When you step into the middle of the circle you have the full attention of every player there. An important question is, "Are you returning that attention in kind?" I have seen highly energetic facilitators with fantastic presentation skills jump into a circle but facilitate blindly. Although they had their eyes open, they were not making eye contact with the players. Instead, they were paying attention to the next facilitation idea in their head. That means that they were facilitating their ideas instead of the musical and rhythmical contributions from the players in front of them.

> **The quality of the music you create is more about relationship than rhythmical expertise.**

I have also seen many a beginning-beginner facilitator help create beautiful music with a drum circle because they worked with the people, rhythms and energy in the circle, instead of from some idea in their head or from one of Arthur's facilitation books.

The most important elements in facilitating a successful interactive rhythmical event are contact and relationship. It is not about us. It is about them.

Facilitation or Manipulation?

by Cameron Tummel

The line between helping the group and manipulating the group can be very, very thin.

Cameron Tummel Playing Bell

As we develop our ability to facilitate successful sequences, we must always maintain our connection with the players, and always help the participants feel appreciated.

Empowerment is a key component for a healthy circle. Your drum circle may contain the most experienced players in the world, but if they feel manipulated or disempowered, the music can turn sour. On the other hand, your drum circle may be full of the most inexperienced players in the world, but if they feel empowered, if they feel confident and connected, and if their spirits are free, they will create the most beautiful rhythms possible. Always cultivate a positive atmosphere of appreciation and limitless potential.

One way to prevent your participants from ever feeling over-facilitated (manipulated) is to thank them for their cooperation with you. Your "Thank you!" can come in words, or in smiles, or in other signs of positive feedback. Don't just dispense orders to your participants, appreciate them for letting you lead. When they are doing what you asked of them, let them know they're doing well.

If you initiate a sequence, especially if it is one you have led a thousand times before, always maintain your connection to the group. Never assume they are enjoying your idea as much as you assumed they would. It is easier to redirect your sequence than to reconstruct a broken relationship with the circle.

Your ability to successfully lead the group will be built upon your relationship to the circle, not your agenda. The more they realize you are attentive to their needs, the more they will let you lead them.

Exercise: Connecting

While the group is in full groove, each player takes a turn, one at a time.
- Stop playing and walk into the center of the circle.
  - Make a slow 360 degree turn on the orchestrational spot while making eye contact with each person playing in the circle.
- Return to your place in the circle and begin playing while the person next to you takes their turn.

It is simple, and as you will see, profound.

Blinded by the Light

To share a few ideas about what *not* to do when facilitating I will tell a composite story based on situations I have encountered, describing a facilitator named Olaf (an alias.)

As an elder in our growing drum circle facilitation community, I am frequently called to facilitate the facilitators during events where a group of us are sharing responsibility for the circle. Sometimes I am asked to help organize and guide an event. Other times I am asked to troubleshoot at a gig to help bypass private agendas. This second task is to help herd individual facilitator egos into a cohesive group vision so that the participants can have the most successful event possible with the least amount of tension. A tradition that has developed for the close of a co-facilitation planning meeting is the 'facilitators' handshake.'

For this story, imagine yourself at an event for five hundred players. I began by making a "presenting facilitators" list much like musicians will make a set list of songs for a show. I scheduled facilitators sequentially, based on their facilitation style, dynamics and abilities.

Each person facilitated for approximately thirty minutes. After each facilitator there was a short Arthurian window of communication where I thanked the last facilitator, introduced the next one and, if needed, facilitated a short sequence to adjust the circle's playing energy.

One particular facilitator, Olaf, has been a drum teacher and performer for years. Even though I know he has some limitations with reading groups, I placed him in the second half of the event, because of his highly charismatic and entertaining facilitation style.

Olaf was fully attentive and responsive to the other facilitators during the program, and after I introduced him to the circle, he jumped in with full facilitator guns blazing. His energy and style were perfect at that juncture in the event, because the previous facilitators had warmed up the drum circle.

The players in the circle were energetic, enthusiastic and responsive.

As a masterful drummer, and a veteran performer with a 200-watt smile, he started an excellent groove with a smooth sequence of facilitation directions. At the end of his first sequence, the circle was in full groove and ready to explore the rhythm further on their own. That would have been the perfect time for Olaf to GOOW and let them enjoy the music until a transition point in the rhythm called him back to facilitate more.

Unfortunately, he did not get out of their way. He stood in the middle of the circle, basking in the power of hundreds of drummers focusing their energy and music to that spot.

The power of the orchestrational spot is very seductive. As facilitators, we have each

 succumbed to it from time to time, and stood in it longer than called for by the players we were serving. When that happens, we become as much of a distraction to the circle as someone who is playing loudly out of time.

Basking in the glory of the music, Olaf still stood in the middle of the circle and let the groove go for only a minute before he initiated another sequence of events, then another, and another. He sliced and diced the group using every facilitator trick in the book, with little time between facilitation sequences for the group to enjoy the groove. For the full thirty minutes of his allotted facilitation time Olaf never

Facilitators' Handshake

left the center of the circle.

It may have been clear to some of the players that Olaf was showcasing himself by using all his fancy facilitating tricks. It was definitely obvious to the facilitators in the circle that he was showing us what he did not know: that the facilitation techniques he was using are designed to help guide the group, with their cooperation, to its highest musical potential.

He showed us that he thought that the facilitation tools are simply a means to manipulate the group, with their obedience, to create the best music that he could force them to make. Olaf's performance was entertaining to the group for a short period of time, but it was not very empowering.

In the thirty minutes that Olaf stood in the center of the circle, he demonstrated the typical scenario of what happens when a facilitator creates facilitation burnout in a drum circle event. Instead of supporting the group's musical intention, and letting them play with each other, he consistently interfered with their rhythms by inserting *brilliant* facilitation ideas that had little to do with the music being created.

As more people felt that they were being manipulated rather than being served, they paid less attention to Olaf. As a group, their responses to his directions got sloppy. Some people deliberately ignored him and even played through his excessive use of signals.

With this kind of facilitator's burnout, it is not the facilitator who burns out. It is the players who get burned out on the facilitator. The circle figures out that they are being pushed around, and stops following directions given to them by anybody who acts more like a dictator than a supportive musical guide.

People seldom stop playing and take a break, en masse, in the middle of a healthy rhythm. They usually wait for the completion of a musical piece and take a break during a window of communication between grooves.

By the time Olaf was twenty minutes into his facilitation piece, over twenty-five people had left their seats. Some left their drums where they were sitting, which meant they would be back. Others took their drums and left the program, not a good sign in the middle of an event, and certainly not good for the facilitators scheduled after him.

Occasionally, at this type of event, when I see this, I make a mental note that if people continue to get up and leave, then I will do something that I only do in extreme situations. I will go to the center of the circle where the facilitator is camped out and tell them to create a situation where they can GOOW and let the group drum for a while without interference.

As host, I am concerned that the high energy and good community feelings created by the other facilitators' excellent work can be negated by over-manipulation of the group.

Looking across the circle at the facilitator who was scheduled to follow Olaf, I could see the same concern written all over their face—that they would be expected to facilitate a group of players with a bad case of facilitator's burnout.

While all this was going on, I became aware that Olaf had created the back of a circle. While you might think it is impossible to create a back to something that is round, all the people on one side of this circle were seeing a lot more of Olaf's back than his face. Whenever Olaf sculpted the circle in half he consistently used the same access line. Even when he did a full group intervention he still faced the same direction, facing away from the same half of the circle.

Olaf used the *back* of the circle as his rhythm *platform,* by having them continue to play the groove as a safety net while he turned his back to them and did fancy facilitation with the front group. During the whole time Olaf stood on the orchestrational spot, he turned around only a few times to tell this same group to keep playing and to flash a smile toward them.

The advantage for the players in the back of the circle was that they were less manipulated so they played more continuously. The disadvantage was that the back group couldn't completely connect with the front players in the circle because there was a body constantly standing on the orchestrational spot between them and the other players.

Your players are the source of the rhythmical alchemy and magic.

Once I became conscious of this strange phenomenon that was being created, it did not take me long to figure out why this was happening. Olaf was playing to a spotlight positioned on a balcony across from where the back part of the drum circle was facing. He was treating one part of the circle as the back stage while the part of the circle he faced became his audience. Instead of facilitating, Olaf was performing to the spotlight.

When Olaf finished his facilitation *performance,* I entered the orchestrational spot and as the host, thanked him and had the circle thank him with a full-group rumble. Because at least forty people stood up preparing to take a well-deserved break, I kept the window of communication short. Instead of introducing the next facilitator, I counted off a group groove with a "one, two, let's all play" and the group started their next rhythm. Being sure to face each section of the circle equally often, I locked the group pulse with my cow bell.

Looking at the next facilitator, I could see that they understood the intention of my actions because they mouthed the words *thank you* to me. I was using the rhythm to wash away the facilitator's burnout by allowing the circle to get into their own groove. Then, when the next transition point came I was planning to bring the groove to a close and introduce their new facilitator. By then I hoped to be handing over a rhythmically refreshed group of players.

Once the group groove was solid, I made a large theatrical gesture while leaving the circle. The message was "I am getting out of the way so you can play your groove." I ran out of the orchestrational spot, up one of the aisles and behind the circle. Some of the people who were standing up to leave the circle sat down again and played, while others who had previously left during Olaf's facilitation returned and joined the groove.

When I ran out of orchestrational spot, many players' bodies faced the center of the circle but their heads turned around backwards like a scene from the movie *The Exorcist*. Their eyes were following me as I left the circle. When I stopped at the outer edge and turned around, I discovered that the spotlight was still shinning down on me. The attention of many of the players had followed me. I had become a major distraction, which was just the opposite of what I intended.

To rectify the situation, I used simple body language to refocus the attention of the distracted players back to the circle and at the same time deliver an important message to the group. I pulled my right arm back behind my head as if preparing to throw a football. Instead I theatrically threw my arm forward and made a point that went up to the second story balcony, past the spotlight, and deep into the chest of the spotlight operator. Then, turning, I pointed with both hands into the center of the circle. The operator immediately shifted the spotlight from me and back onto the orchestrational spot. The distracted players returned their energy to the rhythm and it solidified. My actions were a direct message to everybody in the circle.

A facilitated drum circle experience is not now, and never has been, about us the facilitators. It is, and always will be, about them. Your players are the source of the rhythmical alchemy and magic. It is their rhythmical spirits that we are facilitating.

8 Percussion Ensemble

A percussion ensemble is a group of people who play together with various percussion instruments. They consciously adhere to basic musicmaking principals, including listening to each other and creating a musical dialogue with space in their playing for each other's contributions. In their playing, they express dynamics in volume and intensity while creating musical harmony and rhythmical relationships.

Developing your rhythmical and musical experience and understanding will help you facilitate, especially as your circle jells in its experience as a group. This chapter presents some of these basic technical elements. An understanding of these ideas will help you facilitate and teach without teaching as you direct your group toward percussion ensemble consciousness. These ideas will be useful to you in the following scenarios:

- When you play in a culturally specific drumming circle,
- When you perform in a professional percussion ensemble,
- When you facilitate a rhythm-based event with players who have different levels of rhythmical expertise.

The basic universal principles discussed below explain both the technical aspects and the interactive relationships among players in a drum circle. If you have musical or drumming experience, then many of the elements presented in this section may not come as a surprise to you, but will likely give you a fresh perspective. If you are new to drumming, ideas for gaining experience are described next.

Ways to Get from Here to There

If you are just beginning your drumming and facilitation journey, you can learn a lot as a participant in a drum circle. Pay close attention to the relationships between the players and the instruments they are playing, as well as to the relationships between the players and the facilitator. You can also gain valuable information by attending a philharmonic orchestra concert and paying close attention to the relationships between the orchestra players, their instruments and the conductor.

Taking hand drumming classes will also help you develop an understanding of the relationships between players, instruments and facilitating. Hopefully, as a drumming student, you can find an eclectic teacher who has broad experience studying and teaching different styles of hand drumming from a variety of cultures. She can explain the universal principles of hand drumming that are inherent in all rhythmacultures. I recommend that you seek out and study with such a teacher.

If you cannot find an eclectic teacher, then you can create your own curriculum by studying beginning hand drumming with three teachers who teach different styles from specific rhythmacultures. You can either do this simultaneously or sequentially. By studying in a beginning-beginner situation with multiple culturally specific drum teachers you will avoid the blinders that studying with a single culturally specific teacher can give you. Instead, you will gain an eclectic understanding of the universal principles of hand drumming inherent in all cultures. In the process, you will also gain rhythmical expertise that will help you successfully facilitate rhythm-based events.

You can learn a lot as a participant in a drum circle.

An extensive choice of culturally specific classes are available in and around any metropolis on the planet. Some examples of drumming choices include West African djembe and dunun, Taiko drumming from Japan, Haitian, Congolese, Afro-Cuban, salsa, samba and capoeira. The list is almost endless. The study of drum and dance rhythmacultures permeates many other cultures throughout the world. For instance Afro-Cuban music and drumming is popular in Japan, and samba ensembles are fashionable in England and Scandinavia. West African drumming and dance are popular throughout Europe. Balinese Gamelan orchestras and Zimbabwean-style marimba ensembles provide culturally specific experiences as well, and are beginning to appear in many metropolitan areas and at universities.

Information you receive in culturally specific classes can teach you how to set up a percussion ensemble consciousness in your drum circle participants. This consciousness encourages listening and playing success. In a community drum circle, players will have a wide variety of rhythmical expertise and experience. Many of the participants may not have met or played with each other before your event.

Instrumentation

What is the perfect instrument mix and placement for a well-balanced orchestra? Any answer that I give you will not fit all scenarios. Also, my response for a particular scenario is debatable among facilitators because each has their own preferences for the same event. Each facilitator is free to choose their instrument mix and format. My opinion of the perfect mix and placement for a well-balanced orchestra is one half drums and one half percussion scattered evenly throughout the circle, with the bass drums in the innermost circle.

As a player in a percussion ensemble, one basic performing principle is to have an understanding of your instrument and its role in the group. Then you can use that understanding in your interaction with the other players, while using the universal principles of musicmaking to support the ensemble's intention and interaction.

As a player in an anarchist freeform circle, the basic idea is to express yourself while sharing your rhythmical spirit, with the belief that there are no rules. Expressing yourself is good in any drum circle, but being ignorant of, or ignoring basic natural laws of musicmaking can create rhythmical chaos. While you can live your life ignoring the social roles that permeate our society, there will be consequences if you ignore the natural laws of the universe, such as the law of gravity. It is also true that you can share spirit in a freeform circle while ignoring the natural laws of rhythmical interaction that are understood by percussion ensemble members, but the consequences will likely be a rhythmical train wreck.

As a facilitator, after gaining a basic understanding of how the instrument timbres and pitches interact, support and affect each other, you will be able to pass this information on to your drum circle participants while teaching without teaching. Once you share your understanding with them, the group will be able to play more like a professional percussion ensemble and less like an anarchist freeform drum circle. At the same time, your players will still be adhering to the basic principles of both types of drum circles: freedom of expression accompanied by an understanding of their role in the group.

When I facilitate a drum circle, I usually identify and divide instruments into two general categories based on the timbre of the hand percussion and the pitches of the hand drums. I use triplicities to describe each of these two instrument groups, based on their three most identifiable parts.

The three most distinguishable timbre sounds of hand percussion in a drum circle:
• Wood blocks and claves: sticks on wood
• Shakers: beads on surfaces or inside containers
• Bells: sticks on metal.

The three most distinguishable pitch ranges of hand drums:
• Low
• Medium
• High

Hand drums have varying timbres depending on whether their heads are played with your hands, with drumsticks or with mallets. I divide drums into the pitch groupings listed above when I facilitate because it is easier for players in the circle to identify the drum pitches rather than the timbre distinctions. Although you can distinguish many additional subdivisions, for facilitating it is easier to identify wood, shakers and bells for percussion and low, medium and high pitches for drums.

Once you understand the purpose and use of these six instrument groupings, you can use them when you facilitate to help your circle take the music to higher and higher levels. Hand percussion instruments have easily distinguishable and identifiable timbres. They are usually atonal in nature and have short note durations so you can hear space between their notes. On the other hand, while membrane drums have one general timbre with easily distinguishable pitches, the notes sustain longer than most percussion notes, and, as a result, create identifiable harmonies between the drums. I explain ways to use these differences below.

Percussion Timbre Triplicity

The hand percussion instruments are the non-membrane instruments in a drum circle that players usually shake or play with sticks. I classify them into wood, shakers and bells, as listed above. These instruments are made of many different substances, so each has a distinct and identifiable timbre. Each timbre has its place and use in the orchestral mix of a drum circle ensemble. Ideally, you will have a large variety of percussion instruments distributed throughout your circle so you can achieve a well-balanced orchestra.

The Percussion Timbre Triplicity fits perfectly with the rock-paper-scissors metaphor. Each of the timbre groups does something the other two cannot do. The tripod metaphor for this triplicity also fits well, as each timbre group holds up the others by playing into the sounds of the remaining two groups' instruments. We use all three types of instruments to get a balanced timbre mix.

> I call the hand drums the chicken and the percussion the spices.

I sometimes tell my drum circle participants that while the drums are the meat and potatoes, the hand percussion are the spices. Wherever I go on this planet, I eat chicken, but everywhere I go, the chicken tastes entirely different. The taste of the chicken changes because of the spices used by that culture. I call the hand drums the chicken and the percussion the spices.

Wood: Timekeeper, Precision, Scissors

Most wood instruments are struck or scraped with wooden drumsticks or timbale sticks. Various wooden instruments include wood blocks as well as guiros, claves and the now-popular carved wooden frogs. Some

Wood Instruments

modern-day "woodblock" sounds are produced from instruments constructed in plastic.

The clave is a good example of how wood percussion is used in the music of many cultures. Clave are two hardwood sticks that you strike together to make a short, piercing wood sound that can be clearly heard, even in the loudest drum circle. In a traditional Afro-Cuban drum ensemble, one player uses the clave as the timekeeper. The pattern that the clave plays in the ensemble locks all the players' music together.

Typically, a wooden instrument in a drum circle can be heard and considered as the timekeeper for the music. Even in a one-hundred-person drum circle it is easy to hear the timbre of a single wooden instrument. When approximately one sixth of the players in your circle are playing wood instruments, the result is a well-established rhythm clock.

When you sculpt all the wood percussion in your drum circle, then stop cut the other players and showcase the wood players, you uncover a sound similar to the inside of an old-fashioned wind-up clock. When you listen to the showcased wood instruments, you can hear the sound of the drum circle's clock.

$$+ \rightarrow \emptyset \, W \, G, \; ROC \; \bigotimes = W \; ☆$$

One of the most important characteristics of the wood instruments is the preciseness and shortness of their notes. This space in time leaves room for all the other players. In the international kids' rock-paper-scissors game, wood would be the scissors because their sound "cuts through time."

Frog Circle

Scraper instruments are typically made of wood, gourd or plastic material, with grooves cut into or mounted on their top surface. When you drag a stick across the grooves it makes a frog-like "ribbit" sound. Some enterprising people in Southeast Asia are now carving various sizes of hollowed-out wooden frogs, each with a ridge of grooves on its back. When I went to Vietnam to do a corporate program I found a supplier and brought home a banana box full of different sizes of this type of wooden frog. In addition to using the frogs as part of my instrument mix in corporate programs, I also bring a complete set of frogs and other scraper instruments for each participant in my Rhythmical Alchemy Playshops™. With them, we do a Frog circle that focuses on "dialoguing across the pond."

I facilitated a Rhythmical Alchemy Playshop at the Mt. Madonna Retreat Center situated in the coastal mountains overlooking Monterey Bay, California. Ponds and waterfalls are sprinkled throughout the retreat center, and wherever you find water there, you find frogs. I decided to close the first evening of the retreat with a frog circle. Without setting a specific tempo to start, I let the group create spaces between their frog calls. As the frog pond dialogue started, I slowly dimmed the lights in the room to complete darkness. The only reference points for the participants were the frog calls themselves. Slowly the frog dialogue evolved into an excellent rhythm. As the rhythm began to find its own closing, I facilitated the group to play their frogs softer and softer toward a gentle fade-out. As the group played their frogs at lower volumes, it was obvious that someone in the circle was playing their instrument louder rather than softer. Since the room was pitch black I could not see who it was. But as soon as everyone but that one person had stopped playing, it was obvious to us that it was not a person at all but a real frog outside our window dialoguing with the circle. "Hey, where did you guys go? RIBBIT!"

Shakers: Space Fillers, Environment, Paper 🎵

Shakers come in many shapes and sizes, with containers typically made of gourds, plastic cylinders or tin cans. Sometimes the beads or seeds are inside the shaker container, and sometimes you find the beads or seeds strung on the outside of a gourd in a tied-macramé netting. I also put tambourines in the shaker category because they are imprecise instruments that you shake to play, even though the jingles on most of them are made of metal.

Shakers

Arthur's Favorite Shekeres

You play a shaker by shaking it. Because of the lack of a demand for accuracy, the shaker is considered the easiest instrument to play by the beginning-beginner player. They are also the percussion instrument of choice of some advanced players because of their unique sound and timbre. I like playing the shekere in a drum circle or a band because the instrument is capable playing the pattern being played by any other instrument.

Shakers are the most imprecise instrument in the hand percussion triplicity. Instead of going *doink* or *dink*, they go *swish* with hundreds of beads hitting the instrument's surface in and around some specific point in time. All of these beads never hit the surface at precisely the same time, so you hear a sloppy, imprecise note that is a combination of all the beads hitting the surface of the shaker on one shake. "Swish!"

During the more sensitive songs and dynamic musical moments in a rhythm-based event, you can facilitate the shakers rhythmically or as rumbles, to create different songs and emotional environments. The shakers are the paper in the rock-paper-scissors game. They fill up the space between the notes, covering that space with a *swish*.

Didgeridoo Segue to Trance Groove

The traditional didgeridoo is made of a skinny Australian eucalyptus tree trunk that has been hollowed out by termites. When you blow air through it, you create a very low-pitched sound. The sound is similar to long Bavarian alpine bugle horns, but with a lot more rhythmic variations. Other versions of didgeridoos are made from Yucca cactus, PVC tubing and fiberglass.

While facilitating a community event, I saw one player in the circle playing her didgeridoo. Other didge players stood off to the side, not knowing how to make themselves heard in the circle. At a transition point during an ongoing groove, I placed the plastic top of one of my shipping boxes upside down on the orchestrational spot as a sounding board for the didgeridoos. I then invited the didge players into the center of the circle. They gathered around the box top, placing the horn ends of their instruments into it to increase their resonance, and they began to blow. It was necessary to be right next to the didge players to hear them over the loud volume of this one-hundred-person drum circle. To the drummers, it looked as if I had invited people into the middle of the circle to blow on a bunch of long hollow tree trunks for no reason. They looked like they were blowing over-sized Native American peace pipes without any musical result. I waited for the didge players to connect and play with each other for a while before I stop cut the other players in the circle. I showcased the deep resonant sounds of the didgeridoos, and the subsonic body-shaking vibrations surprised some of the players in the circle.

After the didges played for a while and established their own rhythm, I orchestrated the emotional tone of the musical piece by facilitating the shaker players to create a series of long, quiet rumble waves. The shakers made a sound like ocean waves advancing and receding on the shoreline of the didgeridoos' humming vibration. After signaling both the didge and the shaker players to continue, with a call to groove I gently brought the wood players quietly into the rhythm at half tempo. Then I layered in the bells in a similar way. I took my time, letting the emotional mood of the music simmer between each layer. By the time I invited the drummers into the groove, they were in a trance state, listening to the new

Don Davidson Facilitates Didgeri-crew

environment created by the music. When the drummers joined in, they felt a totally different rhythm than the one they had been playing before the stop cut. The new groove was softer and slower than the preceding one and the drum circle players supported and played with the didgeridoos instead of on top and over them.

$+ \rightarrow$ didg **G** , ROC ! ⊗ = didg ☆ , S ∿ ∫⌒ , didg / S **G** ,

/// W , /// B , /// D GOOW

Bells: Harmonies, Emotion, Rocks ⬤

Bells come in many shapes and sizes of metal. Their timbre is the sharp sound of wood against metal, as we strike the bells with sticks. Their tone and pitch vary depending on their shape, size and thickness.

Bells

The hard metallic sound of the bell rings over the softer notes of the membrane instruments (drums) in the drum circle ensemble. Because the bell has the longest-lasting note of the hand percussion instruments, and due to the range of pitches in a group of bells, overlapping notes create harmonies inside the group song.

(T) When you have ten or more mixed bells in your drum ensemble and you showcase them by signalling for them to continue to play while you stop cut the other players, you can hear an interactive bell song. It sounds similar to parts of a Balinese Gamelan Ensemble—an interactively woven pattern of bell harmonies that can easily shift the emotional mood of the song.

In the rock-paper-scissors game, the bells are the rocks. They are the hardest sound, with a sharper attack than the wood instruments.

Drum Pitches and Drum Families

Unlike percussion instruments, drums have skin membranes stretched over a shell or frame of some sort. Whether the drums are hit with hands, sticks or mallets, their timbre will be generally the same and not as easily distinguishable as their pitches in an ongoing drum circle. This is why I identify the drum sounds by pitch rather than by timbre when I facilitate.

For identifying and facilitating the drummers in a rhythm-based event, classifying the drums into three general pitches is quite sufficient and effective for most situations. Facilitators with a more extensive drumming background can often distinguish more separate pitch ranges.

(T) To help each player identify their pitch in the orchestra, you can play rumble games. For example, have all the drums rumble with their hands in the tonal area of their drum, while listening to each other. Then facilitate each pitch range rumbling separately. If you have unequal group sizes, you can have the medium group rumble and listen again, and then move the lower-medium pitched drums into the low-pitch group. After identifying and establishing the three pitch groups, show the group the body language you plan to use to start and stop a rumble for each group. With flattened palm parallel to the ground, place your hand over your head for high pitches, at chest level for medium pitches and lowered for low pitches. You can create a rumble song by simply raising and lowering your hand. Each group's rumble starts when your hand enters their area and stops when you move your hand out of their area. Be playful. Have fun!

A Family of Conga Drums

Unlike the hand percussion, most types of drums played in a drum circle are tunable. This means that all the same type of drum do not typically get identified in the same pitch group.

A drum family includes drums from a particular rhythm culture that are tuned and played together as an orchestral group. For example, ten or more Ewe drums from Ghana can be played to create a culturally specific rhythm. The three-drum conga ensemble common to Cuba includes a tumba (low), a conga (medium) and a quinto (high pitch). This type of pitch arrangement is typical for hand drum families from many rhythmacultures. The range of low to high pitches helps create the interactive harmonics that become the melody line in a drum song. You can sculpt and showcase drum types, but when you want to facilitate pitches in a community drum circle it is better to ignore drum type. When facilitating by pitch, consider all the drums to be a part of one big drum family.

 When you want to teach players at your event about culturally specific drum families you can sculpt and showcase drum types such as djembes, congas and dununs.

Drum Pitch Triplicity

Low Pitch: Bottom, Foundation, Body

The large double-headed drums are typically the lowest-pitched drums in your circle. Additionally, you can use hand drums such as Cuban tumbas, Brazilian tan-tans, and large frame drums as bottom drums. In larger circles, I set up a sound bowl or concentric circles of chairs with my low drums in the center circle. I place the bass players around the inner circle so they can easily see and hear each other.

I let the bottom players know they are the foundation of each rhythm and ask them to pay particular attention to my body language when they support me while I facilitate. I also invite them to dialogue rhythmically and to pay as much attention to each other as they do to me, to ensure a well connected low drum song.

 Typically during an opening drum call, I sculpt the low drums for showcasing and stop cut the remaining players. This gives the low-pitch drummers an opportunity to listen to each other and fine tune their song before I bring in the other players. When I give the circle a window for listening to the bottom drum song, everyone's musical connection improves after I bring the group back to full groove.

The low-pitched drums have a subsonic physical vibration that you can feel almost as much as you hear. These vibrations speak to the body. If you have a friend who is tense,

Low-pitched Drums

invite them to lie down in the middle of a drum circle and receive a body massage from the vibrations of the low drums. Their tension will often melt from their body like butter melting in the sunlight on a summer day.

When someone in the circle finds it challenging to find the pulse because they are trying to play from their head, I like to give them a shaker and place them between two low drum players. They won't need to look for the pulse. The pulse will find them.

A drum circle can be a scary place for you as facilitator unless you have a few low-pitched bass drum players to hold down the rhythm foundation. I suggest you carry an extra bass drum, such as a surdo or dunun, just in case no one brings a

bottom drum. When you know you will be facilitating mostly beginning-beginner drummers, consider bringing along an experienced drummer to play a bass drum, to ensure a solid bottom for your drum song.

Augie Doggie Peltonen of Brgantine Beach, New Jersey, shares his perspective for a pleasant way to enjoy these vibrations provided by your circle.

Receiving a Full-body Sound Massage

Under the Hawaiian moon, after drumming for hours, that late night atmosphere was fully present. Our fire tender walked into the middle of the drum circle to lie down on the ground, as the drumming was in full trance mode. He stayed there for quite some time. It is hard to judge how long, because late-night trance mode is timeless. He appeared to be sleeping in middle of the circle, but then he arose with this incredible smile on his face as if he had just emerged from some amazing place. After this, others took turns going into the center to lie down. After lying there for some time they each began to smile. It began to look like we might need a "take a number" machine like those they have at a deli.

The next night someone thought to bring a blanket so folks wouldn't have to lie down in the dirt. That night almost everyone at the fire circle took turns going into the center of the drum circle and lying down to absorb the vibrations. Arthur, who was not feeling well due to a flu bug, entered the circle. After lying there for a long time, he too came out of the experience rejuvenated. It was becoming apparent that this new discovery must have a healing effect.

I took a turn lying on my back in the center of the circle. After orienting myself to the surroundings, I noticed the bright Hawaiian starry sky, and the bare knees enveloping drums cast an orange flickering light above me. It was a supporting and nurturing group that almost seemed like a scene from a tribal movie. When I closed my eyes, I became aware of the various timbres—the high pitched, the medium, and the djun-djuns. Especially noticeable were the djun-djuns. The vibrations of the drums came out through holes at the bottom and went into the ground on which I was lying. This was a oneness of the hands on drum skin through the wood, into the ground and up into my spine, legs, torso, neck and head. It was a full-body sound-vibration massage. After a few minutes, I became one with the vibrations, and completely relaxed into a zen-like state of well-being. I knew others wanted a turn, and I arose with that certain look one gets on their face after feeling the effects of lying in a drum circle.

Medium-pitch Drums

Medium Pitch: Harmonies, Character, Heart

Almost all rhythmaculture drum families have medium-pitched drums, such as the Cuban conga, Haitian secunde and Nigerian ashiko. These drums typically define the character of the rhythm being played. When I set up a sound bowl or concentric circles of chairs, I check to be sure the middle drums are placed throughout the circle.

I consider all the middle-pitched drums in a circle to be the heart-part drums, regardless of drum type, for the following reasons:

- Heart-part drums typically play syncopated patterns that interlock with the simpler patterns of the higher-pitched time-keeping drums and the lower-pitched foundation drums. This interlock creates a very discernible and identifiable rhythm song. As a culturally specific drummer, when someone wants me to play a specific rhythm, the heart part comes to my mind and hands first.
- The harmonies between the medium pitches interact and vibrate the heart chakra, helping create emotional release and relaxation in the players.

Whenever you showcase all the medium-pitch drums in your circle, some people will swear that they hear voices in the drumming because they hear the very clear harmonies in the rhythmical interactions.

High Pitch: Accents, Lead Solo, Head

Facilitators find a wide variety of high-pitched drums such as the quinto, dumbeck, talking drum, bongos, small frame drums and tightly-strung djembes and ashikos in their circles. The high-pitched drum players create all kinds of interesting interactive dialogue and patterns.

Depending on the mix of drum types and players in any particular circle, you will hear very different sounds. The high-pitched drums might sound like a bunch of chattering chipmunks or possibly their song could be full of syncopated accents that stimulate the other drummers in the circle.

High-pitched Drums

In some drum families the high drums are used as timekeepers, and in other drum families the high drums are played by lead soloists. Advanced drummers in a rhythm circle can use their high-pitched drums to play lead solos over the existing drum circle groove. When you acknowledge these dynamic players by showcasing them, the soloists can inspire the other players. When you showcase them, you also relieve the advanced players of the need to over-play or solo at inappropriate times.

The quick, sharp notes made by the high-pitched drums are famous for clearing out the thoughts in your head. By doing so they also help to keep you in the *now* of every beat in the music.

The total chorus of drum voices creates a vibration that goes beyond the drum song. The subsonic body vibrations, medium-pitched heart massage and high-pitched thought-clearing notes vibrate our bodies, hearts and minds to lift our souls into a unity of spirit manifest in sound.

Kenya and Gabriela Masala are corporate and community development consultants who create breakthroughs in issues affecting the community and workplace. They share a story of their experience guiding shamanic trance drumming circles.

Shamanic Trance Drumming

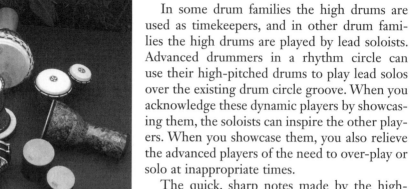

My wife and I participated as faculty, guiding a group of thirty people at a beautiful retreat center in Costa Rica. The program included outdoor adventures, yoga, dance, fitness training and drumming. The joy in the community drum circles was a constant; so was the mystery in the Shamanic drumming sessions.

The Shamanic or "trance" drumming sessions were simple 60-minute meditations utilizing down-tempo community drumming. We began each session with a short, guided visualization for relaxation, then started with a heartbeat rhythm, inviting the participants to join. The only instructions were to relax and feel the flow of the rhythm.

As the participants became tranquil and dropped into the groove, the relaxed state of awareness in the space became palpable. Some participants let go into the rhythm instantly; they closed their eyes, entrained to the beat and soon it was hard to tell whether they were playing the rhythm or the rhythm was playing them.

Others, more unfamiliar with relaxing in a groove, struggled to keep their eyes open, their gaze searching for the right way to do it. Since we know the experience of the drum trance, we trust that eventually the mind lets go into the simple flow of the rhythm. Inevitably these folks relaxed.

Before long, in a place beyond spoken language, everyone lost track of time. Some participants playing smaller percussion instruments were moved to dance and their authentic movement naturally guided them around the circle of drummers.

Then came the magic and the mystery.

No one was chanting, and yet every time we guided these trance-drumming circles, a chorus of low rhythmic sounding and vocalization emerged about 30 minutes into the experience. It's an amazing phenomenon. The overtones of what sounded like tribal, indigenous voices chimed in. They were calm and rolling over the rhythms with a soft, but clearly audible melody. Their sound was ancient yet familiar, and this chanting remained steady until we brought the participants out of the hour-long meditation.

We watched as participants were visibly relaxed, peaceful, deep in themselves and touched beyond words. We gave them time and space to come all the way back to an alert state, and encouraged them to stay with the energy of their experience as they headed off to bed. We asked them to be aware of their dreams as they rested and to share with us in the morning. There was an atmosphere of reverence, honor, gratitude and magic as the group dispersed.

The following morning, without fail, at least a dozen or so participants asked, "Who started chanting?" "When did you all start singing?" "That singing was beautiful. Who was it?" "Was that a CD of chanting in the background?" We smiled and wondered with them. Was it the voice of the ancient ones? Was it the voice of the drum? Was it the tribal spirit magnetized to gatherings of humans in ritual rhythmic offering?

Participants share accounts of inner journeys, healing states, dreams, surrender, visitations, cleansing tears, peaceful joy and experiences of deep peace. We never cease to be amazed by the simplicity of this practice and its ability to facilitate profound shifts of awareness. Our gratitude to the primal mother grooves and all her voices, human, animal, drums and spirit—they are all blessings.

When you listen closely you can hear voices in the drum song of almost any rhythm-based event. They are the angels in the music.

Taylor Rockwell shares a story of Dan Metzger and himself facilitating the recognition of the angels in the music.

Angels in the Music

Dan and I were guest artists at a two-week in-school percussion workshop. We came in to guide drum circles for all the fifth graders who had been having fun making drums and drumming in small groups. During one of those drum circles, we discovered an amazing way to hear the angels in the music. We lifted a hand drum while the drum circle groove was going, and held it gently so that the open bottom end of the drum was a few inches from each player's ear. We made the rounds of the whole circle, letting each person hear the same drum. This slow-walking rhythm "liturgy," full of eye contact and smiles without words, was reminiscent of communion.

Then we invited half the circle to drum, while the other half held their hands just over their drum skins and felt the vibration song. Then those who were not playing leaned down and put one ear just over their drum skin to hear their drum's unique song. When half the group does this, it looks like prayer as they bow down, close their eyes, and tune in with the angels in the music.

Exercise: Rumble by Pitch

 This simple rumble game teaches without teaching and can easily be turned into a foundational rhythm for group improvisation.

1 Facilitate the players as they each identify their pitch group.
2 Show the group the body language you plan to use to start and stop a rumble for each group.
3 Set up a simple rumble rhythm pattern. For example: L-M-H-H, L-M-M-H.
4 Once the pattern of when to rumble is established, encourage the players to make up their own rhythms within their rumble turns, to morph the rumble groove into a rhythm groove.

Portland Rumbles

Patrick Pinson was a rhythmical evangelist long before I met him during my early drum circle pioneering days. He invited me to add a Portland, Oregon, community event as part of my regular west coast drum circle tours. I said yes, of course, and we held the first drum circle in his store, Cedar Mountain Drums. I knew that Patrick's rhythmical focus is centered around Native American drumming and culture, but it was not until I arrived at his store that I learned that his drum shop also is. After that realization, it was no surprise to see that most of the players entering the circle carried a traditional Native American frame drum and mallet. By the end of drum call, two-thirds of the instruments in the circle were frame drums. The resulting sound was a low drone pitch, with a bit of variety from a few djembes, congas and dumbecks.

The frame drummers had a tendency to all play their drums, with their mallets, on the same pulse. Playing the "one beat" is typical for frame drummers participating in a trance-meditation drumming circle. But that style of drumming would not sustain the interest of the moms, dads and kids who came to the community circle to experiment with their rhythmical spirits, celebrate and have fun.

I had to rectify the situation or lose the families and be left with only the trance drummers. Not all the frame drums had the same pitch. I identified and sculpted three basic pitch groups among the players, using a series of rumbles. This dispersed the frame drummers into three groups. I then passed out interactive rhythm parts to each of the different pitch groups, as foundations for musical exploration. Our drum song remained low-pitched, but with a lot of rhythmical and melodic interactions.

After that first circle in Portland, the mix of instruments shifted over time. At later circles, more hand drums and percussion were brought and played, and fewer frame drums. In those early days as I was learning to facilitate, every drum circle was a big experiment, as I experienced the nuances of drum circle facilitation. The drum circles I facilitate today still offer me opportunities to grow. But the wonderful challenge of that first Portland community drum circle taught me a very important lesson about identifying and facilitating pitch in your orchestra.

Patrick Pinson

Drum Circle Song

A Drum Circle Song is music created by the players' rhythmical and harmonic interaction. When you hear the song of your circle, the group has jelled and is cooperating with each other to make music. One of your jobs as facilitator is to use these rhythmical and harmonic contributions to guide the group to play with a unified voice. This drum circle song is usually made up of three basic elements: universal patterns, interactive rhythms and melody lines.

Universal patterns set the foundation that is the basis of an interactive dialogue among the players. This dialogue creates pitch harmonies in the patterns being played on different instruments. Let's look at these elements through the lens of the Drum Circle Song Triplicity and explore each one individually.

Drum Circle Song Triplicity

A group of players can easily come together and create a solid rhythm groove, but the group must be conscious of specific elements before a definable drum circle song will typically emanate from their groove.

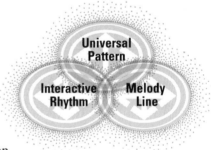

When the players understand how to make music with drums and percussion, in addition to playing rhythmical grooves, you get a drum circle song. You can help your players do this when you facilitate the teaching-without-teaching activities provided below.

Universal Pattern as Foundation

The foundation of any musical composition, from philharmonic orchestras to jazz quartets to drum circles, is the universal pattern that holds the rhythm together as the piece progresses. The players need to agree about the foundational pace and pattern for any sustained rhythmical or musical interaction to happen.

Over the past thirty years I have flown over a million miles around the world, interacting with the many rhythmacultures of different countries. In almost every culture, I hear players using a rhythmical pattern that we Westerners call the clave. Because this clave pattern can be found in the music of cultures all over the planet, I call it a universal pattern. While rhythmacultures use thousands of rhythms, only a handful of universal patterns are found among many different cultures. The clave is one such rhythm.

Universal patterns typically leave open at least as much space as they use. For example, the 3•2 clave has notes that are played during only *five spots in time* in a space with 16 possible 16th notes or spots. Another characteristic is that most universal patterns have two sides: a front and a back. The 3•2 clave has a front pattern that sounds and feels like a question: 1•2•3. Its back pattern sounds and feels like an answer to the question: 1•2. The 1•2•3 question is answered by 1•2.

As facilitator, you can introduce universal patterns into the group's rhythm as a foundation for improvisation. More complicated and syncopated patterns are challenging for the beginning-beginner player to play and leave less room for group or individual improvisation. Remember to KISS!

The pulse is the simplest foundational pattern, the universal tick-tock of the world's music. I can start a rhythm almost anywhere on the planet with a simple pulse-based call to groove, "One, two, lets all play!" Of all the universal patterns, the pulse leaves the most room in the rhythm for improvisation. Even though the pulse does not have two sides, it is a universal reference point for music and rhythm.

Interactive Rhythm as Dialogue

Players need to feel free to rhythmically explore their relationship with each other. Once you introduce a universal rhythm to establish a foundation for a drum circle song, encourage your players to improvise. If they all play the exact same rhythm, such as a 3•2 clave, without any variation, they are not interacting. As rhythm robots playing the same linear pattern without adding any of their own rhythmical character or life force, they would create a very mechanical rhythm with no personal expression.

You need to establish with your players that they have the freedom to rhythmically improvise, explore their relationship with each other and express their rhythmical spirits as they play around the universal pattern. When you use a universal pattern as the foundational platform and free your players to interact in rhythmical dialogue they create a rhythm full of spirit, character and life.

One way to encourage players to use a universal pattern as a foundation for improvisation is to empower them to experiment by taking out or adding one or two notes to the pattern with which you started the groove. This interaction can easily be turned into a rhythmical dialogue when you ask the players to connect with someone across the circle and interact with them rhythmically. Another way is to directly ask players to have a dialogue with the other players in the circle.

Melody Line as Harmony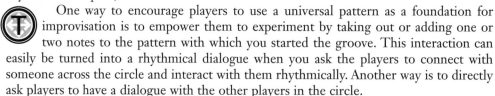

When players listen to the relationship between the pitch of their rhythms, they can create combinations of harmonies that enhance the drum circle song.

While you have an ongoing interactive dialogue in your drum circle, you can focus the group's attention on the pitches of the different notes they are playing on their instruments. Once they become aware of their individual melodies, you can guide their attention to the different harmonic combinations being created by the instruments being played around them. By making the players aware of these harmonies and melodies, you encourage them to make conscious choices about which other players with whom to engage in dialogue.

You as facilitator can help a drum circle song emerge at any recreational rhythm event.

When your goal is a dynamic expressive drum circle song, you want to introduce a universal pattern to the players in your circle. Then encourage them to engage in an interactive dialogue with their fellow players. Finally, help them become aware of the harmonies they are creating. When you help the participants become aware of the potential of the drum circle song, then the quality and sustainability of their music increases.

Lego Drummers Create a Song

Clave Clap Exercise

 This drum circle exercise educates your players about the importance of listening and engaging in a dialogue. Players will want to have a full range of drums and percussion ready, so they can emerge from clapping into a drum circle song.

- Have the group clap the 3•2 clave pattern. When they are all clapping the clave, their foundation provides a rhythm platform for improvisation.
- Have them each improvise their own rhythm relative to the group clave. Now you have an interactive rhythm. Ask them to pay attention to the other players and to play around each others' patterns.

You now have an interactive dialogue clave clap, but with everyone clapping with their hands you have all skin-on-skin timbre and practically no pitch. With only hands as instruments there is little chance to create a melody line with your group of clappers.

- While the group is clapping, signal for them to pick up their instruments by giving them a call to groove signal, "One, two, let's all play." An alternative signal that Cameron likes to use is to sing the call to groove at the clave spots in time as "One two three, let's play."

Their drum circle song will emerge.

Planting the Seeds

I facilitated a program in southern Wales for seventy high school students and twenty high school music teachers from that region. Because the teachers requested a drum circle demonstration, I facilitated the basic universal principles of ethnic drumming, teaching parts for each drum pitch range, and we put the parts together to make one drum circle song.

I taught the group how to use the basic language of rhythm to communicate with each other in a collaborative, improvisational musical dialogue. Using universal drumming principles, they played in-the-moment music with their rhythmical spirits.

Using their solid groove as a platform, I facilitated some

advanced orchestrational ideas into their music. By sculpting and showcasing particular players' parts in the ongoing groove, I encouraged others to join in playing those parts as the music evolved. I closed that piece with a call and response that morphed into a climactic rumble.

Then I asked the teachers to wait outside the building for me. They went out with surprised looks on their faces. Under my direction, the kids then moved closer together to fill the empty seats left by their departing teachers. The students exchanged their drums for any other available drum that they might want to play. I then empowered a couple of the teenagers to come to the center of the circle and facilitate the group using body language they had seen me model in the earlier piece. The two teen facilitators started a groove and facilitated the circle while I stepped outside.

I found the music teachers on their tiptoes, peeking in through the windows. They were aghast that I would leave a group of seventy high school kids playing drums without an adult conductor to supervise. I told them the kids were conducting themselves just fine and that the excitement of the music they were creating would supervise them. Then I stood between the teachers and the entrance to the building and conducted a question-and-answer session. They inquired about how they could use this drum circle technology in their music classes. What kind of low-cost, low-maintenance instruments could they buy that could be played in a variety of situations? I explained that they can create simple hand percussion instruments for their school without spending lots of money. I gave them a copy of my book, *Drum Circle Spirit* to share among themselves, and showed them various exercises from the book that they could use.

While we were outside, the kids were inside self-facilitating and maintaining an energetic groove for ten to fifteen minutes before we adults came back in to join them and bring the session to a close. Sometimes the rhythm can do its own evangelism without me.

"What do you critique?" Triplicity

While Jonathan Murray was President of the Drum Circle Facilitator's Guild (DCFG), he asked my advice, while we were working on the peer review section of their professional accreditation application. Jonathan asked a simple but profound question as we discussed peer review critique techniques that are required for professional DCFG accreditation. "Just what do you critique?" he asked. No one had ever asked me that question, not even me. I received a blinding flash of the obvious. I am not sure how long I held the phone in my lap, but as my mind returned from the all-consuming blinding flash of the obvious, I could hear Jonathan call to me through the phone. "Arthur! You there?" I put the phone to my ear and gave him the answer to his question.

My answer to Jonathan Murray's question is, "A triplicity of triplicities." In Facilitation Playshops, we use the critique technique process to give feedback for both short sequences. When someone completes a short sequence of facilitator interventions we use the "Critique Technique Triplicity" on page 108.

When we have the privilege of critiquing someone facilitating a complete rhythm-based event, we delve deeper. While in the position of being a witness, we take notes and make observations, while applying critique techniques in three major areas: presentation, relationship and results. I define each of these three in triplicities described in this book.

Presentation

I describe presentation in the "Presentation Skills Triplicity" on page 43.
- Vocal Skills—The use of the voice to move and inspire.
- Group Leadership Skills—Directing people to achieve a goal.
- Body Language Skills—The use of the body as a communication element.

Relationship

I describe relationship in the "Trust Triplicity" on page 127.
- Honesty—Devoid of hypocrisy.
- Rapport—Harmony and mutual understanding.
- Congruency—Consistent logical agreement among the community, reflected by their level of participation and engagement.

Result

I describe results in the "Drum Circle Song Triplicity" on page 165.
- Use of universal patterns that are open to interpretation.
- Interactive rhythms that create rhythmical dialogue.
- Melody lines, created using percussion, timbres and drum pitches to enhance instrumental harmonies.

As part of their Professional Accreditation Peer Review program the DCFG now uses a scoring system in each of these three areas. I also currently use these three triplicities as guidelines for peer review critiques during our ten-day Mentor Facilitator Programs held in Hawaii. Once you are comfortable with the "Critique Technique Triplicity" on page 108, you can use these three triplicities as additional guidelines for your critiques. Understanding what to critique opens up the floodgates to a vast amount of information. Remember that there are no mistakes, only learning opportunities.

Rhythmasized by Rhythmaculture

Guto Goffi is the percussionist for the popular Brazilian band Barao Vermelho, which has been touring the world for over twenty years. In each of the fifteen days of my first visit to Brazil, I heard at least one of the band's songs played on the radio. Guto owns and runs Maracatu Brazil, a culturally specific music and dance institute in Rio De Janeiro. Guto is well-connected in the professional drumming community in Brazil, and when he heard that I would be facilitating drum circles in his country he invited me to do a drum circle facilitation *demonstration* at

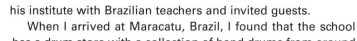

his institute with Brazilian teachers and invited guests.

When I arrived at Maracatu, Brazil, I found that the school has a drum store with a collection of hand drums from around the world that would satisfy any percussionist's dream. The two-story compound even has a small restaurant in the courtyard. Guto walked with me down the school's hallways, lined with sound-proofed rooms. Each time he opened one of the doors we were greeted by an emanating wall of sound, rhythm and culture—Afoxe from one room, fusion Samba from another, and a Batucada played by seventy-five players in the third.

In preparation for my drum circle demonstration, we placed chairs for twenty in the courtyard. We also supplied drums and percussion, but most of the players arrived with their own. Our group included a master Timbale player, the school's Afro-Cuban percussion teacher, a respected elder in the local Candomble community, a Capoeira master, and member of a local Escuela de Samba group.

The variety of instruments that they brought to the circle reflected the variety in the players' backgrounds. The instruments ranged from Afro-Cuban congas to a snare-like samba repique, pronounced "hapeek." After introductions, instead of doing a call to groove, I sat down and started playing a low conga. I deliberately played a very different pattern than any Samba-style rhythm I know, so that I could hear what the other drummers would play as they joined the groove. Pure drum jazz emerged, into one of the most amazing in-the-moment culturally specific drum jams of my life.

The words 'culturally specific' and 'drum jam' do not typically appear in the same sentence in the U.S. Those words represent opposite extremes of the drumming experience. A drum jam implies that rhythmical expression is encouraged, but playing culturally specific rhythms would be frowned upon. Similarly, a culturally specific drum circle does not include improvisational jamming. Playing culturally specific rhythms correctly is a sign of respect to the cultures that are the source of the rhythms we study.

Because each of the players in the circle was a masterful percussionist, an extraordinary rhythm emerged, merging individual rhythmical expressions rather than any specific rhythm from Brazilian culture. We had started a drum jam that most drum circle facilitators would recognize.

Even though it was a jam, the following elements that make a culturally specific rhythm were well in place:

- The use of universal patterns
- Using rhythmic patterns to make space for other players
- Active cooperation instead of competition
- Rhythmical dialogue
- Interactive harmonics

While we were jamming, someone changed their rhythm to a culturally specific Brazilian Afoxe, pronounced afosha. Without stopping, we smoothly moved from a jam to a dynamic Afoxe rhythm, complete with song and chorus.

From Afoxe, the rhythm morphed into a Comparsa rhythm, then into another jam that slowly became a Maracatu rhythm, for which the school is named. While we were playing the Maracatu, which was in 4/4, we slowly morphed our rhythm into a triplet-feel 6/8

Camdonble rhythm.

Whenever someone started to sing, the group played softer and join into the song. At different times the rhythm sped up or slowed down as if we all decided to do it at the same moment. When it was finally time to stop for a break, that is what we did. We brought the rhythm to a smooth close, all on the same note. No one went into the middle of the circle and made a stop cut. We all just stopped, as if we were one player with many hands. "We didn't need no stinkin' facilitator."

I was stunned, amazed and pleased down to the core of my little drummer's heart.

"Maracatu Brasil" Drum

Planting the Seeds

9 Orchestration

The orchestration phase of an event typically occurs during the last third of a community drum circle, with players self-facilitating much of their own music and conscious that it is, in fact, *their* music. Transition points appear less often as each new groove is more solid, has more continuity and lasts longer than the last groove. By this time, you and your players have a positive, supportive relationship that leads to a musically and emotionally rewarding event.

First you facilitate the basic elements into the group's playing consciousness using teaching without teaching. Then, once you complete the ice-breaking community building and develop the technical aspects among the players, you free them to focus less on maintaining their rhythm and *more* on the musical harmonies evolving from those rhythms. Your job description evolves from being facilitator for the group's rhythms to being an orchestra conductor of their music.

Your signal that the event is entering the orchestrational phase occurs when the trust level between you and the players becomes so strong that the group wants you to conduct their music even when they are not at a transition point. This happens once they recognize that your facilitation and orchestration of their music adds value to the drum circle experience that would be lacking if you were not there.

Your facilitation and orchestration of their music adds value to the drum circle experience.

To successfully facilitate any drum circle, you will want to have a solid understanding of the phases that you and your players naturally experience during a rhythm-based event. The "Anatomy of a Rhythm-Based Event" describes these relationships.

Anatomy of a Rhythm-Based Event

Please understand that no two rhythm-based events will ever be the same. If it were possible to facilitate two drum circles on two separate days with the exact same participants sitting in the same seats in the same venue and playing the same instruments, you would still have two very different experiences. There is no preset formula that can precisely predict the process and outcome of an in-the-moment rhythm-based event. There are simply too many relationship factors, exciting variables and wonderful surprises.

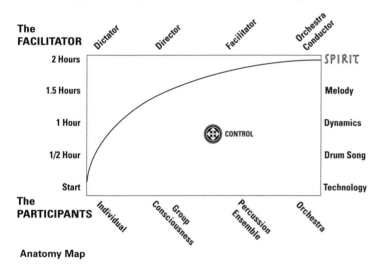

Anatomy Map

That being said, I now introduce my Anatomy of a Rhythm-Based Event. It maps some of the more important interactive and dynamic variables that are inherent in many types of drum circles when you use Arthurian-style facilitation. You can apply this map to both progressive, two-hour family-friendly community drum circle events and to most corporate and conference events, which have a specific group of participants.

While some elements of the anatomy map may apply to all circles, you will not see the same progression for most school events, transient drum circles or programs for kids or special-needs populations. In those cases, time restrictions and other factors often hamper the full achievement of the goals outlined in the map. You still want to facilitate toward Rhythmical Alchemy as the final goal of most rhythm-based events.

In each chapter of this book, I present concepts that parallel the phases in the Anatomy of a Rhythm-Based Event map. I introduce these concepts in a specific order to describe the elements that you need to facilitate as your event evolves and progresses to its conclusion. Each element is an important foundation for the next concept. My map represents an entire program, progressing from the beginning drum call to a climactic orchestral completion. Remember, the map is not the territory!

The Anatomy of a Rhythm-Based Event charts the typical changes that happen over the course of an drum circle event from the following perspectives:

- The role of the facilitator
- The awareness level of the participants in the circle
- The elements you progressively facilitate into the music being made by the group

This map describes the perspectives of participants, the facilitator and the elements they facilitate, as they interact and evolve in an interdependent symbiosis over the course of a two-hour program. All the changes represented on the map take place simultaneously as the event progresses through the steps of its natural evolution toward Rhythmical Alchemy.

The map is not the territory.

The Facilitator

Your job as facilitator is ever-changing, morphing as your role evolves while the rhythm-based event progresses through its musical journey.

Your facilitation process develops from the beginning of a rhythm-based event to the end; you begin by dictating to the group, then you direct them, then you facilitate the players and, finally, you conduct an orchestra.

You can see the facilitator's roles listed across the top of the Anatomy of a Rhythm-Based Event map.

The Participants

Over the course of an event, and with the guidance of you as facilitator, participants' awareness evolves through a progressive series of identities. Their role evolves as their perspective of their identity changes. Players start with the perspective of individuals, then develop group consciousness, which later evolves into percussion ensemble consciousness. Finally, they become an orchestra.

People drumming together naturally progress from having an individual perspective to becoming part of a group consciousness. Except in long-standing drumming communities, rarely does a community drum circle evolve into an orchestra without the guidance and teaching without teaching of a facilitator.

The Anatomy map charts how a player's role changes in parallel with your evolving role as facilitator. You can see the participants' roles listed across the bottom of the Anatomy of a Rhythm-Based Event map.

The Elements

Elements that you progressively facilitate into the group's playing consciousness:

1 A technical understanding of drumming
2 A drum circle song
3 Dynamics and sensitivity
4 Melodic musical relationships
5 *Spirit*.

The Anatomy of a Rhythm-Based Event map shows the elements to be facilitated, in order, from the bottom to the top along the right side.

At the beginning of the event, you need to dictate a technical understanding of the basic components of drumming, such as how to play the drum, listening to the whole circle, and how to leave space for other peoples' musical contributions. I present these aspects in detail in Call of the Drum on page 115.

A drum circle song uses universal patterns, interactive rhythm dialogue, and an understanding of harmonies and melody lines. I present this aspect of facilitation in detail in Drum Circle Song on page 165.

You facilitate volume dynamics and sensitivity into the group's playing using the tools and techniques described in "Arthurian Facilitation Triplicity" on page 51. That chapter also provides ideas for facilitating the melodic musical relationships that occur within the rhythmic and harmonic interactions of the players.

As the relationship develops and changes between participants and the facilitator, so does the expectation each has of the music they are creating. During this process, different elements present themselves to be facilitated. When you facilitate by progressively moving from using basic directions and body language to using more advanced tools and techniques, you and the group co-create an evolving series of successful musical pieces.

Follow your group as much as you lead it.

Teaching without teaching helps ensure the successful evolution of any rhythm-based event. You want to continually read and quantify the group's progress and potential so that you know what to teach and when to teach it.

You as facilitator, your participants and these elements are the foundational, interdependent ingredients for creating Rhythmical Alchemy. For the progressive changes from drum circle song toward spirited music to occur, both the facilitator and participants' roles and perceptions must evolve together.

This evolution presents a "chicken and egg" question. Which changes which? Does the evolution of players from individual to group consciousness to percussion ensemble change the facilitator's role from dictator to director to facilitator, or does a change in the facilitator's behavior act as a catalyst for the change in the players' perceptions? For example, if while dictating you notice the players become more conscious of being part of the group, then you will want to change to directing the group consciousness. Alternatively, if you perceive that individuals are expressing ego more than noticing each others' contributions, you can dictate changes that help them notice and support each other's playing. Remember to read and follow your group as much as you lead it.

Interrelationships in a Rhythm-Based Event

We will now follow the facilitator, the participants and their facilitated musical elements as the three evolve together through a two-hour rhythm-based event, from its beginning to its conclusion.

From drum call, through to the completion of your event, the successes you help create along the way can be thought of as progressive platforms. As dictator, you build the technical platform that you can then use to direct the group as they build a drum song. Then you can facilitate musical dynamics from this drum song platform. Finally, as orchestra conductor, you can use their dynamics as you build a melody line for musical spirit sharing.

Dictate Technology to Individuals

At the beginning of a drum circle, people enter as individuals and begin to play. During this time, you educate the players about your body language signals and basic drumming and playing technology. You show them how to play the drum without hurting themselves and you explain basic drum circle etiquette, as discussed in Call of the Drum on page 115. By dictating to the group, using basic facilitator body language signals such as starts, stops and speed ups, you help individuals begin to listen to and play with each other.

In the beginning of a program, while you are dictating basic drum circle technology to the players, you control most of the music and dynamics. By using full-group interventions, everybody learns at once. You want to use this controlling style of facilitation for the shortest amount of time possible, to move the group from playing as individuals to group consciousness. One of your invisible allies in this opening drum call is the rhythmical entrainment that naturally happens in the music. If you dictate a well balanced instrument placement in the circle, then rhythmical entrainment will automatically appear in their playing. This entrainment will become your ally as the individuals play toward group consciousness.

Entrainment will become your ally.

Direct the Group's Consciousness toward Drum Circle Song

Once the players understand your facilitation body language, they start to play together and respond to both their music and your facilitation directions more as a group than as individuals. When this happens you can drop your role as dictator and become the director of their group consciousness and rhythm groove.

After they reach group consciousness, you can add to their understanding of basic drum circle technology and direct them as they create a drum circle song. They are taking responsibility for the foundation of their music as they self-facilitate the elements that you introduce into their playing consciousness, using teaching-without-teaching techniques. Once they are playing their drum circle song, you are well on your way to creating percussion ensemble consciousness.

Facilitate Dynamics in a Percussion Ensemble

Your job evolves as you facilitate the music they are creating. The rhythmical and musical foundation of their drum circle song becomes the platform from which you facilitate the dynamics of the group. *Now* you can fully facilitate the group's interactive collaboration and emotional contributions into the drum circle experience.

Using teaching-without-teaching methods you can help your participants discover their instrument's relationship to other instruments in the circle. This will help your players gain percussion ensemble consciousness, whether they are experienced drummers or beginning-beginners.

Once your players become a percussion ensemble, their rhythms are more solid and self-sustaining, and the group's rhythmical transition points happen less often. They self-organize. For example, an individual may switch from a bell to a shaker or a drum to help balance the musical song being created. This percussion ensemble consciousness provides space for the players to discover and explore much deeper rhythmical and musical relationships. With this sensibility, the group is ready and willing to go on a musical adventure with you as their guide.

Conduct the Music of the Orchestra

When you add musical and emotional dynamics to a drum circle song it turns into music.

Your percussion ensemble becomes an orchestra, and you become an orchestra conductor.

When the players are fully engaged in their music, self-facilitating and attuned to your facilitation style, they are an orchestra ready to be conducted. You will know it is time to conduct when you feel from the group that they want you to go into the orchestrational spot and play with their music, even though there is no transition point in the rhythm. This implied invitation is a privilege to be respected. You want to avoid overstaying your welcome.

You must have as much trust in the players as they have in you.

Mutual trust is important at this stage. Before you conduct their music, you must have as much trust in the players as they have in you as their facilitator. The Trust Triplicity, discussed in detail in "Establish Trust" on page 127, must be functioning both ways. With trust in place, your orchestra expresses its personality through its music. When you conduct rhythmical alchemy, the music you create together in the moment expresses the personality of your group's spirit.

Spirit as a Facilitated Element

Each person walks into a drum circle with their own spirit. When they align their rhythmical expression with other spirited players they become part of a single vibrant voice. This voice expresses fun and excitement, as they each contribute their spirit to the whole song. They create in-the-moment music together, sharing their rhythmical and emotional spirits. With this sharing, the drum circle becomes a living, breathing entity that is interdependent on all the different parts of itself. You can hear the spirit of this entity speak through the music.

During the orchestrational phase of an event, the energy of the circle encourages lots

A Drum Circle Orchestra in Hong Kong

of spontaneous expression. When you facilitate these expressions, you experience their ongoing, ever-changing Rhythmical Alchemy. Your flexibility as a facilitator will support your intention to educate, empower and inspire the group's spirit.

Who is in control when?

As a drum circle unfolds, participants take on more responsibility for themselves and their music. This is represented in the Anatomy of a Rhythm-Based Event Control Map by the long curved line starting at the left hand side of the map, near the bottom. The curve arches up to end on the upper right hand edge of the map, representing the end of a two-hour event. The space below the line represents the amount of control that the participants have.

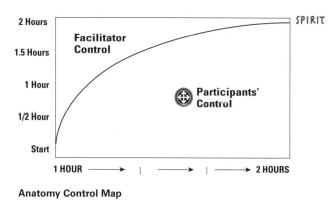

Anatomy Control Map

The space above the line represents the amount of control that the facilitator has. Note that the facilitator is never completely in control of the drum circle at any time.

This curved line represents my overall intention for the facilitator to give control of the event to the participants and empower the group to create their own experience. If the facilitator maintains a lot of control over the drum circle throughout the program, thus keeping the line close to the bottom of the chart, then most likely percussion-ensemble consciousness and certainly orchestrational consciousness will not emerge and the group's spirit will be stifled.

These concepts apply to many but not all rhythm-based events. As we discussed when I introduced this map, it applies to both progressive, two hour family-friendly community drum circle events and to most corporate and conference events, which have a specific group of participants. But you will likely be unable to run through the full anatomy during a transient-population event where people are constantly coming and going at will. Instead you will be continually facilitating drum call to the new additions to your circle. Also, although the chart may not apply to a forty-five minute school program, keep open the possibility of percussion ensemble and orchestrational consciousness appearing out of the blue. Remember to always leave room for unexpected surprises and magic to appear and they will.

Leave room for unexpected surprises and magic.

When to Apply Which Tools and Techniques

In summary, specific facilitation tools are appropriate at each progressive stage of a drum circle event.

- **Dictator:** At the beginning of drum call, direct the individuals in the group toward group consciousness using full-group interventions with these basic facilitation tools:
  - stop cuts
  - speed ups

- volume up and down
- call and response
- accent notes
- rumbles
- **Director:** By the middle of drum call, the players will understand your body language, and you can direct the group toward percussion ensemble consciousness by sculpting, using these teaching-without-teaching techniques:

  - Full timbre song sculpts—for example, all the bells, all the shakers or all the wood toys
  - Full pitch song sculpts—for example, all the low-pitched, medium-pitched or high-pitched drums
  - Full drum-type song sculpts—for example, all the dununs, all the djembes or all the congas
  - One-half circle platform sculpts for listening, clapping, call and response, and rumbles.
- **Facilitator:** Once your group achieves clarity in their rhythmical interactions, you can direct the percussion ensemble toward orchestrational consciousness by following the people who are following you. Use what they give you.
  - Sculpt songs with mixed timbres and pitches.
  - Sculpt a partial circle, such as half, or one-quarter of the circle as a platform for more sophisticated musical interactions.
- **Orchestra Conductor:** As the group focuses more on the harmonies they are creating, they achieve musical synergy. With their permission, play with and orchestrate the group's music using everything you've learned.

Achieving Alchemy

As facilitator, you observe your players' potential during the beginning drum call. As the program progresses, this initial potential manifests itself and the group presents even more possibilities.

As the group evolves, so do their intentions and their potential.

In the beginning of a rhythm-based event, the facilitator uses big body movements to communicate with the circle. During this time, the circle goes through very big positive and readable changes on many levels. As the group progresses from percussion ensemble consciousness toward becoming an orchestra, the relationship between the facilitator and the players also progresses. The facilitator's body language signals become more subtle and sophisticated and at the same time, carry more impact. Meanwhile, the group becomes more sophisticated in their use of the information provided. This positively impacts the music being produced.

By the time your circle participants become aware of themselves as an orchestra, many of your beginning players often surpass their highest expectations of their rhythmical playing ability. They become able to distinguish instrumentation and orchestrate their own sound while being conscious of the group's synergy, even though they may not have been aware of the idea of group consciousness when they entered the circle.

As the group evolves, so do their intentions and their potential. Your ability to read the group must evolve to meet and support those intentions. You want to constantly read and adjust your techniques to support the group. While ascertaining their current level, consider how you can facilitate them as they progress toward their next rhythmical and musical success. When you constantly quantify their evolving potential, you will be better able to choose what techniques to use to guide them to their highest level of Rhythmical Alchemy.

Instrument Alchemy

To create Rhythmical Alchemy at an event, you need both players and the instruments for them to play. Two sources of instruments are participants who bring their own instruments into the event, and a facilitator who provides instruments for players.

For events with a closed population for which you provide all the instruments and have choice of instrument placement, you have total control over both which instruments become part of the circle and where they will be placed. I like to place a drum in every other seat and a hand percussion instrument in the alternating seats, with bass drums and large frames in the centermost circle of seats. I call this placement of instruments by type, pitch and timbre *orchestral integration*. When you balance your instruments by placing them in an orchestra-like setup before participants arrive, you enhance the likelihood of attaining instrument alchemy. Even though your players will not have orchestral consciousness when they sit down, by the end of your successful event, they will have become a well-balanced orchestra.

In an open community drum circle, everyone brings their own instruments and sits wherever they want, creating a situation in your circle that I liken to a "blind date." On this date, you can instigate instrument integration by inviting people to sit where they help balance the placement of drum and timbre types in the circle. As the program progresses, a deeper level of instrument integration can be achieved as you teach without teaching.

Instrument Placement Example

When you facilitate community drum circles you will want to bring along your own drum circle kit of supplemental percussion instruments. You can use this extra emergency equipment to provide instruments for people who don't bring one and to balance the mix of drums and percussion in your circle. A useful mix for your kit is a few bells, shakers and wood instruments, one or two bass drums, and a few frame drums with mallets for players who might be intimidated by the idea of playing drums with their hands. I like to bring my set of REMO nesting drums. They nest compactly and provide a full range of drum pitches so I can add whichever pitch range might be under-represented in the circle. I also include in my supplemental kit a few ambient-sound instruments such as a rainstick, REMO ocean drum, and REMO thunder tube for rhythmically challenged participants. Gongs and chimes are also excellent additions to any kit. In particular, when you facilitate any special-needs players, you will need non- rhythmical instruments that create ambient sounds.

In any open community drum circle, some regular recreational drummers will bring more than one drum and a bag of percussion toys. As you teach participants about the

Non-Rhythmical Instruments on Remo Ocean Drum

instrument sound mix while they are playing, they will become more conscious about their choice of instruments. As the group becomes more aware of the different pitches and timbres of a well-balanced percussion orchestra, some of your players may choose to stop playing their drums and reach into their percussion bags for an instrument of a timbre not well represented at that moment. When you successfully teach them about their mix, their sound orchestration evolves toward Rhythmical Alchemy.

You can often recognize veteran players who are aware enough to help create a balanced percussion mix and are ready to help when you ask. I call these people *playing shills*. In the days of vaudeville theater, performers and comedians paid a few people to sit in their audiences to laugh at their jokes or applaud at appropriate times. These covert event supporters are called *shills*. Whenever possible I find and acknowledge any playing shills in my larger drum circles. Then when I need a particular sound support they are there for me and the circle, ready to help.

An open community drum circle is part of our graduation ceremonies at the close of each Village Music Circles Facilitators' Playshop. Typically the circle has at least as many walk-in players as graduates. Peer-selected graduates of the playshop take turns facilitating the event while the remaining graduates act as shills for whoever is facilitating. Each playing shill has a drum to play and places a bell, a shaker and a wood block or clave under their chair. At any moment, each shill plays the instrument they think will enhance the overall sound mix of the orchestra.

Shills can become models for newer players in any circle, providing an opportunity for you to do less teaching without teaching to instill consciousness of instrument balance. This helps the group achieve its orchestrational potential.

Playing Alchemy

Rhythmical expertise is the technical knowledge and the language of rhythm, as applied to playing percussion instruments. Playing expertise is the ability to apply your rhythmical expertise to cooperative music-making with other players in a drum circle. Some drummers have very good rhythmical expertise but very little playing ability and other drummers have great playing ability even with limited rhythmical expertise.

One of your overall intentions as a facilitator is to help people express their rhythmical expertise. While you will typically see some measurable improvement in a beginning-beginner player's rhythmical expertise by the end of a two-hour event, the rhythmical expertise of an intermediate or advanced player will likely improve very little. Without turning your event into a drum class, you can share simple playing technology through teaching without teaching. This gives first-time players in your circle information they need to play their drums without hurting themselves.

I use a metaphor to show beginners how to play their drums. I say, "Hold up your hand and point to it with your other hand and repeat after me." Then I say, "This is a small child" and the group does and says the same thing. Then I say, "Now point down to your drum and repeat after me, "This is a trampoline." Once again the group does and says the same thing. Then I say "Yippee!" while repeatedly letting my hand fall down onto the drum and bounce off the drum head. All the drummers do the same thing with gleeful yells of "Yippee!" Then we bounce a "Yippee" rumble with both hands. Beginning players learn how to bounce their hands off the drum and get the sounds I am modelling without hitting the drum so hard they hurt themselves.

Playing expertise includes the ability to listen and participate successfully in a collaborative rhythm exchange, creating melody lines and harmonies together. You can raise the group's playing level by facilitating various teaching-without-teaching techniques described in "Percussion Ensemble" on page 151. These techniques help you create musical experiences together that solidify players' new knowledge as they play. Each partici-pant's playing expertise expands as they learn more about sound and instrument orchestration, and the mixture of instrument timbres and pitches. Independently of any individual or group rhythmical expertise, with a facilitator's guidance, the overall ability of a group to play successfully together will improve markedly over the course of a two-hour event.

A group always has more potential than they realize.

A group always has more rhythmical and playing potential than they realize. Helping them develop their rhythmical and playing expertise as you guide them toward Rhythmical Alchemy is a challenge and a joy for any facilitator.

Spirit Alchemy

Many people walk into a drum circle with an acute awareness of self. "How do I look?" "Am I the only beginning or advanced player in the circle?" "Does this rhythm that I am playing sound right?" "Am I sitting in the right spot in the circle?"

Meanwhile, drum circle veterans consciously come into the event to merge into group consciousness through rhythmical and musical entrainment. Their thoughts might flow along these lines: "Am I playing too loud to be able to hear everyone else?" "Is there someone across the circle with whom I can rhythmically dialogue?" "Where are all the other bell players and how can I blend my bell pattern with theirs?" "Oh! There are too many bell players. Maybe I will put my bell down and play a wood block."

Once players begin to play in-the-moment music together, group consciousness is one of the first elements that needs to be in place for the group groove to be self-sustaining and successful. Like a gathering of people who collaborate together on a project, the development of group consciousness is a natural result of their intention to work together to achieve a goal. You can guide your players to group consciousness simply by using your windows of communication to make references to listening to and cooperating while creating a group song together. Once the group's grooves are self-sustaining, they become the platform for musicmaking.

Group consciousness develops as a natural result of their intention.

Once the group achieves group consciousness, then by facilitating a bit of instrument and playing technology, you can raise their playing sensibility to percussion-ensemble consciousness. By doing so, you move the group's intentions from wanting to play together to hearing enough that they want to play their parts in ways that interact well with each other. Once the group is playing with this level of interaction, you are more able to guide them toward orchestrational consciousness. As you facilitate, their playing evolves beyond musical and rhythmical conversations to deeper interpersonal connections. These connections create excitement and energy in the circle that go beyond playing consciousness. I call this "spirit consciousness." When spirit manifests in the group's music you successfully meet your objective to empower individual contribution and spontaneity. You are fostering an emotional and playing environment where Rhythmical Alchemy can emerge.

Drums don't lie. It is almost impossible to pretend to be someone other than your true self when you are playing a drum. The energy that you express through your drum reflects your personality. Combining this individual expression of self with a group of other players doing the same thing will often manifest as a very palatable group spirit.

Generating group spirit is sometimes the conscious goal of the players in a circle, such as in shaman, prayer or healing drum circles. Alternatively, sometimes in a recreational drumming event where attaining group spirit is not the conscious goal of the players, you can still facilitate a group's playing consciousness. This helps them play together successfully so that their spirit consciousness manifests through their music.

As a facilitator you cannot force spirit to appear, but you can certainly facilitate a group toward the expression of their spirits. The group spirit that manifests belongs to the whole circle. Often they will offer their spirit to you as an element which can then be facilitated.

At this point you might ask, "How do you facilitate spirit?" My short answer is, "With spirit." The long answer is expressed throughout this book.

The Pyramid

At one of our annual week-long East Coast Facilitator Playshops, my students offered this revised version of the *Anatomy of a Rhythm-Based Event Map*, to me. They made an Anatomy Pyramid, to be read from the bottom up to Spirit.

As the event progresses the facilitator has different job functions, as shown in the "Anatomy Pyramid" on page 185:

- Dictate to the individuals, leading them toward group consciousness using technology.

SPIRIT

Conductor	Orchestra	Melody
Facilitator	Percussion Ensemble	Dynamics
Director	Group	Drum Circle Song
Dictator	Individual	Technology

Anatomy Pyramid

- Direct the group consciousness toward percussion-ensemble consciousness using the drum circle song.
- Facilitate the percussion ensemble toward orchestrational consciousness using dynamics.
- Conduct the orchestra toward the expression of spirit using melody.

Rhythm Church Is Always Free

While facilitating a team-building program for the thirty sales and marketing staff members of a small start-up company, something clicked in the drumming. We went to *that* place in the music—a place all of us veteran drum circle participants constantly try to achieve. Maybe it was the full-moon energy we saw reflected off the Monterey Bay, at the foot of the Santa Cruz mountains. Maybe it was that the dinner was good, and just the right amount of wine had flowed into the group to relax them before my program.

Maybe the company was small enough that its corporate culture was already oriented toward empowering relationships. Maybe the participants were comfortable enough with each other that the normal corporate physiology, that I usually must melt off of them before I can get them to play with each other, simply wasn't there. Maybe the *team* showed up before I

arrived and they really did not need a team-building exercise. Whatever the maybe, or combination of maybes, something clicked. When it did, they all went to *that* place in the drum circle that we veteran drummers seek whenever we play. This group of executives went to that magic place.

It made no difference that there were only three experienced drummers in the group or that they had only a surface understanding of the universal principles that make a drum circle work. It also made no difference that they were beginning-beginner drummers. It just happened.

I was seated in the circle, playing with them when it happened. By my plan for the program, it was time to find a transition point with my radar, and facilitate the completion of the musical piece. This would set up a window of communication for delivery of the next corporate metaphor.

But something clicked, as if somebody flipped a switch, and suddenly they all went to *that* place. We were halfway through the event, and we were *there.* We had an hour left and there was no place to go, because we were already there.

They got it. Their heads were up. Our hearts were into it. We played as one voice, one energy, one vision, one entity with sixty hands on thirty drums as one body. We had stopped looking for the one in the beat, and had become one in spirit and music. We had gone to that magic place where time stops.

One drummer can go to that magic place by herself, but a group of drummers must focus and cooperate together to achieve the infinite nowness beyond the beat, beyond ego, personality, rhythmical expertise and musical ideas. *That* place exists beyond time itself, in the "be here now" of every musical and rhythmical moment of the experience.

We drummers constantly throw words at that nameless place, trying to describe it, but we are only able to cover its surface with words, like throwing flour on a ghost. You can describe its shape and surface with words, but you cannot describe its essence.

The group arrived at *that* place so fast that it surprised me. The usual step-by-step facilitation of small successes that slowly changes a group of individuals into a percussion ensemble was not needed. We simply fell into a deep solid groove, stayed there and then went deeper. We all recognized it, as squeals and shouts of delight emanated from around the circle.

There were no longer executives in the room, just people. The transition point would not happen for a long time, and when it did, the group would be calling me into the orchestration point to take them to the next level, instead of closing the piece. This metamorphosis changed my role from facilitator of an experiential event, used to deliver corporate metaphors, to an orchestrator of pure spirit. Our groove was as deep as late night, no-curfew, Hawaii grooves. I live for these moments.

It was another twenty minutes before the transition came—a "where do we go now?" transition rather than a 'we're done' moment. The music never stopped until I brought the groove to a close by slowly bringing the volume down. As we played softly, I told the group that this was what they might hear if they were walking away from a never-ending drum circle.

When we were finally drumming over our drums without touching them, every face reflected a deep trance. With our silence we acknowledged the magic place we had visited. This silence lasted long enough that I saw some people starting to feel uncomfortable.

Before someone decided to break the silence with a joke, I said with a quiet but strong voice, "Thank you for coming to rhythm church. I hope you enjoyed the sermon." Some people laughed, but most of them looked at me and nodded their heads with understanding.

After the president of the company thanked me and we *all* applauded each other, nearly everybody joined a thank-you line as they left the event. They *all* had that look I typically see in the eyes of one or two participants who have been touched deeply by the drumming in a corporate program. I was overwhelmed.

I kept saying, "It wasn't me, it was us,"—something I often say to people who come to me to give praise at the end of a community drum circle. I offer it as a way to help them understand the power of the group to create magic beyond anyone's facilitation.

My facilitation had little to do with what we experienced. We all contributed equally to the magical musical space. So by saying "It wasn't me, it was us," I made a plea to them to believe that each of us was responsible for creating the magic. I could see in their eyes that most of them did not believe me. They wanted to point to a source outside themselves who made it happen, so they pointed at me. I knew better.

One man came to me with the same starry-eyed look as everyone else, but with concern on his face. He said to me, "I am a deeply religious person and so I must ask you about this experience we just had." He looked down at his feet, took a breath and looked back me, saying under his breath, "Did we get possessed?" I smiled and said, "Only by your own true spirit freely and fully expressing and sharing itself." He smiled back at me and said "All right, I can accept that."

As I was packing the instruments, the company president came to me and said, "This was a lot more than I expected." I said, "Me too." Then he said, "No, what I meant was that you met and exceeded my expectations. How much extra do I owe you for…" He paused and then said "Rhythm Church?" I said, "Rhythm Church is always free."

Sky King!

Why I Facilitate Drum Circles

Mikael Khei, a drum circle facilitation pioneer in Scandinavia, shares his bliss.

When I facilitate drum circles I want to create moments that expand beyond space and time. I want to bring out good experiences, warm feelings and clear non-verbal communication. In a drum circle, you know beyond any doubt that the good things you experience are a result of everyone sharing their bliss, their spirit and their good intentions. This empowers people and they feel it for days and even months after they have drummed together. Drum circles, where magic and beauty unfold in both wild and subtle ways, change peoples lives and change communities for the better.

Drum circles transform! People might have had prejudices against each other before the drum circle, but once it's cooking, this attitude melts away. You can hear it in the music, you can feel it in your heart and you can see it very clearly in their faces. People from every continent, of all ages and from all the major religions have participated in my open community drum circles. Even in institutions, schools and corporations, I encounter different kinds of people, but the booms, the bangs, the schick and the clangs link them together in a way that is beyond language and culture. Drumming gets straight down to the core: we are all brothers and sisters! We are stuck on this planet and the best we can do is to use our diversity to enrich each other.

10 Professional Aspects of Facilitation

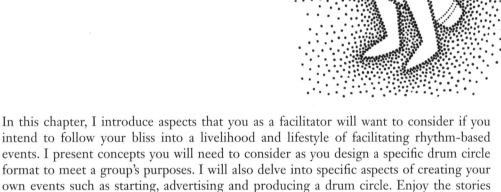

In this chapter, I introduce aspects that you as a facilitator will want to consider if you intend to follow your bliss into a livelihood and lifestyle of facilitating rhythm-based events. I present concepts you will need to consider as you design a specific drum circle format to meet a group's purposes. I will also delve into specific aspects of creating your own events such as starting, advertising and producing a drum circle. Enjoy the stories along the way!

Developing a Career as a Rhythm-Event Facilitator

Facilitating rhythm-based events can be developed into a career. For most of us, it begins as a sharing of our rhythmical bliss or as an extension of the service to the community with which we are already involved. As we are discovered by different groups within our community we are asked to apply our rhythm-

Share your Rhythmical Bliss

Serve your Community

Develop Business Skills

event facilitation skills to serve different populations. To develop a successful career as a rhythm event facilitator, you will need to develop a business, while serving your community and sharing your rhythmical bliss.

Share Your Rhythmical Bliss ☙

A foundation for becoming a rhythm event facilitator is a desire to share your rhythmical bliss with other people and guide them to experience their own rhythmical bliss. I call a person who is doing this a "rhythmical evangelist." I believe that rhythmical evangelism needs to be at the core of a drum circle facilitation career or it will be just another job. Why be a rhythm evangelist unless you like rhythm, or be a salesperson if you don't like selling, or be a chauffeur if you don't like driving?

Before choosing a career as a facilitator, consider whether experiencing and expressing your rhythmical bliss is an easy and natural act for you. I believe that most people would only want to develop a lifelong career doing something about which they are passionate. Why be involved in any career unless it is a natural extension of your life's path and you are having fun doing it?

Rhythmical bliss is the foundation of the experience. Learning how to share your rhythmical passion with others in a way that encourages them to express theirs is an art form that you want to develop if you plan to make drum circle facilitation your career.

Most people who create a career for themselves, who focus less on making money and more on experiencing and sharing their bliss, are living basically happy and fulfilling lives. A good question to ask yourself as you consider facilitating as a career: "Would I do this if I didn't get paid?" If the answer is yes, then you are on the right path.

As a rhythm event facilitator I have a job that I love to do that also makes a positive difference in the world. It gives me purpose, and many opportunities to share my spirit while I follow my bliss and get paid for doing it. What more could I ask of a career?

Serve Your Community ☙

By its basic nature, facilitating a group of people toward achieving a common goal is an act of service. When you serve your community as a rhythm event facilitator you will make a positive difference where you live. If you are dedicated and sincere in your community service then career development will be a natural by-product. Your community will support you in your service to them in many ways.

When you make service the engine that drives your facilitation, success is usually the outcome.

Most of the people who come to participate in one of my Facilitator Training Playshops are already deeply involved in their chosen service career. Drum teachers, priests, pastors, school teachers, kids-at-risk counselors, music therapists, personal growth facilitators and well-elderly care personnel each serve populations with special needs. They come to the program to adapt facilitated rhythm-based events to meet the needs of the specific population they are already serving as professionals. While service is their foundational focus, facilitation of rhythm-based events is only one of their tools.

Service is a skill that can be learned and developed. When you make service the engine that drives your facilitation, success is usually the outcome.

Develop Business Skills ⊚

To make rhythm-event facilitation your career, it is helpful to recognize this service as a business. Then develop and use business skills as you organize yourself. It is hard to do the good work you want to do as a facilitator unless this work sustains your lifestyle.

In addition to facilitating well, you want to develop outreach skills. You need to let your community know what you have to offer them and that you are available. Develop a good business relationship with your community and brand your style of facilitation services by creating an organizational identity, and you will be well on your way to developing a professional career in rhythm-event facilitation.

A scarcity consciousness will make your work more challenging.

As you develop your organizational identity in your community, avoid having a scarcity consciousness, as it will make your successes feel less fulfilling and your work more challenging. While it is common sense to trademark your organizational identity, remember that you cannot trademark the spirit your service offers to your community. Instead of seeing other facilitators in your area as competitors for market share, recognize that you are part of a community of facilitators. Look for ways to collaborate with them to create win-win situations.

Evolution of Awareness

During the years I was writing my earlier book, *Drum Circle Spirit,* my understanding of my audience matured. I progressed from writing for drummers, drum teachers and musicians, to writing for facilitators serving many different populations. I originally intended to shift the perspective of rhythmatists toward using their performance and teaching skills to serve their community as facilitators. During the writing process, I realized that a drum circle is a tool that can be used with almost any group, regardless of their rhythmical skill level and even their physical or mental challenges. I also learned that rhythm event facilitation can be taught to people with minimal rhythmical expertise in a way that empowers them to successfully use drum circles with their specific populations.

By the time *Drum Circle Spirit* was completed, it was designed to meet the needs of all types of people who could use rhythm-based event facilitation technology. The book was written for people who cared about their community in many ways.

During the writing of the book we held our first week-long Facilitators' Playshop in Hawaii. That first training was based on two sets of my experiences:

- A facilitators' apprentice program I had been teaching to my advanced students at the University of California, Santa Cruz
- Short facilitation trainings I had developed for the music therapist conferences to which I had been invited.

At this first Hawaii training, two thirds of the attendees were drummers, who brought their rhythmical passion and one third were people who brought their passion to serve.

Most of the drummers were there to learn how to facilitate the publicly accessible community drum circles that were just beginning to appear all over the U.S. at the time. These recreational circles consisted of people of all ages and rhythmical skill levels, from beginning-beginner drummers to professional performers.

The caregivers had seen me facilitate rhythm-based events in the populations that they serve. They came to the Hawaii Playshop to add rhythm-event facilitation to their repertoire of tools, so they would be better able to serve. They saw the value of rhythm circles as an interactive process that could enhance the lives of their constituency. Most of these caregivers brought minimal rhythmical skills but maximum service skills to the drum circle facilitation trainings.

Three times as many people attended the sixth annual Hawaii Facilitators Playshop, but the demographics had changed from two thirds drummers and one third caregivers to half drummers and half caregivers.

By the tenth annual Hawaii Facilitators Playshop, one third of the attendees were drummers and two thirds of them were caregivers, including people who serve special-needs populations all over the world.

The drummers, drum teachers and performers learned from the caregivers that it is more about serving your community than performing for a rhythm event. If you invest your facilitation energy into service to community rather than in a performance, the world will beat a path to your door in search of the service you have to offer.

Professional Development Triplicity

Jim Boneau trained corporate trainers before becoming a drum circle facilitator. He shares his triplicity in this section.

To fully develop yourself as a professional drum circle facilitator, you will need to attain a wide range of skills that go beyond basic drum circle facilitation. If you plan to create a business and use drum circle facilitation as your primary source of income, consider developing skills that allow you to manage your business and sell yourself to a wide variety of populations. These skills can be viewed through three lenses: business skills, group process facilitation skills and event design skills.

Business Skills ☙

If you intend to create a business as a drum circle facilitator, you must prepare yourself for the challenges of running your own business. As sole proprietor, you will be responsible for all aspects, including product, finances and marketing. You must determine what you are selling and to whom you are selling it. You will need to go through a process of deciding what it is that you do.

Determine what type of population best responds to your abilities as a drum circle facilitator. Are you focused on specific groups, such as kids, elders, physically challenged, workplaces or associations? You will also need to know what types of rhythm events to offer. You can use events for celebrations and team building, as well as for specific intentions of a client. For example, does the client need to raise his group's level of awareness about diversity, communication or organizational alignment? Educate yourself on the language of your potential clients to learn what they need.

You will need to set your fees, bill clients, and follow up with clients who do not pay their bills. Running a business costs money and you must be able to track your finances so that you can pay your own bills.

How will you market yourself? Websites, brochures, business cards and ads are all costly. As a sole proprietor, you must manage your finances, spending your money where it can provide the biggest payoff. Word of mouth is your best marketing tool. Be sure to request references when a rhythm event goes well. Follow up with each client for whom you work, as a good business practice. Remember, it is usually easier to get more business from an existing client than to try and find new clients. Running your own business is challenging. You will need all the business skills you can learn to be successful.

Group Process Skills

A drum circle is a powerful group experience. As part of your professional development as a drum circle facilitator, you need to assess your abilities as a group process facilitator. These abilities go beyond the basics of drum circle facilitation, directly to the heart of how you manage what happens in the group while they are drumming together. Each individual may potentially shift their thinking, learn something new about themselves, or be reminded of something they are currently experiencing in the world. As an effective group process facilitator, it is your job to hold the container for all of that to happen, for everyone in the circle.

As part of your initial discussion with your primary contact, educate them on the potential impact a rhythm event may have on the group. Then have a discussion about how much group processing they would like and for what purpose. Do they simply want to see where the group goes, or do they have a specific goal in mind? These decisions will define how much or how little sharing occurs in the group during your windows of communication. It is your challenge to draw out the appropriate metaphors for each player. The direction and goals of the group need to be determined by you and your primary contact, the person who is paying you.

As an effective group process facilitator, recognize that each individual will come into the rhythm event with their own story of life. Some will want to share about how this affects them on a personal and professional level. Others will have a reaction to those who share. It is your job as group process and drum circle facilitator to balance the needs of your primary contact with the wants of the individuals attending the rhythm event. You will need to decide when to speak and when to listen. Be clear on your intent and the intention of your primary contact. Use those intentions as a continual filter as you provide the metaphors of the drum circle to the attendees. That is your job as group process facilitator.

Event Design Skills

Professional drum circle facilitators provide a complete rhythm event, not simply a drum circle. Each experience has a beginning, a middle and an end. You want to design a package that will meet the primary contact's expectations and have an impact on the group. Include various activities to use as metaphors, open drum time to deepen the experience, windows of communication to talk about the experience and planned interventions for specific purposes. Deepening your understanding of how to best design the event will increase the impact on the group.

All groups that come together experience common feelings. They may be resistant at first to try something new. As they overcome that resistance, they may move into a state of total acceptance of you as a facilitator. At some point, individuals usually exert their independence if they feel they are losing too much of their own identity to the group. Finally, the group comes together and performs as an orchestra. If you understand these cycles of groups, you will be able to design events that utilize those common characteristics. For example, you can plan interventions in the beginning that will help overcome resistance rather than asking for a great deal of personal sharing.

> **All groups that come together experience common feelings. They may be resistant at first to try something new.**

Use metaphors to deepen the group's awareness of the concepts requested by the primary contact.

Many events last up to two hours. Will you use big drums right away or start with small percussion or Boomwhackers™? Will you separate the group into smaller groups? How will you end the event? How will you start? Having a plan for the opening and the closing is essential. Consider these concepts as you deepen your awareness of how to design a rhythm event.

Drum Circle Format Triplicity

You can design rhythm-based events for a huge range of group sizes, kinds of groups (populations) and their various purposes for utilizing a facilitator. Your set of event criteria will help you decide which of the myriad possible formats to use for a specific event. You will want to develop your particular presentation so that it addresses the needs posed by the group's intentions.

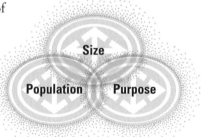

Size: Will there be 50, 100 or 300 participants at your circle? The group's size will define the venue size, amount of equipment needed, and the seating arrangement for your event.

Fabiana Bandeira leading a Corporate Training in Brazil

Population: Are they teachers, executives at a corporate off-site, music therapists, school students or a mixed group from the community? The type of group will help you choose nuances of language and facilitation style to match their culture.

Purpose: Are they celebrating, doing community building, team building, or hoping to motivate workers or students? The group's purpose will help you specify what type of metaphors you want to impart and therefore what activities you choose to use to convey those ideas. Your choice of equipment for the event will depend on which activities you decide to use.

For example, consider what your design would be if you start with the idea of creating an event for twenty corporate executives who have invited you to do an experiential team-building exercise using a drum circle. Knowing who they are, how many of them will attend your event, and the purpose of their meeting gives you the basic info you need to design an experience that will meet their needs.

> If the group size, type or purpose changes, your design format will need to change.

If the group size, type or purpose changes, your design format will need to change. For example, consider what happens if you receive a call from the meeting planner who hired you for the corporate gig. He apologizes and tells you that now two hundred corporate executives want to attend the experiential team-building exercise. You will need to redesign the logistics for your program. Some of the rhythmical activities that you planned for twenty participants may not have the intended effect for two hundred players.

As another example, the kind of format that you would design for an opening celebration for a one-hundred-person corporate sales conference would be considerably different than an opening celebration for one hundred people attending a personal growth conference. Even though the physical logistics may be the same for both populations, the messages you would be asked to deliver and the appropriate language would likely be entirely different.

Your client contact will tell you what messages to deliver and what words to use to best deliver that message. Also, doing your own research about a specific population will acclimate you and help you understand their history, culture and use of language.

I Did My Homework

Baba Ram Dass, a noted author and spiritualist, teaches about the nature of consciousness and about service as a spiritual path. His best known book, Be Here Now has sold over a million copies. As a leader, teacher and lecturer he is an internationally sought-after keynote speaker on the personal growth circuit. My drum circle celebrations are often scheduled as the final event of the opening night festivities for these events, so I have often have had the privilege of following Ram Dass's keynote address. Sometimes he has stayed after his presentation to drum in the celebration, making it possible for us to develop a casual relationship over the years.

Over the years, I have worked with John Grinder, co-founder of Neuro Linguistic Programming (NLP), as his rhythmasizer in programs from Australia to Moscow. During the seven years that I facilitated rhythm events in John's trainings, I also received my NLP master tracker certification. I was very surprised when I heard that Baba Ram Dass was to be the keynote speaker at the same NLP conference whose celebration drum circle I would be facilitating. It seemed to me that asking a spiritual leader to be the keynote speaker for the opening of a technically focused psychology conference was like trying to mix oil and water.

I was well acquainted with the two very different types of populations: the scientifically technical NLP approach to relationships and the spiritual heart-oriented approach of the personal growth movement. The two groups speak very different languages and have very different cultures. NLP talks about tools and techniques, while the personal growth community talks about the path of the heart, with compassion and love.

From the very first word out of his mouth at his NLP keynote address, Ram Dass talked like he had been an NLP master practitioner for years. I had never heard Ram Dass use the types of words and phrases he used in this presentation. By using all the very technical NLP jargon at the right times and places during his presentation, he identified himself to his audience as one of them. He praised the NLP practitioners for developing the amazing tools and techniques that they were using to help people. But at the same time he admonished them to use their tools from the heart-centered point of view of compassionate healers instead from the scientific viewpoint of many doctors.

I became aware that Ram Dass was using NLP technology in his presentation to sway his audience to add heart consciousness into their use of NLP. By the middle of his keynote, he was adding words into his presentation that came from the personal growth movement. And by the end of his talk, he had subtly switched completely from NLP jargon to the vocabulary of the spiritualist that I know and love. As we say in the theatrical profession, he had the audience in the palm of his hand.

At the All One Tribe Conference the next month, Baba Ram Dass was the keynote speaker who presented me with a Drumming Education Award. During a chat before the ceremony, I told him about my NLP history and how surprised I was to see how well he was able to put on the NLP costume in order to give his NLP keynote speech such an impact. I bluntly asked him how he did it. With a wink of an eye he said, "I did my homework."

Considering a Career?

If you are considering a career as a professional drum circle facilitator, the Drum Circle Facilitators Guild (DCFG) offers many resources to help foster professional development of a DCF career including internet exposure, educational resources and tools for business development. You will find more information about the DCFG, including contact information, in the resource section at the back of this book.

Adapting Facilitation Principles to Business

Mary Tolena and Steve Anderson are graduates of multiple Hawaii facilitator Playshops. They have invited me into their manufacturing plant more than once to facilitate team-building experiences with their whole company. The commons meeting area for their plant is open to all the offices, as well as to the manufacturing floor. To call their employees together for a meeting, Mary and Steve play their drums in the common area until everyone comes to the meeting area. In her story, Mary shares insights of ways she and Steve adapted the Arthurian drum circle facilitation principles to help lead their company to success.

Waking Up in the Role of Corporate Leader

I met Arthur and learned about drum circle facilitation while I was teaching and consulting about leadership and organizational change. I was immediately captivated by Arthur's drum circles and his facilitation model as powerful illustrations of effective leadership principles and healthy teamwork development.

A few years later, my husband Steve and I suddenly found ourselves on the front lines of management. We jumped into leading a manufacturing company in a rather dire turnaround situation. As co-owners, we were very motivated to transform the company into a vibrant, successful organization, satisfying to both customers and employees. We responded to the challenge by working 80-hour weeks for 22 months straight.

Though we put most of the rest of our lives on hold, drumming remained a vital anchor for us. Arthur and the drum circle facilitation community inspired us. As we faced the fact that our work pace was not sustainable and had to change, we realized that, in the intense busy-ness of work, we had forgotten the lessons of the drum circle. We had been operating like facilitators who race around the circle—from the center to each instrument and back again—trying to prop up each section.

We wondered why it seemed so hard to get even positive changes to stick. We forgot to "Get Out Of the Way", let alone "Stay Out Of the Way." Our employees did not have a chance to find and explore their work groove and make it their own. When we compared our business approach to what we would do in the drum circle facilitation context we saw not only what was wrong, but also what to do about it. Here are some aspects of our comparison.

- **Roles for co-leaders:** We clarified our roles as co-leaders covering the two most critical jobs: the facilitator and lead dunun player. By identifying who had which role, our staff was clear about which of us to follow. Also, the facilitator felt supported by the steady beat of their partner.
- **One, two, let's all play!** We had been operating in a pattern of doing too much rather than encouraging our employees to learn new tasks. Though driven by worry about over-imposing on employees when our staff was so lean, by over-functioning we were saying, "Put your instruments down and sit while we entertain you." No! The healing power of the drum circle is in the spontaneous co-creation of music together.
- **Group learning:** As in a drum circle, a workgroup's skills and cohesion develop over time so that they work together more easily and with less facilitation. For example, starting with a task of workflow mapping (akin to handing out parts), the team's processes evolve and they are able to add their creativity.
- **It's a wonderful, long song:** Re-awakening to the lessons of the drum circle helped us settle in for the long circle around the campfire. There's urgency, yes, but progress will happen over time. Realizing we could not fix everything at once, we approached change as a series of orchestrations. By allowing each sequence to develop before facilitating the next one, we built the infrastructure and skill platform so that the next steps would come more easily.
- **GOOW:** But stay close and hold the space. The facilitator's presence around the edge of the circle, enjoying the rhythm with a smile and body pulse, is important to a group trying something new. Less doing, more being.

The leadership lessons of the drum circle came to us at a critical time for the company. They reminded us that the company's level of success is reflected by how well we live the lessons day to day, hour to hour.

Although I ended my daily role at the company to pursue rhythm and drum circle activities full time, Steve is carrying on with these principles, especially with the most important one.

- **Be in Service:** Especially as an owner, have an attitude of service to the confluence of life energy your company represents. Just like a drum circle, the experience that employees, customers and suppliers have with each other, as well as what their company becomes and creates, ripples out and helps make the world a better place.

Rules of Gold

Cameron Tummel is an internationally known very successful drum teacher, facilitator

Cameron and Arthur Drumming

and performer. I had the good fortune to mentor him as he served as my apprentice during the early days of his facilitation career. Here he shares his Rules of Gold.

One of my ongoing meditations is the balance between career and passion. As a full-time facilitator, it has become increasingly important to keep a healthy perspective on the money stuff. Here are a cosmic rules which seem to keep resurfacing.

A. If I focus on the money, something always goes wrong.

Yes, we all need to make a living, and so, yes, we have to consider the financial reality of our endeavors. But it has been my experience that whenever I become too caught up in thinking about the financial compensation, something goes wrong. Perhaps I forget an essential tool I should have remembered to bring to the gig, because I was daydreaming about getting paid. Or perhaps I let personal financial concerns enter my thoughts while I am in the circle, and I become distracted, which can have disastrous results. I once lost touch with my group, because rather than staying fully aware of all their needs, I just plowed through my format, thinking about the reward before earning it.

Rule Number One: It Ain't About the Money!

Do it because you love it, and you will always succeed.

B. Whenever I give it away, something unexpected and wonderful always happens.

I make it a habit to donate my time as often as I can. By offering my services free of charge, it enables me to focus purely on the event, without any distractions about my personal compensation. And y'know what? Every single time I facilitate a drum circle free of charge, or at a drastically reduced rate, there is ALWAYS an unexpected reward!

If it's a kids' birthday party, and they really wanted to drum but didn't have any money for an event, and I decide to do the circle for free, or for birthday cake, or whatever, Bingo! The next thing I know, one of the kids' parents just happens to be the director of a local organization, and she or he loves the drum circle, and wants to hire me to work with their associates. Or maybe it's a group that doesn't have enough funding to do the event of their dreams, but I offer to do their dream circle at a fraction of the price. Those are often the best situations to suggest a work trade of some kind, such as, "Would you be willing to write me a letter of recommendation after the circle?" or, "Do you have a network of associates to whom you would be willing to recommend my services?" The next thing you know, it leads to a very lucrative project. Every time I give it away, I receive a reward I hadn't even imagined.

Rule Number Two: Give It Away!

This idea is nothing new. Spiritual teachers throughout history share this concept.

C. Love is the answer.

Love is its own reward. Do it because you love it.

The more I focus on doing the jobs because I love them, and the less I worry about financial compensation, the more jobs I seem to get. More jobs lead to more experiences, which develop my skills, which result in better drum circles, which then result in more jobs, which develop my skills further, which leads to more jobs, and then I don't even think about the money at all. I just love my life, and the drum circles of which it is composed. If I focus upon doing it because I love it, that is when I am able to do my best work.

Rule Number Three: Love Is Its Own Reward. Do It Because You Love It.

Hawaii Lineup

To prepare for the beginning of each of my Facilitator Playshops, I ask participants to write their mission statement, as described in "Create Your Own Mission Statement" on page 78. Even though they come from different parts of the world, and represent different populations that they want to serve, most of them express the same basic elements described in the Intention Triplicity. They each reflect the same ideas in different ways: creating and serving community, following their bliss and rhythmical empowerment. Some of their writings include creating a career orientation that supports them financially while they do what they love to do. But career orientation is low on the priority list for most people.

These writing assignments help Playshop participants understand who they are in relationship to drum circle facilitation and why they want to learn to facilitate. The assignments set a framework for their learning experiences.

When I read their mission statements I am reminded of why I am teaching and who I am serving in that workshop. I am there to serve those people and their mission. I get misty-eyed every time I read their mission statements.

It was the opening night of the very first Hawaii one-week intensive training. The program was over for the day and most of the attendees were at the beach fire circle, participating in their first late night drumming session. Meanwhile, I sat off to the side of the circle reading their mission statement writing assignments by firelight.

As I read through these powerful statements of intention, all teary eyed, I came to a particular assignment that stunned me. It was a short paragraph statement saying something to the effect, "I want to take this thing and make lots of money with it, and be rich like you, Arthur." At the bottom of the statement it read, "Oh, by the way, share my spirit." Boy, I stopped crying. I thought, "What is this person doing here?" In that same batch of mission statements, I came across another person—an experienced drummer, with little facilitation experience—who wanted to learn to facilitate in a week and then go facilitate rhythm events in the corporate training world.

This was my first inkling that there were people who had gotten as far as coming to this Hawaii training whose main reason for being there was to learn a skill quickly and make money.

The next morning I gathered the fifty participants and asked them to organize themselves in a half circle, with beginning-beginners on one side of the circle, in a sequence based on how long they had been drumming. Veteran drummers positioned themselves on the far side of the semicircle.

Among the many drummers, some were respected elders in the community and professional performers. They were the people who can be seen endorsing products for large drum companies. When you open a music magazine they smile at you, while holding up an autographed drumstick or drum. These people had been drumming most of their lives.

I explained to the group that this lineup represents how long it takes to develop a career in the world of rhythm. I asked them to listen carefully to each others' responses to the following questions.

I asked the people standing on the beginning-beginner side of the circle, "How long have you been playing?" These were some of their answers:

- "Well I haven't started yet, but I'm a kids-at-risk counselor and I want to offer drumming to the kids who can't talk to each other without hitting each other."
- "I've started drumming after I attended a conference with you a few months ago."
- "I have drummed occasionally at a women's circle, for the past year."

I asked each participant along the semicircle. By the end of the row the answers shifted. For example: "Well, let's see, I've been playing twenty-five years, teaching for fifteen. I've published two videos that teach how to drum, and I endorse products for a major drum company."

After the last person answered I stood back and said, "I would like for anyone who has been serving their community by teaching hand drumming to please take one step forward."

About a quarter of them, mostly from the more experienced half of the semicircle, stepped forward. As I went along the row of people who had stepped forward, I enquired about each person's teaching history.

Near the beginning of the row I heard, "I just started teaching what I know to some friends of mine last month." Halfway along the line someone said, "I've been teaching about a year." It wasn't until the end of the row that I heard, "I've been teaching hand drumming fifteen years."

I thanked the teachers and invited them to step back into the original semicircle.

Then I asked, "If you have been facilitating rhythm-based events please step forward." Only among the most-experienced third of the players, a few people stepped forward. I heard, "Well, I've been facilitating kids-at-risk programs for two years," and "I've been facilitating community drum circles for four years."

I thanked the facilitators and asked them to step back into the semicircle.

I then asked them, "If your total income now comes from serving your community through drumming, teaching rhythm or facilitating circles, please step forward." Four people stepped

Kids in Drum Conversation

forward. Then I asked, "How long have you been totally supported by what you do in that rhythm service?" One answer I heard: "While I have been drumming, teaching and facilitating rhythm events in the community for the last fifteen years, I quit my day job five years ago and started teaching and facilitating full time."

By listening to each other's answers to my questions, they learned that creating a facilitation career is a lifelong process. It is not about taking a class from Arthur, or reading his book, and then taking his ideas into the world and trying to make money. I helped them understand that creating a career in rhythm event facilitation is about learning how to serve community while sharing their own bliss.

Creating a career begins by acting on your specific mission intention and serving your community through that mission until the community begins to support you in that service. Only after many hours of facilitation does your mission and intention begin to serve you by feeding your family, putting shoes on your kids and paying your rent.

It is interesting to note that at the time of the first Hawaii Playshop, after facilitating thousands of drum circles since the *Summer of Love,* I was still teaching drum classes, drumming for dance classes and performing in World Beat bands to make ends meet.

So what were those people doing in that first Facilitation Playshop and what happened to them later? Since that first Playshop I have had the great pleasure of reading their later mission statements from subsequent Playshops. After wanting to learn to facilitate in a week and to make lots of money, they came to the realization that it is over time and through sacrifice that we create our careers and share our rhythmical bliss. Each of them has evolved and matured as a facilitator. They have grown into respected elders in our community. Like me, they are still trying to make ends meet.

Prelude to Creating Your Own Events

You will want to have a clear understanding of community drum circles and the ability to express yourself clearly before you search for a physical location for your event or start advertising it. With the help of REMO, I developed and distributed a booklet called "Prelude to Drum Circles," to hundreds of facilitators and store owners. The topics described in the next sections, for advertising, starting and producing drum circles, evolve directly from my experiences over a twelve-year period, as we regularly updated that booklet.

What is a facilitated community drum circle?

Before you start on your journey, you want to be clear about how to communicate to the people in your community who are not yet drummers. Before you can get their cooperation and support, you need to help them understand the answer to the first question they will likely ask you, "What is a facilitated community drum circle?"

In a community drum circle we value each person for his or her unique contribution to the group song.

When you are talking to a person who is *not* part of the recreational hand drumming community you need to communicate to them at their level of understanding. How would you describe a drum circle to someone who has never experienced one?

A facilitated community drum circle is a fun family-friendly rhythm event. Participants express themselves by playing on a chorus of tuned drums and hand percussion. They create a musical song together, while being guided by a rhythm event facilitator. These community drum circles are accessible to all ages and all levels of rhythmical expertise, including beginners.

At community drum circles, participants make in-the-moment music, expressing their collective rhythmical spirit. A community drum circle is *not* a drum class.

When a community comes together to drum they unite in rhythm and harmony to celebrate life. Their interactions create a supportive, interdependent relationship. In a community drum circle, we value each person for his or her unique contribution to the group song.

The facilitator is a guide, whose intention is to create community through group rhythmical empowerment. They are there to help facilitate the group's collaborative musical effort.

Why do people drum?

People go to drum circles because they have discovered that rhythmical expression is an important aspect that has been missing from their lives. Drumming awakens them to self-discovery and helps them to see the world with the eyes of a child. Drumming affects each person differently, stimulating creative expression, as they explore, experience and express the rhythms of their lives. Although people drum for musical expression, to reduce stress and to create community, most people come to community drum circles for the pure fun of it! That is why we call it recreational drumming.

Most people come to community drum circles for the pure fun of it!

Who drums?

All kinds of people drum. Children in schools, well elderly, corporate executives and health care practitioners drum. Physically challenged men and women, people in prison, and kids at risk drum. Men, women and children of all ages participate in rhythm-based events.

Men's groups and women's groups each use drums for ritual bonding and empowerment for their genders. Spiritual groups such as Quakers, Lutherans, Episcopalians and Catholics use drums as part of their worship.

Over the past thirty years, more and more people are studying with African and Afro-Cuban drum teachers. These people, who study dancing and drumming of other cultures, are creating ethnic arts networks. These local networks are merging into regional and national networks.

Advertising, Starting & Producing Drum Circles

This section provides step-by-step suggestions for successfully starting and running a community drum circle. This simple comprehensive discussion explains how to set up, advertise and start your circle.

Drum Circle Logistics

Here are the steps to take to create, advertise and hold a successful community-based recreational drum circle event.

Venues

Find the Site

Before you hold a drum circle, you must find a place where you can avoid disturbing the neighbors with your loud joy. You will want to secure your site months in advance, to give yourself plenty of time for planning, preparation and outreach. Here are some ideas and examples of possible venues for your event.

> **Secure your site months in advance, to give yourself plenty of time for planning, preparation and outreach.**

- A community center is a place where the members of a community come together to meet. Approach your local community center with the idea that a drum circle is a family-friendly community-building activity and they may be willing to give you access to their auditoriums or rooms.
- Music stores are viable options as possible drum circle venues in some countries. Holding a regular drum circle in a local music store or percussion shop would be mutually beneficial to the store owner, the community and you. In "Partnering with the Music Industry" on page 216, I share ways to communicate with and educate store owners about the possibilities and advantages of holding drum circles in their stores.
- Churches and temples often make their recreation rooms available for community events. The Earth Drum Council, in Cambridge, Massachusetts, currently holds what is now the longest-running drum circle in the U.S. in a church.
- Rooms in city-owned buildings may be accessible through your city's parks and recreation department. Some parks may also be available for community events.
- Many coffee shops, in metropolitan areas all around the U.S., hold weekly drum circle events.
- Some schools are willing to allow access to their available space in exchange for drum circles for their students. I have occasionally provided my service of facilitating a school assembly in exchange for the use of a school room for a community drumming event.
- Personal growth bookstores and centers and yoga centers are willing hosts to many types of drum circles. Sometimes these venues work better with quieter timbres, but many of them are fine with the full sound of a frolicking drum circle.
- Recreational music centers (RMC) are the latest innovations in community drumming spaces. When the REMO drum company moved into their new plant north of Los Angeles, California, Remo Belli kept one of their old factory buildings in North Hollywood and has been using it for an experiment in recreational musicmaking. The REMO Recreational Music Center hosts many types of rhythm-based events. The REMO RMC has been an inspiration and model for entrepreneurial facilitators who are creating their own RMCs around the U.S.

Drum and Dance Church

Jimi and Morwen Two Feathers are elders in a drum and dance community that was functioning long before the modern-day drum circle movement started. They founded Earth Drum Council in 1990. Here they share their perspective on venues.

Jimi and I were asked to take the reins of *Drum and Dance Saturday* in Cambridge, a circle that had been ongoing for ten years, under the leadership of several different people. When we began facilitating the circle in 1991, we moved it back to its original location: the First Church Congregational in Harvard Square.

This church is next to the Cambridge Common, where local drummers (including Jimi) first began to gather in the 1960s and formed the core of what became the Boston area drum and dance community. Fifteen years later, we still drum there every month, drawing between 50 and 100 people each time. Church administrators and pastors have come and gone, and we are still there!

Aside from our being a reliable source of rental income, there are a few reasons the church continues to embrace our presence there. Our community has become involved in helping the church on several occasions, including when a fire broke out in the sanctuary and Jimi brought in a generator and helped clean up the smoke damage. When the floor in the hall was refinished, we took it upon ourselves to minimize dents and scratches by providing cardboard to go under people's drums. It's very important to leave a place better than you found it. Each year at Winter Solstice we take a collection and donate funds to the homeless shelter the church runs in the basement, under our feet as we drum and dance.

Maintaining a positive relationship with this church is important to us. As is true with any event, the three most critical factors for success are location, location and location. In Harvard Square, we often have curious people, including lots of college students, walk in off the street to investigate the source of the music. Some of them stay. Also, we are accessible to public transportation. Perhaps most important is our sense of being grounded in the history of the modern American drumming movement. About Harvard Square, Jimi says, "I am a guardian of that place, and I'll always be there. We expect to keep Drum and Dance Saturday running in this space for many years to come."

Over the years, while the location has stayed constant, the setup within the space has changed. When we first started organizing Drum and Dance Saturday, the drummers' chairs were set up in a circle. Soon we noticed that when the drummers were in a circle there was no good place for dancers. Either the dancers were outside the circle where the drummers could not interact with them, or they were inside it, blocking the drummers from hearing and seeing each other. In response, we changed the architecture of the circle and made it a semicircle of drummers, bringing them together on one side of the room and creating space for dancers. Then the drummers and the dancers could function as two parts of a single energy system.

Not long afterward, we began to integrate additional elements of the Fire Circle work we were doing outdoors in the summer months. At the Fire Circle we had begun arranging drummers on one side of the fire while dancers moved around the fire. We brought this arrangement indoors to Drum and Dance Saturday and began setting up a candle altar in the middle of the floor to simulate a bonfire. We also learned from trial and error that a semicircle with arms spread wide left the drummers at the ends out of the loop. The people at one end of the semicircle could not hear the people at the other end. Brainstorming with members of the community that was forming around the Fire Circle, we evolved into a drum setup that was more like a V than a U, with the bass drums clustered at the point of the V, laying down the pulse. Pulling the two wings closer together to face each other, a zone was created between the two lines of drummers that invited dancers to come closer to interact with drummers, then return to the open dance space. We've come to call this the gratitude zone, because dancers regularly express gratitude there, in their interaction with the drummers. And the drummers are grateful, too, for their rhythms are fed by the dancers, who in turn are fed by the rhythm. We're not a drum circle: we're a drum and dance circle, even if we're only actually a circle when we take a break in the middle of the evening and join hands for introductions and announcements.

These days, a core group of people help organize Drum and Dance Saturday in Cambridge. We get together periodically to assess what is working and what could be improved. So far we have not found a new improvement to the setup. If you visit us on the first Saturday of the month, you'll find the drummers cooking and the dancers riding the rhythm. That's how we like it!

The Sound Space

When you are choosing a venue for your drum circle, remember that each physical space will have its own special acoustic and logistical challenges. The physical space that holds your circle always affects the sound quality of your circle, whether you are using a small room for twenty drummers or a ballroom with fifteen hundred players.

One way that I assess the acoustic qualities of a room is to give a short loud boisterous yell, and then listen to the resultant sound. I warn people who are accompanying me that I am about to do this, so I don't scare them. For rooms with lots of glass or cement or metal and high ceilings, the sound comes back as more of an echo than a reverberation. Rooms with lots of cloth, thick rugs or acoustic ceiling tiles or walls absorb the sound so an echo is not kicked back to you. The reverberations blend with the sounds being created by your players.

Gymnasiums are a drum circle facilitator's nightmare, because the delayed echoes of the drums, bouncing off the hard walls and ceilings, are almost as loud and strong as their source. The middle of the gym is definitely not where you want to set up the center of your drum circle. When I give a shout in a gym, I typically hear several echoes coming from multiple directions. I walk around, giving shouts and listening to the resultant echoes until I hear a sound that is more of a reverb than an echo. The ideal location is typically approximately equidistant from two walls near a corner. I call this creating a bandshell effect. The reverb supports the groove and the echoes from the more distant walls are late enough that they are drowned out by the other sounds, so these echoes have less effect on the circle's sound.

At a park near the Diamond Head crater in Honolulu, we planned to hold a celebration drum circle with Baba Olatunji and four hundred people, just outside the giant symphony-sized bandshell. When I yelled to check out the acoustics, a huge echo bounced back from the bandshell like a megaphone, almost as loud as my original yell. We set our drum circle inside the bandshell to avoid having the kickback. Due to the effects of the bandshell, hikers were able to hear our sounds from the top of the crater, even though it was a mile away. They came to find the source of the rhythms and to join in the fun.

Holding a rhythm event outside poses a very different challenge. The sounds of the drum circle go up and out in all directions. Without any sound kickback off any walls or ceilings, people on one side of the circle have a hard time hearing the players on the opposite side. The bigger the circle, the harder it is for the circle to connect with itself. To help players connect with each other, encourage them to move in as close as possible to each other. You can also think of your standing players around the outside perimeter as a type of sound wall.

At an event I facilitated in downtown Los Angeles, I had been told that I would be facilitating a group of about two hundred players at an outdoor drum circle. I prepared myself for the usual outdoor logistical sound challenges, but when I arrived at the site I discovered that the organizers had put a large canopy over the circle of chairs, to protect the players from the summer sun. It had no sides so the circle was open to the outdoors. Our canvas roof was four large triangular awnings that met at a point in the middle, above the chairs. From the outside, the roof looked like a suspended pyramid. It was high enough above the drummers to give players the sense of still being outside. Due to the angles, each awning reflected the sounds coming from the drummers below, over to the players on the other side. I was both surprised and pleased. We had a great outdoor downtown drum day in the shade under the sound dome.

Music 101

I was hired to facilitate an international group of 150 human resource professionals, as part of a corporate training program whose theme was "Going back to school." The program was held in a Chicago arts complex physically adjacent to Orchestra Hall, home of the world-famous Chicago Symphony Orchestra.

The professionals became students and the presenters were their faculty. At the end of each presentation, the organizers rang a portable school bell and their assistants, dressed in fluorescent school-crossing-guard vests, escorted the students to the next classroom to receive their next presentation. My class was entitled Music 101. All that the students knew about my class was the title and that the presenter was Arthur Hull from the University of California, Santa Cruz.

They did not know that all the classrooms they had been using were rehearsal rooms located just next to the famous Chicago Symphony Orchestra Hall. When the crossing guards escorted the students through the door marked Music 101, they found themselves walking into the mezzanine seating area of Orchestra Hall, into the area just above and behind the stage. Their vantage point provided a bird's-eye view of the beautifully ornate, plush music hall as would be seen by the symphony players. Standing in front of them on the conductor's podium, holding a long white tapered conductor's baton, was the Arthurian Elf himself, me.

My stunned students were directed to their seats, where a vast array of drums and hand percussion awaited them. Seeing in their body language a fear of being discovered and embarrassed as rhythmically challenged people, I let them know that the quality of the music they were about to produce would be based, not on their rhythmical expertise, but on their relationship with each other.

By the end of our hour together, I was facilitating the group with the basic elements that help a symphony orchestra play together successfully. I was orchestrating beautiful, intricate in-the-moment music being performed by the *Human Resources Percussion Symphony*. Because they were seated just above the orchestra stage in the Chicago Symphony Orchestra Hall, the sound was as well balanced and as beautiful to me as the hall was to them.

The Loud Whisper

I facilitated a full day Rhythmical Alchemy Playshop™ at a yoga retreat outside Florence, Italy. Including my facilitator trainees and their yoga staff, sixty of us played together that day.

The retreat was being held at an old villa. We held the Playshop outside all day, but the threat of rain moved us inside for the final climatic drum circle, so we set up the closing drum circle in the empty wine cellar under the villa. How many hundreds of years old this villa was, I don't know, but the stones of the curved walls looked hand hewn. Like a silo sliced and laid on its side, the stones formed an arch that became the walls and ceiling, placing our drum circle of sixty people inside a large stone half cylinder.

While the group was moving chairs and drums into the room, I asked my host why they call this room the *inner ear?* She explained that because of its special acoustic qualities, local groups do most of their chanting and meditation here. She asked me to sit in a corner on one end of this rock cylinder, facing the wall. She then went to the far corner of the room and sat down with her back to me, and quietly whispered, "Arthur, this room is magic." I was astounded to hear her quite clearly over all the chair scratching, drum tuning, and people-talking noise. It was as if she were right next to me whispering into my ear, instead of forty feet away.

The sound dynamics sixty drummers created in that room made it feel like we were playing inside a rock drum. Because it was impossible for our group to play loudly without hurting our ears, we were forced to play very softly. We could hear every nuance of every drum and instrument. This allowed us to play for long periods of time while exploring subtle timbre relationships and sound dynamics. We played ourselves into a deep drum trance, then into finger tapping and drum-head scratching and finally into a silence-filled room lasting ten minutes before anybody moved or even sighed. It was a perfect closing for a great day. That room was magic.

When to Hold the Circle

Saturday afternoon is an excellent time to get full participation from families and people of all ages. Weekday evenings are also better than Friday evenings. The changes of the seasons marked by the solstices and equinoxes offer excellent opportunities to create community drum circle celebrations. Many communities throughout the country do this as a tradition. Any community celebration is a good excuse to hold a drum circle.

Let Your Circle Grow

If you are planning to facilitate a weekly or bi-weekly drum circle, then use the same time and place for each event. Have patience as it takes time to build a supportive and committed group of participants. Remember that three or more drummers make a drum circle. It is all about quality rather than quantity. If you have five to seven players come to your first circle, GREAT! Facilitate them from your seat in your small circle rather than from the center. Thank them for their support at the beginning of the event, and at the end ask them to bring their friends to your next scheduled circle. Over time you can slowly but surely build a local recreational community. Perseverance furthers.

It is all about quality rather than quantity.

In some communities, facilitators schedule a beginning drum class just before the drum circle event. This enhances the playing skills of beginning players and gives them playing confidence. As facilitator, you can also support your growing hand drumming community by sponsoring visiting drumming teachers and advertising drumming workshops.

Network in Your Community

Do basic research about your community and meet people who are not typically in your sphere of influence. As you build relationships with local musicians, dancers and community organizers, they can help you find people who may be interested in your community drum circle event.

Do ethnic arts networking. Dance classes and drum classes are good places to share information and advertise your event. In most metropolitan areas, you can find at least one dance studio that features ethnic dance classes with live drumming such as Afro-Cuban, Senegalese, Congolese or Brazilian Samba and Capoeira. Check with dance centers and dance studios for classes where groups of drummers play specific rhythms for each culture's dance. You may find open-minded, open-hearted drummers or dance teachers who are willing to provide access to their community resources, such as newsletter email lists.

Each drum teacher is a communicator for his or her drum classes. Drummers play in each others' circles to support the dance classes. The dancers in the ethnic arts community will be attracted to an open drumming event, so put dance teachers on your email list. You may also find an ethnic arts network that serves the communication needs for the community. If so, they will have a mailing list and possibly a monthly or weekly newsletter in which you can advertise or insert your drum circle poster.

Do not be discouraged if established drummers and teachers show little interest when you first contact them. You may want to reassure them that a community drum circle is not competition for their dance and drum classes. As your circle grows, these teachers can see the benefits of supporting your event as an entry-level experience that encourages the interest of novices for their ethnic drum and dance classes.

Be a detective. Visit your local percussion store to learn who plays in local drumming groups. Ask about hand drumming teachers and drum circle facilitators in the area. Contact these teachers and facilitators to find out how you can each support each other's events. Also find out if there are any freeform drum circles meeting at the local parks on the weekends. Go to your local anarchist drum circle and befriend drummers who would be happy to play in a facilitator-guided drumming event. By doing this outreach you will find players willing to create a supportive drum circle community.

Create a Poster

Create a poster or flyer for your event using the following ideas:
- Come and experience a fun family-friendly community drum circle.
- Share the spirit of your community by drumming together to create unity.
- All levels from beginning-beginner to advanced are invited and welcome.
- Bring your own drum or other personal percussion instrument. Some extra drums and percussion will be provided.

A picture is worth a thousand words! Put pictures of drummers, drums or a drum circle on your poster.

Advertise

Generate and maintain a mailing list and email list of all your contacts that you can use to send out flyers or posters that can be put on fridges or handed to friends.

Put activity announcements in the calendar of your local free paper as well as your local for-profit newspaper. Most communities now have a personal growth newsletter or New Age newspaper. Be sure to confirm the release date in advance when you put ads and announcements in those types of periodicals, as they may be published sporadically.

Poster for an Arthurian Facilitated Drum Circle in China

Create a website that promotes your drum circle events. You can also subscribe to and advertise on regional internet drum circle dialogue lists. Start your own if the idea is new in your area.

Put your posters in music stores, coffee houses and personal growth and independent bookshops two weeks before the event.

Provide your handouts to dance classes and place your poster on community center bulletin boards.

Hang your poster on local college campuses, especially around the bus stops, coffee houses and the dance, arts and music departments. Advertise in local college newspapers the week of your event.

Go to local Reggae, ethnic-specific and World Beat concerts and ask the organizers' permission before handing your flyers to concert-goers.

You can find a local posting company in nearly every community, if doing the posting by yourself seems daunting. But remember that until you generate a supportive drum circle community with volunteer advocates, everything that you have someone else do will add to your COT.

There are many ways to advertise your services to the community, including word of mouth. Be sensitive with your timing if you choose to advertise your event at other drum circles. Tell all your friends to tell their friends.

Encourage Media Coverage

Two weeks prior to the event, contact the entertainment editor of your local newspaper, and ask to be interviewed for an article that promotes drum circles and your event.

Find the local World Beat, Reggae, and ethnic arts radio programs in your area. These programs are now permeating the air waves of many communities in the U.S., especially local college radio stations, and publicly sponsored stations. It wold be helpful for your drum circle promotion to set up a live interview at each of these stations during the week before the event. Hint: bring a bag of percussion and have the radio staff join you in a live radio jam. There's a story about jamming in "A Reality Check for the Merchants" on page 217.

Write 15-second and 30-second public service announcements, called PSAs, about your desired drum circle and send these announcements to the radio stations mentioned above. Add a note, "Attention to the DJ who runs the World Beat or ethnic arts music program." If you know the names of the World Beat programmers, personalize your notes.

PSA Examples

- **15 seconds:** Come celebrate community by sharing your rhythmical spirit with others. Participate in this facilitated family-friendly community drum circle at PLACE, on DAY at TIME, DATE. All levels of rhythmical expertise welcome. Extra drums and percussion will be provided.
- **30 seconds:** Come celebrate community by sharing your rhythmical spirit with others. You can participate in this facilitated family-friendly community drum circle at PLACE, on DAY at TIME, DATE. All levels of rhythmical expertise welcome, from beginners to advanced players. Bring your own drum or other personal percussion instrument. Extra drums and percussion will be provided. Bring your friends and share the spirit of your community by drumming together.

Large community drum circles are good photo opportunities for TV and newsprint media. Numerous drum circles have been featured on the 10 o'clock news the evening of the event. Invite the media for interviews prior to the event and with participants during the event. Generate a media package that includes photos, a biography, news articles and magazine reprints that can help you prepare them for your event. Even though most of these media appearances happen after your event, it is good local educational outreach for future events.

What to Bring to the Event

Bring extra drums and percussion. Create a "loaner kit" consisting of at least one bass drum or dunun, a few *kid-proof* hand drums, and a bag of hand percussion: bells, shakers, wood blocks and claves. Include at least one non-rhythmical sound, such as a rain stick, Tibetan bell, or REMO Thunder Tube, for the physically challenged or rhythmically intimidated.

If you expect a large turnout of a hundred or more players, then invite some rhythm-evangelist volunteers to be welcomers. These helpers will distribute your extra instruments to those who arrive empty-handed. Also if you expect a large turnout, you will want to have at least one large double-headed bass, dunun or surdo drum for every ten drummers. Some facilitators bring a player who is sufficiently musically talented to keep the beat and help the other bass bottom drummers stay connected.

Make physical copies of the ideas expressed in "Drum Circle Etiquette" on page 118 and give it to first-time participants. Alternatively you can create a sign that lists the basic Drum Circle Etiquette guidelines and post it at the entrance of your event. (Please credit this book.)

Bring cameras. Ask a friend to take photos and videos of your event that you can use in future promotions and on your website.

Bring paper, a clipboard and pens for your mail and email networking list. Place the clipboard at the entrance of the venue, as part of registration. Your mail and email lists will be very important tools for your continuing networking efforts, so you will want to keep these lists updated.

Bring posters or handbills that advertise your next drum circle to give to attendees.

Christine Stevens brings 3" x 5" cards to events and at the end of the drum circle, she asks the participants to write one sentence about their experience. She also asks them to include their first name and age. These quotes become useful sound bytes for advertising and press releases.

Setup for your facilitated drum circle can be low maintenance. You will be the drum circle facilitator, and you will need your loaner kit and chairs. If you expect thirty or more people, set up either a sound bowl or concentric chair seating, as shown in "Take Responsibility for the Physical Circle" on page 122. If the circle is more than two hundred people, you might need a small riser or platform, approximately two feet high, so players can all see the facilitator. You can make a simple platform: duct tape four milk crates together to support a 3' by 3' piece of half-inch plywood.

Follow-Up

If you plan to sponsor regularly scheduled ongoing drum circles, stay in touch with your community by creating and sending a monthly newsletter. By providing a "World Beat & Drum Circle" newsletter you become an asset to your community. Add value by printing schedules for any World Beat performers coming into town and any other ongoing rhythm events available in your area. Include notices for specific beginning-beginner drum classes and ethnic arts dance classes to help connect your larger community. If you are organizing your drum circle in conjunction with a music store, your newsletter can help generate new traffic for the store if they choose to advertise with a coupon in your newsletter.

You can distribute your newsletter using either email or snail mail. Other ways to make it available to your community include providing copies to the music store and bringing copies to your rhythm circles to share.

Checklist

Find your Drum Circle Site
- Community centers
- Music stores
- Churches & temples
- City-owned buildings and parks
- Coffee shops

- Schools
- Personal growth bookshops
- Yoga centers
- Recreational music centers

Community Networking
- Local musicians and dancers
- Dance teachers and their classes
- Hand drum teachers and their classes
- Ethnic arts organizations
- Percussion store customers and owners
- Freeform drum circle participants
- Other drum circle facilitators (win win)

Advertising and Media
- Posters and handouts
- Public service announcements for radio and TV
- Announcements on your website
- Announcements to your snail mail or email list
- Announcements in local newspaper calendars
- Radio, TV and newspaper interviews before and during events

Poster and Handout Locations
- Drum department of music stores
- At the site of the circle, at least two weeks prier to the event
- Dance and drum classes
- Personal growth shops and bookstores
- Local college campuses
- World Beat, Reggae and ethnic concerts
- Local posting company
- Mail packages of posters or flyers to your supporters.
- Mail poster to your local ethnic arts organization for their next newsletter mailing.

Growing Media Awareness

The recreational hand drumming movement has grown large enough to be regularly noticed by the media. Feature articles published in *Newsweek, Yoga Journal, the Wall Street Journal* and *The New York Times*

Arthur & Mickey Facilitate Rhythm for Life Celebration

provide evidence of this scrutiny.

The first national media awakening to the recreational hand drumming movement happened when CNN, a national television news channel, covered a benefit drum circle for the Rhythm for Life foundation. Mickey Hart, Airto Moreira, Santana, Sheila E., Hamza El Din and I shared facilitation responsibilities for sixteen hundred players at the largest community drumming event, to date. I refer to that event as the Woodstock of hand drumming.

The Woodstock of Drumming

Interview with John Avinger, by Simone Welsh.

On February 28, 1992, sixteen hundred people filled a college gymnasium in Marin County, California, for the purpose of making rhythm together. Among them was John Avinger, owner of John's Music in Seattle, Washington. John drove down there with some friends, relatives and drums, spending about thirty hours on the road to take in the two-hour program. The event, called "Rhythm for Life," was the brainchild of Mickey Hart and was created to raise funds for his Rhythm for Life Project, which employs music therapists and drummers in healing capacities in nursing homes, prisons and other institutions.

SW: John, that w as a heck of a trip to make for a two-hour program. Why did you go down there?

John: Frankly, it was a gamble. I had talked to Arthur Hull who was facilitating the whole thing—trying to make it work as a jam—and he described it as "possibly the Woodstock of drumming." So I said to myself, if it is truly the Woodstock of drumming, I better be there. Also, it was just a way of finding out how they were going to pull this off with a huge mob of people so there would be someone up here with some direct knowledge of how to do it—so when we do it, we can really do it!

SW: Can you describe the scene? What was it like when you got down there?

John: There was a big parking lot full of people. There were young people in vans and people who looked like they still had their VW buses from twenty years ago. It was a total mix. There were people in suits, people in rags…an incredible cross-section. Men, women, kids, old people, young people. There was a long line outside the gymnasium and people were playing in line, jamming, all kinds of things going on.

Just about everybody had something to play—everything from djembes to coffee cans to plastic jugs to congas to bongos, shaman drums…anything you can think of. So there was a big lineup and people hustling tickets—a lot of people came who didn't have tickets 'cause they sold out the tickets at $15 a pop.

SW: OK, so you walk into this gym. What was the sight that greeted your eyes?

John: There was a small, low stage in the center of the gym, just a couple of feet high. They had mics and stuff on it, and there was a circle already set up around the stage of surdos [a very large Brazilian drum played with a mallet; normally plays the basic beat for samba.] I didn't count them but I estimated 25 or 30 surdos in the inner circle. And then people just going out from there on the floor. There was one side with bleachers, which were packed, but there were people just kind of packed onto the floor of the gym emanating from the circle.

SW: Were they performers?
John: No, just people. There really weren't any performers. There were leaders who [happened to be] stars: Sheila E., Airto, Flora Purim and Carlos Santana and Mickey Hart. And Arthur Hull, of course. These guys were there, not to perform but to simply support the event and to help lead the playing. Many grabbed a bell or shaker and just faced different areas of the crowd to help lead the playing.

SW: How did it get started?
John: Mickey Hart came out and talked about what this was all about and his Rhythm for Life foundation. Then he introduced the stars and Arthur Hull. Hull had it all figured out, what he was going to do. He was the guy they were looking to. They started out with a basic samba, a surdo thing...

> I recall being swept away by the whole thing.
> —John Avinger

SW: The audience isn't playing yet?
John: No, they're quiet. They're really depending on the surdos and the surdo guys were really working. They were watching Arthur. They were the "plants," picked because they could hang.

SW: They were really together, that many surdos?
John: Yeah, they were workin' at it. The circle was depending on them to hold the whole thing together. And then he [Hull] set up a very simple rhythm to go with that and got it started, got everybody playing. Then they set up an alternative rhythm—very simple, just a skeleton, trying to get two sides of the room going. Sometimes Mickey would come up with something—but Arthur was definitely working with the surdos and running all around. He's the guy with the super mondo energy. He was something else, trying to keep it all going and kind of conducting the crowd. He had a way of just punching his fist into the air. Being in the middle of it, it felt quite exciting.

SW: You told me this is the first time you've been in a place where this many people were playing percussion at the same time. What was the overall effect? How were the acoustics?
John: All I remember is it was so huge—just the size of the event—I'm usually kind of disturbed by "thunder drumming," it's mildly irritating in a lot of ways. But I don't recall being irritated. I recall being swept away by the whole thing, actually. And I'm a good test case for that because I'm a guy who would tend to resist that. I think part of what did it was having that underpinning hanging the thing together so that whatever people were doing was OK. The energy and the feelings were quite good, the vibe and spirit were very good because everybody was really into the thing. I think the secret of this working is that it was set up with the surdos and with Hull having a specific idea of what he was going to do. Just very simple stuff; he'd done it with hundreds of people at a time although I don't know if he'd ever worked with this many people before. But he knew how to go at it...

Partnering with the Music Industry

The music industry is becoming more aware of the growing recreational drumming movement. But many people, from facilitators to music store owners to drum shop managers do not know the difference between a clinic and community drum circle. Understanding the differences between a drum clinic and a drum circle will make it possible for you to educate and partner with local music store owners. The potential benefits to you as facilitator, to the merchants and to your growing recreational drumming community can be enormous.

As you learn *music-industry-speak* you will find key words and phrases that you can use to gain the store owners' interest and support. You will be able to approach store owners and drum shop managers. You can use this information to prepare yourself to describe the benefits to a store owner or to generate a letter of introduction.

Drum Clinics

Drum clinics are events that music store owners and drum shop managers regularly promote and host at their stores. The clinician is an artist who has usually mastered a given musical instrument and is often nationally recognized and endorsed by a name-brand music instrument maker. The clinician gives a demonstration or performs on their instrument for the audience, answers questions and signs autographs.

The people who attend a store clinic are usually professional musicians, or people who are striving to become professionals. They come to listen to the artist, get autographs and pick up tips on developing their musical and performance abilities. The people who make up this audience tend to be frequent store customers who hear about the clinic through the store's mailing list, newsletter or an advertisement posted in the store or seen in a local magazine.

Drum Circles

Drum circles are events that can be hosted by and held in music stores. The artist is a facilitator who orchestrates a group of people, regardless of their expertise, into a fully functioning, improvisational percussion ensemble. The people who come to a drum circle are from all walks of life, and are not typically professional musicians. They come, not to perfect their musical skills, but to express themselves at a recreational percussion event.

These people come prepared to participate, rather than be an audience. The store provides percussion and drums for some of the participants. Others bring their own instruments, which the store tags at the entrance. Most hear about the event through the community hand drumming grapevine or network, instead of through the store's advertisements.

When a store owner invites facilitated drum circles into their world, they "widen their customer base," and "create new traffic" for the business. By networking into their local hand drumming community, store owners and managers become an active part of one of the fastest growing segments of the music merchant industry: recreational rhythm instruments. This will have a definite positive effect on the store's financial bottom line.

You can help the store owner or manager start an entry-level drum circle that is accessible to anyone. By doing so, you involve people who are new to drumming circles, giving them an opportunity to experience the fun of rhythmical expression. When you facilitate your event at the store you introduce the participants to all the percussion instruments and other goodies the store has to offer.

You can encourage the store to become increasingly active in the nonprofessional hand drumming community. This will generate new ongoing traffic into the store and broaden their customer base. If they host a regular drum circle, they will develop a mutually supportive relationship with the growing recreational drumming community. In turn, the community will empower and support the store.

Hosting a Drum Circle in a Music Store

To host your facilitated community drum circle in a music store you will need to prepare, by considering the following elements:

- Parking accommodations
- Cleared area large enough for a circle in the store, and choice of how to organize participants; For small stores with limited space you can use the floor-to-standing sound bowl described in "Take Responsibility for the Physical Circle" on page 122.
- Drum stools or chairs or benches, preferably without armrests
- Turn off all the snares in the drum department.
- Tags to mark the personally owned drums as they are brought into the store
- Security to be sure players leave the store with only their own tagged instruments.
- Sound system. If you expect more than 75 players, you may need a sound system with a mic available. I prefer a wireless headset mic, but you may also use a wireless lapel lavaliere mic or handheld mic. For large events, you may also want to ask for an extra handheld mic to showcase some of the players during the event.
- A mailing list on a clipboard with a pen attached to a string. During the event, pass the mailing list among the participants. Then, place it on the information table by the store entrance before the end of the event.

A Reality Check for the Merchants

On one of my REMO England drum circle tours, the Nottingham drum shop agreed to participate in the tour only two weeks prior to their scheduled event. With so little time to advertise, these music store owners did not receive a copy of "Prelude to Drumcircle" and therefore received no community drumming education. So they did what they would do for any clinic. They posted "Master Class" drum clinic flyers at their shop and sent a mailing to their drum customers. They also set up interview for me, with the BBC radio station for the day of the event. That interview saved the day.

On the day of the event, I was listening to the car radio as I was riding through Sherwood Forest (as in Robin Hood and his Merry Men) into the town of Nottingham. The BBC talk show host announced that the American drumming master Arthur Hull would be a guest on his show in two hours. I cringed when I heard the words "drumming master," because I knew that, out of respect to my master drum teachers, I would need to correct this misplaced title when I was interviewed. The talk show host described the drum circle that I would be facilitating that evening. He read a public service announcement (PSA), given to him by the owners of the drum store. As he promoted my upcoming interview, he said that the program that evening would be a master drum class. Ouch! By using the words "master drum class" he was saying to his audience, "If you can't drum, don't come." Hearing this I panicked. If I did not intervene, the result would be a typical clinic that evening, attended by only a few professional drummers and drum students. It would not have been a community drum circle.

If that happened, then neither the community nor the merchants would get to see the possibilities of community-accessible recreational drumming. No one would benefit from my visit except a few drummers. I immediately called the radio station and asked the announcer to change the words on the PSA from master class to "a family-friendly community drum circle where anyone can participate." He made the change and made extra announcements of the updated PSA, as the time for the interview grew closer.

When I arrived at the radio station, I carried a bunch of REMO drums into the studio. I told the announcer that I would prove to him that anybody can play a drum if he would let me gather volunteers from the radio station. With his help, we recruited reluctant volunteer drummers, who gathered around the studio microphones. I facilitated an impromptu community drum circle, on the BBC program, as a live introduction to the interview.

The second that we were live on the air, I started the group with a few calls and responses and then counted the group in to play with a call-to-groove, "one, two, let's all play." The groove was solid and the melody line was good. We could have played for quite a while before encountering a natural transition or closing. Knowing that we were live on the radio, I was time conscious and kept my eye on the announcer for any sign from him to stop the groove and start the interview. He gleefully pounded on his drum with the rest of the group. When I finally caught his eye I pointed to my wrist and drew my finger across my throat with a questioning look. With this gesture I asked with my body language "Is it time to quit?" His smile got even larger as he shook his head no, and kept playing. When he finally gave me a stop signal, I did a call and response to a rumble closing. He then asked me to describe and talk about each of the REMO drums, and asked the group to wait in the studio so that we could play again during the interview. We did three in-the-moment drumming presentations during the half-hour interview. I explained to the listening audience that even though I am not a master drummer, some of my drumming teachers are, and then talked about the role of drums in relationship to community. My message was that the program that night at the Nottingham drum shop was not going to be a drum class, but a community drumming event where anybody could show up and play. I announced to the listening audience that we would have plenty of extra REMO drums and percussion available for mom, dad and the kids.

After I left the radio station, I listened to the program on the car radio. The announcer kept talking about his experience in that little impromptu circle. He said he was so excited about what he had experienced that he might even attend the drum circle that night, and he kept plugging the event. Even though he did not appear that night, the community did. The population was one-third drummers and drum students, and two-thirds people from the community who responded to the radio interview.

With that mixture, we had a very fun and exciting community drum circle. It was fun to watch the store owner's mouth fall open and his chin drop when a whole new potential customer group that he had never seen before appeared at his store. But for the opportunity given us by the BBC radio interview, our successful community drum circle experience would have just been yet another professional drumming clinic. Another rhythm seed has been planted.

Leading the Way to Learning

When an organization calls and asks me to facilitate a rhythm-based event in a situation with a scenario that I have never attempted before, my policy is to say yes, hang up the phone and exclaim to myself, "Oh my God!" Then I do the research needed to figure a way to successfully meet my new challenge. I share one of these experiences in this next story.

Meeting planners from the NSA had seen me facilitate an experiential keynote conference presentation and called to see if I would be available to be the opening keynote speaker at their annual conference. I said yes, of course, and told them that I would need to know more about the NSA organization, its personnel demographics and the theme of the conference to plan my presentation

> I think of a group I am facilitating as participants in a cooperative endeavor to create a group vision in sound.

They informed me that NSA stands for National Speakers Association and that I would be doing the opening keynote presentation for an audience of eight hundred professional keynote speakers. Hearing that, my ears started ringing, my head started spinning and my legs became weak in the knees. I needed to sit down to finish our phone conversation. After confirming my availability and negotiating some preliminary details, I hung up the phone, took a deep breath and said, "Oh my God!"

Although my rhythm-based events have increasingly been placed as keynote openings at conferences I have never thought of myself as a keynote presenter. I do not typically think of the group that I am facilitating as an audience, but instead as participants in a cooperative endeavor to create a group vision in sound. In addition to the conference theme I have been assigned to deliver, I see the musical activity as a body of work we are creating together. The cognitive message of the presentation is the clothing and costume that I put over the musical body.

Now my assignment was to stand on a stage and make a 45-minute keynote presentation to eight hundred keynote presenters. I would feel like a duck out of water if I made a presentation that did not involve any interactive rhythmical or musical components, so I decided to add some water to my presentation. I understand that keynote speakers usually focus on three basic talking points in their presentations. I decided to facilitate an interactive sequence with the audience between each of the three parts of my presentation, to reinforce my talking points.

Many events I have facilitated over the years have been scheduled around keynote speakers, so I have watched them in action. As I considered what talking points to present to support the conference theme of "Leading the Way to Learning" for these keynote speakers, I recalled basic presentation elements that I use when I facilitate. Some of these elements would be as important to a facilitator of a drum circle as they are to the quality of a keynote speaker's presentation.

Following is a synopsis of my keynote presentation, rewritten as though I were doing a keynote presentation for eight hundred drum circle facilitators instead of keynote speakers.

Facilitating on the Edge

As facilitators we lead the way to learning for the players in our rhythm-based events, independently of their playing expertise or of the specific reason for the gathering. By leading the way to learning you help facilitate a group of individuals who may never have participated in a drum circle before, become a synergized group of players creating one voice through rhythm.

The following three elements will help you be successful as you lead the way to learning through facilitating:

1. Be all that you can be.
2. Use your strengths.
3. Facilitate on the edge of your abilities.

Be All That You Can Be

If you want participants to leave at the end of your circle with a positive and lasting experience, then in addition to sharing your facilitation expertise, knowledge and wisdom, you

When all is said and done, your participants do not care how much you know as a facilitator, until they know how much you care about them as people.

will want to share your passion and beliefs. When you bring these personal elements to the center of the circle, you are also bringing an honesty and authenticity to your drum circle facilitation that the participants can feel.

By being "all that you can be" as a facilitator, you are being real with both yourself and your circle. When you do this, you also open yourself up to a vulnerability that makes you as human as the people you are facilitating. When all is said and done, your participants do not care how much you know as a facilitator, until they know how much you care about them as people. By being "all that you can be" you communicate your caring and your facilitation becomes more real.

Use Your Strength

We are facilitators because we are capable as rhythm guides and communicators who have valuable information and experience to share. Most facilitators use some specific personal strength as a vehicle with which to transmit their message to their group during a drum circle. Some of these personal strengths for bliss sharing are humor, drama, movement and playing expertise. For most presenters, our personal strength is also connected to how we share our bliss.

Obviously my strength, as well as my bliss, is my elfish sense of theater. Through elf theater I am able to guide a drum circle through their experience to learn that there is no such thing as a rhythmically challenged person.

Recognizing, developing and fine tuning your personal strength as a message delivery device can only improve your facilitation skills. This also gives you the benefit of "being who you are" while sharing your bliss, as you lead the way to learning. What is your strength or bliss and how can you use it to be all that you can be in your own facilitation presentations?

Facilitate on the Edge of Your Abilities

Facilitating on the edge of your abilities means exactly that. You will continue to become a better facilitator if you always facilitate on the edge of your abilities. It is a delicate balance to push the edge of your facilitating abilities, while experimenting with how far you can go before you get into trouble. If you play "over the edge," you can easily facilitate your drum circle into a rhythm train wreck, creating panic in the group and embarrassing yourself. This is why I encourage playing on the edge, instead of beyond your facilitation abilities. You are taking the chance for both a facilitated train wreck and a big learning experience to happen when you play "on the edge," but that is what makes life exciting and worth living.

Alternatively, you can easily facilitate inside your comfort zone and still impress the circle with your skills. But when you facilitate in your comfort zone you are playing it safe. If you do not take any chances, make any mistakes or test your abilities, then you are not using your strengths to the best of your ability, nor are you presenting to the circle "all that you can be."

I have seen ho-hum performances by some facilitators who deliver their programs from their comfort zone, but I also have seen many dynamic programs facilitated by those who deliver their spirit from the edge of their facilitation envelope.

Independently of what kind of group I am facilitating, as a rhythmical evangelist my personal intention is to share my rhythmical bliss, whether the focus is team building, community building or spirit building. The best events, for both the players and for me as facilitator, have happened when I have met both my own and the circle's objectives, while playing on the edge of my facilitation abilities.

When we use our strengths to the best of our ability while being all that we can be as facilitators, we lead the way to learning, not just for our circles, but for ourselves as well.

What Comes Around Goes Around

There is an old saying, "What comes around, goes around." This axiom represents the karmic law that states that every energy you put into the world, good or bad, will come back to you.

My Village Music Circles organizational trademark represents this axiom. As you look at the white arrows pointing out from the center of the symbol, you can see that they create the black arrows pointing back into the center of the symbol. This represents the idea that the kind and amount of energy that you put into the world will be the kind and amount that you will get back.

As a Capricorn, I expect some form of return for any advice, service or energy I give, but what that return might be, and how soon I might expect it to come back, does not affect the quality of my giving. Babatunde Olatunji taught me that you want to "get even" only with the people who have used their good energy toward you.

What do you expect for your facilitation service to your community? What is the payback for your hard work? Payback is often not in the form of money. Currency comes in many different forms: community support, the right advice at the right time, or someone creating a new opportunity for you in your life. Sometimes this currency is priceless, and unless you are using a business contract, who is to decide when in your life that payback will come to you?

Long after I leave this planet, I believe that some of the returns for my hard work and service will come back to me by coming to my children's children in the form of a rhythmically enabled culture for them to live in and explore.

Follow your bliss, do what you need to master it, start sharing it as a service, and what you share will come back to you manifold.

Arthur Facilitates Hawaii Inter-island Community Drum Circle

11 Facilitating at the Edge of Chaos

This chapter explores the science of complexity as it relates to a drum circle. Gaining a basic understanding of complexity theory will show us, as facilitators, a fresh perspective of how different elements interact dynamically in a rhythm-based event.

Complexity theory implies that when we observe nature in all its diversity, an underlying unity is revealed through an infinite variety of patterns. These patterns emerge out of chaos. By studying them, we can learn how the complex system of an interactive rhythm-based event works. We can use the science of complexity to observe and describe how the many different parts interact with each other.

Emergence

An *emergence* is a spontaneous combustion.

Because a drum circle is a living, breathing, interactive entity with many different forces functioning together at the same time, its natural dynamic is to self-organize. Due to this tendency toward self-organization, the circle can use a facilitator to help give it a direction and a focus—someone who guides the independently-functioning forces as they interact.

The participants at an event either consciously or unconsciously use their natural rapport skills to play with each other. This rapport creates synergy in the music, even while each participant is playing their own individual rhythm. When this process of self-organization is successful, enlivened music emerges. Using the language of complexity theory, we call this an emergence. You can recognize the following elements that indicate an emergence in a rhythm circle:

- The music evolves and goes through changes on its own.
- Players leave more space between the notes, creating possibilities for more group creativity.
- The quality of the experience for the participants rises. This is visible in the players' body language as an increase in interpersonal interaction, and audible as an increase in their musical spontaneity.

A group's self-organized process can produce new and unique rhythmical and musical structures that cannot be predicted. Your visual, auditory and kinesthetic peripheral sensibilities will help you identify emergences as they evolve into existence. As the group self-organizes, the evolving music becomes quantitatively better with each successful emergence.

As a facilitator, you want to look for and encourage self-organization and synergy in the group as it plays. Emergence most naturally occurs whenever you encourage spontaneity and improvisation in the group's process. You cannot force it. It can only be facilitated. You want to avoid controlling the circle, or over-facilitating with tools and techniques. When you facilitate the spontaneous, improvisational music that the drum circle gives you, then the magical moment of emergence can happen. Spontaneous combustion happens when the right elements come together in the right environment at the right time.

If spontaneity or improvisation is missing in the mix, spontaneous combustion will not happen, and then you'll need to light a fire instead. You as facilitator have the tools and techniques to light that fire in a drum circle event, but a fire lit by a facilitator is an entirely different kind of fire than one that comes from the group's spontaneous combustion, and most people in a drum circle can tell the difference.

For beginning-beginner facilitators, I emphasize the importance of transition points—how to look for and identify them, how to wait for them, what to do when they do appear, and what tools to use when they do. You and the drum circle are co-producing music. Meanwhile, an emergence can happen right at the end of the transition point. If you feel, hear and see a transition point coming in the music and you jump into the middle of the circle and orchestrate the group through the transition point before it reaches its peak, then you might take away an opportunity for the group to emerge through that transition point with their own enlivened music.

When you and the group have enough space in the music and in your facilitating, and when you have a vibrant musical dialogue among participants, you have what the group needs to create a spontaneous combustion fire. You will want to give it the opportunity it needs to light itself. It is important for you not only to GOOW, but to also to STOOW, thus giving them the opportunity to self-organize their own music. In that process of self-organization there's always the chance for an emergence.

Many times I, as a facilitator, anxiously wait on the edge of an ongoing drum circle as a transition point begins to develop in the music. I consciously hold myself back from jumping into the circle to fix it before the time is right. Especially toward the end of a drum circle event, I wait because I know there's a possibility during a transition point that the circle will self-organize and enlivening music may emerge.

When I hold myself back until the very last moment before the transition point reaches its equinox, a time when the quality of the music can begin to degrade, I am literally facilitating on the edge of chaos. As a facilitator in a drum circle, you know what awaits on the other side of an unfacilitated transition point, the scourge and bane of any facilitator—the dreaded train wreck.

By dancing on the edge of chaos you, as facilitator, allow the group the opportunity to experience the one-mind consciousness they need to self organize and emerge through their transition point into an exquisite musical experience.

Elements that Foster Emergence

The music in a facilitated drum circle constantly fluctuates between chaos and order as it evolves to its highest rhythmical and musical potential. A turbulent rhythmical environment is more conducive to emergence than an overly controlled environment. As explained by complexity theory, diversity, fodder and a healthy tension must be in place for emergences to happen. You as facilitator want to foster these three basic elements, described below.

Diversity

A diverse selection of drum types and percussion instruments provides the variety of pitches, notes and timbres you will want for improvisation. If all the players had the same type of drum it would be a pretty dull song, and it would limit the level of interaction possible among the players. With a wider variety of sounds, you can encourage spontaneity and musical emergence.

Fodder

Fodder is raw material for artistic expression. You want to verbally encourage players to improvise, experiment and explore during any rhythm they play. What comes out of the group's process is the fodder from which magical music can emerge.

A Healthy Tension

When your group is playing on the edge of chaos, you and they experience a healthy tension in the music, with an accompanying risk of falling into total chaos. This risk-taking happens at different levels and at different times throughout the event. To dance delicately with your rhythmical ensemble on the edge of chaos, where the musical magic is, you must allow yourself and your circle to take risks.

Expanding your facilitation techniques and letting your circle take chances creates that healthy tension so that you can be *on the edge*. Playing on the edge encourages players to deeply listen and fully participate with a *be here now* consciousness. When they are not on the edge, they sit back in their seats, enjoying the ride, but are unlikely to experience the magic of emergence.

Chaos Is Your Friend

The total opposite of order is chaos. They are two sides of the same coin. A community drum circle needs both. The paradox of this organic system is that both order and chaos are present at the same time. If you exert too much control to facilitate order, then your group will be unable to experience musical spontaneity. A totally linear, predictable process will eliminate the opportunities for individual improvisation and spontaneous drum jazz, making emergence and magic unlikely to happen in the music. Total order and control sit at one extreme end of the facilitation spectrum.

The other end of the spectrum is total chaos, with no control. A circle with only individual spontaneity and improvisation, and no order, is totally nonlinear and will tend to slide toward chaos and a train wreck. There might be a moment or two of music, but without order there will not be enough continuity to create musical magic.

A healthy rhythm circle needs good doses of both chaos and order. A skilled facilitator will balance the amount of chaos in the circle with the amount of order they put into the circle through their facilitating techniques.

This balance between chaos and order in an ongoing musical event needs to fluctuate in a wave, sometimes even wildly. This fluctuation expands and contracts the spaces between the notes, creating rhythmical movement. These spaces allow the group to self-organize and to adjust to the ever-evolving music they are creating. If the balance is facilitated to a constant level of fifty percent order and fifty percent chaos at all times, then there is no fluctuating wave between order and chaos. Without this rhythmical wave tension, the spaces needed for improvisation, spontaneity and emergence are missing.

Chaos is a friend that can present itself at any time in a drum circle. It is an element to be facilitated, and brought into play at appropriate moments. Chaos that is not recognized and facilitated can lead to the demise of a rhythm groove. You want to facilitate this delicate balance between order and chaos to foster the emergence of magical music.

Magic at the Edge

Picture an ongoing drum circle, a large body of people playing. When you look closer, you see individuals, each one adding random factors to the groove. At any given time, some participants are making small rhythmical diversions, perhaps getting distracted and losing the beat or stopping playing to rest their hands or to scratch their noses. Each of these small, independent diversions contributes to the level of chaos. At the same time, other players are connecting with the people around them, fully engaging in moments of cooperative rhythmical entrainment. These connections add order to the circle, as participants consciously create synergistic rhythmical rapport. Somewhere between this chaos and order is the magic. Listen for it between the notes as you facilitate on the edge of chaos.

Governing Elements of an Ongoing Circle

Chaos is a part of the study of non-linear dynamics that explains complicated behaviors of organic systems. Using chaos theory, simple equations can predict complex outputs. Often systems can be described using simple rules. An ongoing rhythm circle is an organic system with the following simple governing elements.

Time Signatures

The time signature represents how a rhythm is structured. A signature of 4/4 refers to four quarter notes per measure, and 6/8 refers to six eighth notes per measure. You need not understand music theory to continue reading from here.

4/4 is the most common time signature found in facilitated drum circles. When carefully introduced, 6/8 can be played even by beginners.

For music to happen, agreement among the players about the rhythm's time signature is necessary. Even though each individual player introduces a random factor within the rhythmical system called the drum circle, a common time signature governs the groove.

Space

The more spaces you make between the notes being played, the more room there is for creativity. As the facilitator, you can encourage the players to use the placement of their notes in time, to make space for other peoples' creativity. By doing this, players will find space for their own creativity as well.

Melody Line

A facilitator can demonstrate a universal pattern for a group to use as a foundational melody line. Players can then use the pattern as a model from which to play, and later from which to improvise.

Even though each individual player is empowered to interpret the melody line, the demonstrated pattern provides a starting point for a self-organized piece of music.

For each rhythm played by a group, the melody changes based on the combination of pitches, notes and timbres. Pitches vary with the tuning of the drums. Notes change with the hand techniques used to produce slaps, bass and tones. Timbres vary depending on which drums, bells, shakers and wood instruments are played. Each combination of timbres, notes and pitches creates a unique melody line in the music.

Intuitive Skills Triplicity

As a facilitator, you facilitate the creation of group mind. As the group mind begins to self-organize its music, you gradually release your control of the circle to the group. This releases your attention to technical aspects of the group, so you can intuitively look for places in the ongoing dynamics of the circle where you can make a positive difference. For example, you may choose to sculpt and stop cut an individual louder player along with the people nearest him, so the players around him can hear the group's

Awareness

Adaptation   Rapport

groove. Then, even when that group re-enters the groove, the whole circle of participants can hear the groove and play together more easily.

Successful facilitators gain perspective for guiding their circles using several specific skills, which are described below.

Awareness

By being present with each moment, and letting go of what has passed, you allow yourself to "be here now." This attitude stimulates your awareness. Consciously using your peripheral sensibilities will help you maintain this facilitation awareness as you support your drum circle's intentions.

As a living, breathing entity that is interdependent on all the different parts of itself you will find that there are hundreds of factors affecting a drum circle at any given moment. Trying to consciously deal with all of these elements at any one time can put you into facilitator crisis mode. When you focus your attention where you can make a difference you avoid crisis mode as you work with the most critical factors affecting the circle.

Any change can have large effects. Each small change initiated by circle participants can have a large effect on the music being created. Small changes created by you as facilitator can also have large effects on the circle's music.

Adaptation

A facilitator needs to be able to adapt. When events change, you need to be able to respond to the dynamic flow of the group's energy. Keep your plans flexible. Being rigid and controlling can keep the group in a linear groove without much chance for the magic in the music to evolve. Encourage and welcome the spontaneous surprises that appear in the moment at rhythmical events.

A facilitator needs to be able to adapt.

When your plans are flexible, you are more likely to recognize the gifts coming from the group's creative energy as the presents they are, instead of as interruptions to your plans. Being able to adapt to any situation in an ongoing drum circle is a kind of flexibility that you want to develop as a facilitator.

Rapport

To build rapport means to facilitate harmonious, mutual understanding among the participants of the circle and with you. It is up to you as the facilitator to give the players both broad directions and the space they need for creativity. That delicate balance between giving directions and giving freedom is best conveyed when you have good rapport with the group both as individuals and as a single entity.

Smaller group interactions grow into group responses and group music. When you as facilitator listen deeply, then spontaneous happenings appear as gifts, rather than shocks. When you attune your awareness, the group's feedback will help you facilitate a positive difference in the music, and thus, the drum circle's rhythmical alchemy experience.

Hidden Order

Hidden order is another aspect of the study of chaos theory. It is buried inside the randomness of any organic system. In a drum circle, that hidden order is created when participants, either consciously or unconsciously, play their random patterns in relationship to universal musical principles. As facilitator, you can guide participants to help them become aware of these principles. With awareness, players begin to consciously apply the principles and the music becomes more organically organized. The paradox is that by creating more order in the musical chaos, both you and the participants create more space in the music for independent improvisation, and as a result, offer more space for chaos.

Out of chaos, patterns emerge.

Out of chaos, patterns emerge.

Drum Council

Community of Drum Circle Facilitators Snuggling

12 A Cross-Country Conversation

Babatunde Olatunji is the father of the African drum and dance movement in the U.S. Baba spent most of his life tirelessly building community using African rhythmaculture as a model for living together in love and peace. He was, in the true sense of the word, a rhythmical evangelist, helping birth our grassroots drum and dance community. With his passing in April of 2003, he leaves this community as his legacy.

As a musician, Olatunji introduced African musical elements, delivering an immediate and lasting effect on American jazz. For example, John Coltraine came to Harlem to study at the Olatunji Center for African Music. Babatunde Olatunji created World Beat music generations before the term had even been conceived. Olatunji and his *Drums of Passion* was a highly sought after act.

Fans have bought over five million copies of his *Drums of Passion* recording, which was the first of many recordings Baba completed during his career. He was also part of the Grateful Dead musical family. For example, he contributed generously to the 1992 Grammy-award-winning Planet Drum CD, produced by Mickey Hart.

As a teacher, Olatunji brought to us a deeper understanding of African culture through his workshops in dance, music and song. He also helped other great African drummers and dancers come to the U.S., including Titos Sompa from the Congo and Papa Ladji Camara from Senegal. He guided them in New York in his *Drums Of Passion* dance and drum troupe before they established themselves in the U.S. ethnic arts community.

As a community builder, Olatunji was a man on a mission. With his inspiration and guidance, this drum and dance community has developed into an international network.

Sakaras in Arthur's Studio

In 1995, I was asked by *DRUM Magazine* to interview Baba for their fall issue. That interview was pieced together from long conversations shared with Baba while I drove him to our various *Drums of Passion* gigs during that year's west coast summer tour. Even though I was a member of his west coast ensemble, I quickly discovered that the only dependable place where we could talk without being interrupted was in my car. The moment we reached our destination, Olatunji would be surrounded by many people, each with different needs. He would happily jump into the fray, multitasking as stage manager, band leader and community elder as he facilitated each event into a magical experience for everyone involved.

Baba was very curious about the newly developing cultural phenomenon known as a facilitated drum circle. Many of our conversations that summer centered around his interest in facilitated circles, as you will see when you read the interview.

The year following our interview, Baba and I co-facilitated a non-culturally specific rhythm empowerment event at a personal growth conference. This was Baba's first experience facilitating an in-the-moment drum circle. Using his old teaching tools, he masterfully facilitated the group's music into magic using new facilitation tricks.

Later that year, Baba flew to our annual Hawaii Facilitators Playshop, to both watch and talk with the players who were training to become the next generation of drum circle facilitators. His interview captures the message he shared with us – his clear far-reaching vision of the evolution of rhythmaculture, drum circles and recreational drumming.

When Baba shared his perspective, the facilitation community was in its infancy. The ideas he shared with me years ago about drum circle facilitation are even more appropriate now that we have a fully developed rhythm event facilitator community. As we move closer to Baba's dream of a drum in every household, may we honor Babatunde Olatunji's memory with every beat of our drum.

The sakara, a drum that Baba refers to in the beginning of this conversation, is a small hand drum which has the form of a tambourine, without the jingles. It looks like a goat skin has been strung over the lip of a clay pot and then the lower part of the pot was removed. I have a few sakaras in my studio and when Baba saw them he picked up one and played it like an old friend. He made it sound like a talking drum by using the thumb of his "holding" hand to press on the inside of the drum, changing the pitch as he played it.

Hull: Let's talk about when you first came to America.

Olatunji: I was playing the hand drum when I was on the boat, coming here in 1950. I remember the engineer on the boat, the M.V. Eluru of the West African Boat Line that brings all the cargoes from West Africa to the United States through New Orleans. It wasn't a passenger boat. It had a few cabins that they would sell to passengers, but it was actually a cargo boat. The engineer said, "A strange man in a strange land shouldn't sing a strange song" because every morning I would play my hand drum just to amuse myself. It was a sakara–a small hand drum which has the form of a tambourine. I came over to become a Rhodes Scholar, studying to become a diplomat. I was hoping to be able to one day represent Nigeria in the U.N., or as a diplomat or an ambassador to some country.

Hull: Instead you became an ambassador of African culture in the U.S. How did you make that transition?

Olatunji: Circumstances led me to doing what I'm doing now. When I arrived on the campus of Morehouse College in Atlanta, I saw a lot of African Americans, brothers, who looked like people I know very well at home. I saw people who looked like my cousins, or my uncle. I saw women who looked like women I liked very much. And I said, "You look like friends of mine." And they'd say, "Oh no, I'm not from Africa. Don't you ever tell me that. I'm a Negro and I'm from the United States." I couldn't believe my ears. I said, "Your ancestors are from Africa." They were very sincere, but I could not fully understand why they said that. They asked me questions about whether we had lions running the streets. I was not discouraged, though, because I had discovered the sincerity in their voices, in the way they asked the questions. They wanted to learn. Then I discovered Hollywood's unholy war on Africa – the betrayer of Africa. Movies I saw in the 1950s portrayed Africa with Tarzan and Jane swinging from tree to tree, people sleeping in trees, head-hunters, as if nothing good could come from Africa. So I really wanted to identify myself with Africa, and say, "Let me educate you about Africa." That is how the first program was put together. The first dance company, the first production, that's how I started. Then after graduating, I moved to New York. I decided to move there on my first visit to New York in my freshman year. I saw Harlem and said, "Oh, this is where my people are. This is the place to come to continue the program."

Hull: How long did it take before the public began to take notice of your work?

Olatunji: That started just after the release of the Drums of Passion album in 1959. It was right there on Billboard's Top Ten for weeks and weeks. That started getting us national attention. Then also it was during the 1960s, a period when social change was happening in this country, which also gave me an opportunity to participate in this change.

Hull: Young people were looking for and discovering a new way of living and recreating their culture.

Olatunji: That's right. So I was credited with the cultural awareness that was going on, of the African Americans and all young people both black and white. How many black radio stations did you know then? Very few if any. There was one in the New York area, WLWU, with a very wonderful man Murray the K, who would always open his shows with "Akiwowo." And he would play it and say, "Well the chief is here today. The change is coming. Look out you guys." The young people on college campuses both black and white would listen to Drums of Passion.

Hull: That's basically where I first heard Drums of Passion, in college. It paved the way for the workshops you did throughout the country. And that began the birthing process of the drumming communities that we see today.

Olatunji: We first introduced African dancing and drumming on college campuses throughout the United States. We traveled the length and breadth of the United States and visited over a thousand colleges and universities over the last twenty years. Probably any college in the East to the Midwest, Minneapolis to California. In the 1980s we opened with a jazz band at the same time we were running the dance company. The jazz band consisted of people like Yousef Lateef and Charles Lloyd, and the manager of Birdland would always give me thirteen weeks to open all the big bands that came there. And then we opened the Troubadour in Los Angeles and another club in San Francisco in 1963 before the march on Washington. When we would go to places to perform, I'd also take the opportunity to say, "Do you have a center where people go? Let me go and give a lecture there." That was very important because it became more than just people coming and doing a concert for the students. I'd give them a workshop in drumming and dance. It was an opportunity to sell the act, but also an opportunity for people to have an understanding of what we are doing. It's important to let people get a little closer. So that they can see and experience and feel what you are doing and what you are a part of. It's also okay for someone to perform and for people to clap their hands at the end, then leave. But to really be a part of it, to know that they can be a part of it, is more.

Hull: Why do you think people from all walks of life are picking up a hand drum and getting involved in this hand drumming phenomena that is sweeping the United States today?

Olatunji: Well, they are going back to their roots. We're people who started with body percussion, with clapping of the hands, stamping of the feet. I guess it's the way we started to amuse ourselves. That's how we learned to imitate sounds of birds and all kinds of things we hear around us, because of man's capacity to imitate. That's how we figured out how to make different instruments. So we started way back, and now we are going back to just ourselves. Rediscovering ourselves. And from there on we can move forward. We are trying to put together the great things of the past with the present for the future. You know the sky is not the limit anymore, it is space now. We are discovering that we need to come back down to earth, from where we started. It's as if we are trying to balance things, in essence.

Hull: We are trying to balance the technological society that has taken us away from…
Olatunji: That has taken us away from the reality of the earth that supports us.

Hull: …the reality of our connection with the earth and our connection with each other as people.
Olatunji: It gave birth to us in the first place. We need to recognize that it will always be there. It's there for us to use, replenish and leave for forthcoming generations, so we cannot afford to destroy it. We are learning to do that now. We are also finding the simple things that people can do together. All people from all walks of life, all colors, have various things that they can do together, and it's the simplest thing to make music and sing together.

Hull: Let's talk about your workshops. They do more than just educate people about

African Culture. They are basically a place for a community to come together. You address a tremendous amount of your work to building and feeding a healthy community though the dances, songs and rhythms that you teach. Do you always try to convey such a message through your workshops?

Olatunji: Well, I must confess that I deliberately make sure my presentation is geared toward the message that emphasizes togetherness, the one that promotes love and the one that makes everyone feel important. I know I must think about what I'm going to say, and I know also that my actions speak louder than my words. So I also try to practice what I preach.

Hull: Such as "getting even"?

Olatunji: As the old Chinese proverb says, the only people that we should really get even with are those who have done us a good turn. So I don't let go of anybody who has done something good for me. Those are the people that I spend my time and energy with. I have no time or spare energy for anything or anyone who is being detrimental to my spirit, or keeping me from my goal. When you think about it, it's true. The energy that you put together trying to get even with people who do unpleasant things to you can kill you. But the energy that you put together to get even with people who are nice to you gives you more power, gives you joy, and that accelerates you.

Hull: You often hear people talk about the spirit of the drum. This phrase is used a lot, but hasn't been well defined. We as a group feel that something happens when we gather to drum together, and people say "Oh, that's the spirit of the drum." But what is it?

Olatunji: [laughs] A great teacher of mine once said, "There are some questions that can never be answered, and would be useless if known."

Hull: [laughs] And this is one of them!

Olatunji: Not totally. It is answerable. The spirit of the drum is something that you feel but cannot put your hands on it. You feel when people come together to play. It does something to you from the inside out, but you can't really put your hands on it. You feel it while you're playing and after you play for a while, sometimes for 24 hours, sometimes for two or three days. It hits people in so many different ways, that to try to define it would just be a matter of semantics, the use of words. But the feeling is one that is satisfying and joyful. It is a feeling that makes you say to yourself, "Yes, I'm glad to be alive today. I'm glad I'm here. I'm glad I'm a part of this world." It stays with you until other things come and take your attention away from it, but you will always remember it.

Hull: Another part of your mission is to be the focal point for orchestration. As a facilitator, you bring people together to express their rhythmical spirit in a community drum circle. As our drumming community grows so does our need for more facilitators. And as new facilitators crop up, the question is, what priorities should they have? I think as long as they are promoting the community rather than themselves, they are learning a basic and very important aspect about the mission.

Olatunji: First of all, whoever is given the opportunity to be a facilitator must realize that it's an opportunity to develop our own talents. It's true, drum teachers might have certain knowledge that probably will prepare them to facilitate a drum community. But you cannot allow self-interest to supersede the goal. I'm not playing a double role. I have to play the role of the facilitator, not the teacher, to bring out the common ground to all of the people in the community – that is the goal.

Hull: So a drum teacher can have good facilitation tools, which you can use in a drum circle. But if you put them on top of the hierarchy of priorities then all of a sudden you're teaching a drum class rather than facilitating spirit in a drum circle.
Olatunji: That's right.

Hull: But, if you don't use the tools that you've generated as a drum teacher then of course...
Olatunji: You fail.

Hull: I've seen some people who aren't good drummers become good drum circle facilitators.
Olatunji: Yes.

Hull: Because they understand the importance of the mission.
Olatunji: Because you are not there to teach or to show people how well you can play. You're there because you know how to bring music out of them. You have to say, "Look, you've got something that you probably don't know you've got. I will prove it to you that you can do it by just doing it." That's what we're talking about.

Hull: You taught me a great lesson. A few years ago while I was being pushed out into the national drum community circuit, you took me aside and said, "You come into town and get them all excited and leave. What are you leaving? You have given them inspiration, but have you introduced them to teachers in the area?"
Olatunji: Where can they go after you're gone? What are they going to do tomorrow or next week?

Hull: Now wherever I go, I contact all the drum teachers and facilitators in the area that I can, and have them come to the drum circle so they can be introduced and acknowledged.
Olatunji: So that the community will know, "Oh yeah, we've got these people in our community."

Hull: What would you like to say to the growing number of facilitators who are coming forward and fulfilling this need in the community?
Olatunji: The great teacher said, "Blessed are the peacemakers, that they shall inherit the earth." Facilitators have to rejoice in the fact that they are messengers. They are given an opportunity to be the ones who are called upon to help build the bond that exists between people. They're the ones who go around telling it to the world, "Don't you forget. We all have a job to do. We need to heal our community and heal the planet." They become the servants of all. Because of that assignment, they will be provided for automatically. Because it has been ordained that the flock will always take care of the shepherd. So the shepherd has to be there for the community to remind you that you are just as important as everybody else.

Hull: No one is any more or less important in a community drum circle. Everyone has something to give to bring the community song alive and to make the magic.
Olatunji: That's what makes it become an irresistible force that can evolve and become an immovable object.

Hull: The media is calling this grass roots movement "the hand drumming phenomena." It's really the beginning of something that is going to affect the culture of the United States in some big ways. I'd like to put you in a time machine and send you ten years into the future. Based upon what you have seen happening within the U. S. since 1950, where do you think hand drumming will be ten years from now?

Olatunji: Well, it depends on how we promote it. I think we will have to teach it to our school children as part of their education, like football or basketball. That way it will not be a fad. We don't want all of them to be musicians, but they will know it because they have touched it.

Hull: It will be a part of our culture.

Olatunji: Yes. It needs to be a part of the culture for the simple reason that the world is here in America. And because the world is here, the world has brought its culture here. The world culture then must be preserved here as well. There will be people who know how to play sakara in Berkeley even if it's not being played in Lagos, so at least it's being preserved.

Hull: That's why it has to be integrated into our cultural expression.

Olatunji: It's happening now. This is a mosaic. It's what makes this country great. There is no other place in the world like America, right? People come from all parts of the world to make America what it is. Cultures must be preserved for that reason. Let me tell you what's going to happen. We are so lucky that some of the people who are now in our drumming and dance classes and our workshops can become executives. So they're going to use it. It's a good thing. They are young now, and are interested in what's happening, and they are going to make sure that this thing survives. They are going to be different than the CEOs that we have now because of their exposure to multi-cultural situations. It is a quiet cultural revolution that will unite all people. It will solve many of the problems that seem so impossible. I have a great hope for this happening in the future. That will be a wonderful thing to see.

"From what culture is this rhythm?"

The highest compliments that I have ever received in my life as a facilitator have come from "people of source." Such people are experts in the musical genre of their culture, as well as being well versed in other rhythmacultures. On two distinct occasions two specific people spoke the exact same words to me. They warmed the cockles of my heart and let me know that I am on the right path.

In downtown Kuala Lumpur in Malaysia, I met Abdoul at a community drum circle I facilitated. He had heard about the American drum circle movement and had come to see it in action. After the event he introduced himself as a drum teacher and as a traditional as well as a contemporary musician. We immediately felt comfortable together and spent two hours taking turns teaching each other rhythms from many cultures around the world, as we are both eclectic rhythm collectors. One traditional Malaysian flirting rhythm Abdoul taught me is almost exactly like a Nigerian party rhythm I know, so I, in turn, taught the rhythm back to him with a few Nigerian twists.

Abdoul plays traditional Malaysian drums in a culturally specific music group, and plays anything he can get his hands on in his contemporary jazz ensemble. I have been told that he is considered a master drummer in his country.

I invited Abdoul to come and watch me facilitate a fifty-person corporate team-building event that evening for the Malaysian Government Human Resource Department.

Adhering to the Malaysian tradition of "rubber time," sometimes called "village time" in the west, Abdoul arrived late, more than halfway through my team-building program. By the time he arrived, the program had progressed so that the basic elements of a successful drum circle had been facilitated into place. The fifty Malaysian government executives were making their own beautiful music. I stood outside the drum circle giving them the space they needed to enjoy themselves. It had evolved from a corporate team-building event into an orchestra of the type you can find in well-facilitated drum circles all over the planet. The rhythm they were playing had a strong groove, with a lot of space between the notes for improvisation and dialogue. The group was consciously making music. They were a drum orchestra.

I was being mesmerized by the harmonies in the music the players were creating. Their music was beckoning me to join them. Because they had successfully identified and self-facilitated their two most recent transition points, I began to make myself invisible so I could take my seat in the center row of chairs and become one of the players. Just then, Abdoul came up behind me, put his hand on my shoulder to get my attention and asked, "From what culture is this rhythm?"

At first I couldn't speak. Although I heard the question, the essence of its implications bypassed my brain and shot straight down into my heart. I felt a warm fuzzy glow start from the bottoms of my feet and the top of my head at the same time. They met somewhere in the middle of my body.

Even though I had just met Abdoul that day, I had a lot of respect for him as a person and for his extensive knowledge of rhythmacultures. He was able to hear and recognize, inside the group's in-the-moment rhythm, the basic components of a two-hundred-year-old culturally specific rhythm that had been handed down from generation to generation.

Hearing this cleanly played clearly harmonic group rhythm, Abdoul assumed that it was something that I had taught these executives from my culturally-specific repertoire as a hand drum teacher. His innocent question was an affirmation to me that I had been able to guide these beginner drummers past their freeform rhythms toward using many of the basic universal drumming principles present in culturally specific rhythms. What they were really doing was successfully sharing their rhythmical spirit.

After I took three full breaths, the warm fuzzy feeling dissipated but Abdoul's unknowing compliment still rang in my heart. "From what culture is this rhythm?" I smiled with a deep satisfaction and said, "The Malaysia Human Resource culture."

His mouth dropped open in amazement as he stared past me at the in-the-moment drum circle. "You mean that this is their own music?" he asked. "Yes," I said.

A few years later, Babatunde Olatunji was the opening keynote speaker at a Noetic Science Conference held near Miami, Florida. As Baba often explained, his message is in

Arthur and Daughter Maraya with Baba

the music, so at least half of his presentation was musicmaking. Because I was to facilitate the community drum circle that would follow, I had the privilege of playing with Baba. After we played a few rhythms as part of his presentation, Baba said that he would take a 15-minute break and join me later at the drum circle. After studying and performing with Baba for many years, I knew better. I expected Baba to be on "village time" and he was.

Because of my ongoing relationship with many of the conference attendees over the previous years, many members of their community were committed recreational drummers. Additionally, Miami drum community members came to participate, honor Baba and assist me. Both parts of the group I was to facilitate that night knew my body language. This was a drumming community rhythm gathering. Much like my experience in Malaysia, the group became an orchestra of self-facilitating musicmakers. Theirs was a cleanly played clearly harmonic drum circle song, only this time we were several hundred strong. As far as I was concerned, I had died and gone to facilitator's heaven.

After the opening drum call, I had worked with the circle participants to plan what we would do to honor Baba whenever he appeared. We planned to open a path through the drummers for him to enter the center of the circle. At the same time, we would switch whatever rhythm we were playing to Baba's Fanga welcoming rhythm from Liberia.

About halfway through the event, I was signalled by one of his entourage that Baba was waiting for me outside the ballroom. The self-facilitating Miami drum song was solid and beautiful so I was comfortable leaving the room to greet Baba. When I met him at the doorway Baba greeted me with "Ata, (Nigerian for Arthur) what is the plan?" As I described the overview of how the group planned to greet him, I noticed that he wasn't listening to me any more. He was listening to the beautiful music filling the ballroom. Babatunde Olatunji had tilted his head back. His eyes stopped focusing on anything particular. He was mesmerized by the harmonies that the players were creating in their drum music. Putting his hand on my shoulder to stop my blathering, he said to me, "This is very sweet. From what culture is this rhythm?"

At first I couldn't speak. Although I heard the question, the essence of its implications bypassed my brain and shot straight down to tickle the cockles of my heart. I felt a warm fuzzy glow start from the bottoms of my feet and the top of my head, at the same time. They met some where in the middle of my body.

Hawaii Playshop Participants Partying

Finale

You know more than you think you do. Trust yourself, and the experiences that you create for yourself while facilitating drum circles will help you discover and access your own inner wisdom. As your understanding and judgement evolve, you empower yourself as well as the people you facilitate.

This is a learning-how-to-learn book. One of my goals in writing it is to share ideas that will teach you ways to learn – both about facilitating and about yourself. Although reading *Drum Circle Facilitation* is a learning experience, facilitating a drum circle is a kinesthetic learning process. In addition to reading this book, you must create and facilitate rhythm-based events and get feedback from your experiences. Then you can see what works for you and your drum circle participants and what you need to fine tune next to be a better facilitator.

In the center of the circle you will find your true self.

Whatever you do is a learning experience. As you learn to facilitate, you go through more than a technical process. You experience thoughts and feelings as part of the facilitation. By choosing to create an event, then designing and facilitating it, you learn as much about your intentions, personal agenda and

241

emotions as you learn about facilitating.

Drum circles can be never-ending learning experiences. Each time you step into a circle to facilitate, you build on your knowledge. If you treat each event as your next learning experience, you gain wisdom as well as more knowledge about facilitation. You can then use your growing wisdom to turn an everyday drum circle event into Rhythmical Alchemy. As part of that process you will grow as a person, while you enhance your facilitation skills. In the center of the circle you will find your true self. Self-discovery awaits you.

Angel Song

I had just finished exploring the magnificent Mayan temple ruins of the ancient city of Copan in the northern jungles of Honduras. I walked across the road from the ruins, over to some very small shops full of trinkets for sale to tourists. It was the end of the day and most of the shops were empty of customers. Some were already closed.

From one of the shops came a short soft burst of grace and beauty manifest in sound. It was what I imagine an angel would sound like. The pure, soft, sweet melody beckoned me to find its source. I found it behind the sales counter of one of the shops, nestled on top of a stack of Honduran cloth pillows. *It* was a four-year-old little girl. She was lying on her side facing the wall, playing with a macramé wall hanging. She hummed her short sweet melody lines between every three or four breaths. Each little song was totally different from the one before and lasted the length of one long relaxed breath. Then she would contentedly breathe a few more breaths before humming a new melody line. My heart melted.

Each of the little girl's songs seemed to wash away a bit more of my fatigue from walking around the Mayan ruins all day. I meandered through the store, pretending to shop while listening to her contented breathing-out songs. When I walked up to the sales counter and faced the little girl's mother waiting for me on the other side, she greeted me with a smile, "Buenos diaz" (good afternoon). I smiled back at her while I put my index finger up to my lips. I pointed with my other hand to the girl behind her, and then to my ear. She gave me an understanding smile and we each leaned on one elbow on our respective sides of the tall counter as we watched and listened to the little girl express and explore her rhythmical humming sounds and melody lines.

After one particularly beautiful angel song, I heard myself softly humming the same sequence of notes back to the little girl. I froze and held my breath to see what would happen next. Although it was an automatic response to her song, I felt upset with myself for interfering. I was afraid that I had broken the magical, private musical space that the girl had created for herself. I was concerned that after hearing the strange voice behind her, she would stop singing, turn her head to see the customer at the counter, jump up from the pillows and run and hide in her mother's skirts. Instead the child held her breath for only a moment. Then she continued to play with the wall hanging and breathe her usual set of breaths before humming her next song.

That song was the same song as her last one, and the one I had sung back to her, except she changed the pitch of one of the notes in the middle and changed her song by humming a new note at the end. Her last note softened and faded into her breathing. The mother and I looked at each other with wide eyes and big grins. My heart skipped a beat and I stifled my impulse to jump up and down with glee.

An improv song game was afoot. I had been accepted by the girl and invited to play. I hummed the exact same song back to her, except I changed the last note from a hum to an open-mouth sigh that became slowly softer and faded into my breathing. The four year old stopped playing with the wall hanging and brought her hand down, but she did not turn around. After a few extra breaths, she started her next song by mimicking my sigh. Her sigh shifted to a hum, and then into other open-and-closed-mouth notes. By changing one of her humming notes into a sighing note and singing it back to her, I gave the girl permission to go beyond her humming pitch exploration into vocal exploration.

What ensued next was a long series of calls and responses between us. As we improvised each song, we were getting our next idea and rhythmical melody from the sound dialogue that we had just created together. As this song improv exchange continued to develop, I could no longer tell who was calling and who was responding. We were weaving sound magic between us.

By the middle of our song game, I could tell by the shadows on the wall, that people had entered the shop behind me. The mother, looking past me, quickly held up one hand palm out, like a policeman stopping traffic. With her other hand she put her index finger up to her lips – universal body language for Shhhhh. Then she pointed to her little girl, who was in full song, then to me and then to her ear. Once the girl finished her turn, her mom motioned to me to continue. I was glad, as I was mesmerized by the song dialogue I was having with this beautiful child. She was not afraid to explore and express her rhythmical and musical spirit through her voice.

Toward the end of our game, we had evolved from song improv to soundscape improv. The child's short angel songs had turned into clicks, honks, shouts and sighs. We were playing in the sound sandbox that we had created for ourselves. Finally, in the middle of one of her soundscape calls, she added a *bazort*. Press your lips firmly together and then blow air between them. When you hear the sound of flapping lips you will know what a bazort is. The bazort that she made surprised her, stopped her in mid-call, and caused her to go into uncontrollable body-shaking giggles. I responded by exactly reproducing her last call, including the bazort and the giggles. She giggled and wiggled even harder.

The Game was over. She turned away from the shop wall, pushed herself up from her pillows onto her knees and, still giggling, looked at me for the very first time. She had her mother's beautiful Mayan eyes. From the very bottom of my heart I thanked her, "Gracias senorita." She stifled her giggling enough to respond with the same tone that I had used, "Gracias señor." I looked at the mother. She didn't have to say anything. Her thank you was in her eyes and smile and she knew it.

The mother's greeting at the beginning of our angel song improvisation and the thank yous between the little girl and me at the end were the only words spoken. All the other sounds were notes and songs that we explored, expressed and shared from a much deeper place than that of our social selves. It did not matter that I was many times older than this little girl. During our in-the-moment musical exchange, we shared our age-less rhythmical spirits with each other – transcending gender, culture and language. We exchanged pure essence through sound. I left the shop before they could see me crying. They may not have understood. But if you have read this book, you do.

In-the-moment music and rhythm exchange is a safe, powerful and magical way for two people to share their spirits. When multiplied by the number of people in a facilitated rhythm event, the experience can be even more powerful and magical. This is the rhyth-mical spirit that I want to share with any person with whom I am playing in a drum circle. I hope and pray that this is the same sharing of spirit that you foster whenever you are facilitating a rhythm-based event. All I ask is that you share your Spirit.

That is all for now.

Drum Circle Facilitation

TRIPLICITIES

Rhythmical Empowerment
Community Building
Health & Wellness

Intention
Triplicity

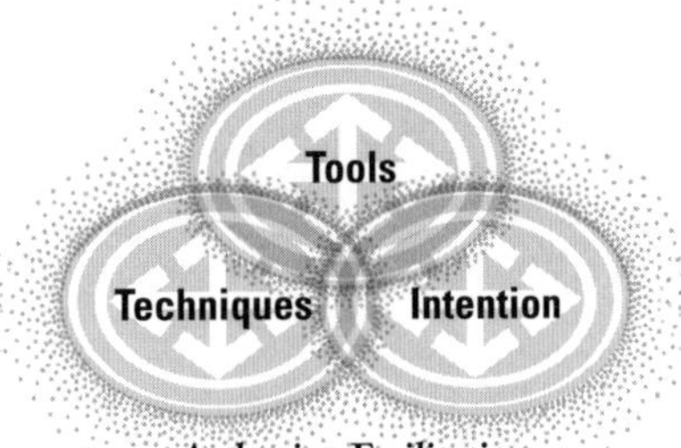

Tools
Techniques
Intention

Arthurian Facilitation
Triplicity

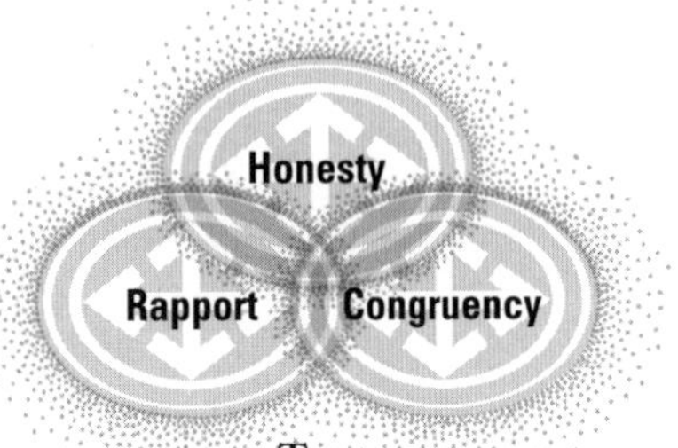

Honesty
Rapport
Congruency

Trust
Triplicity

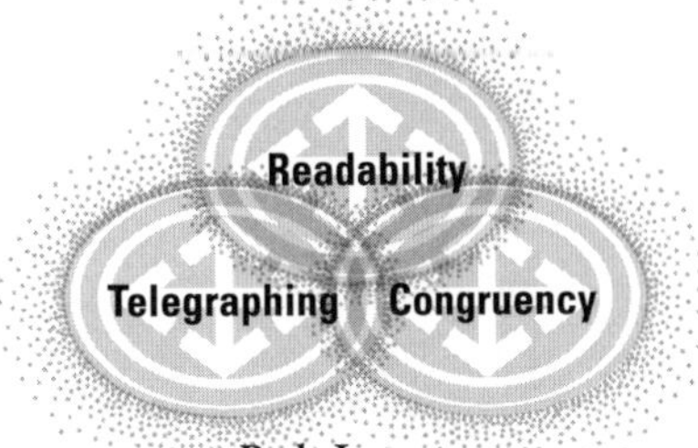

Readability
Telegraphing
Congruency

Body Language
Triplicity

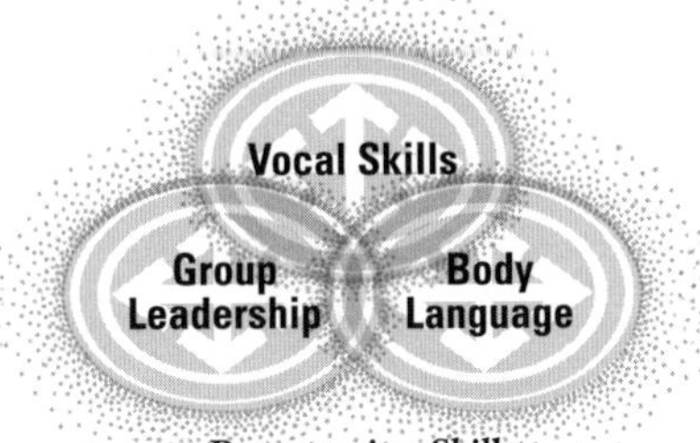

Vocal Skills
Group Leadership
Body Language

Presentation Skills
Triplicity

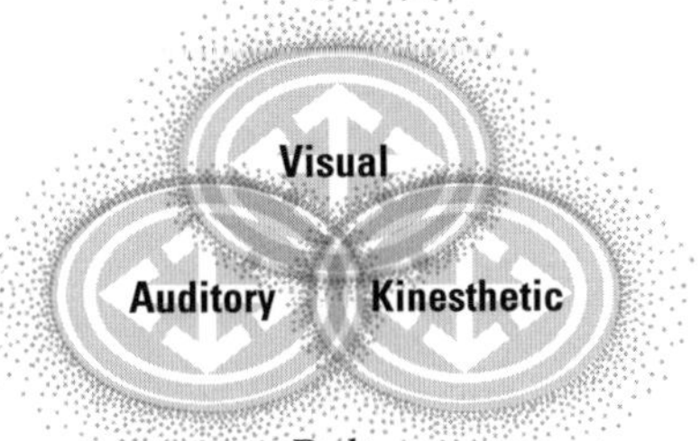

Visual
Auditory
Kinesthetic

Radar
Triplicity

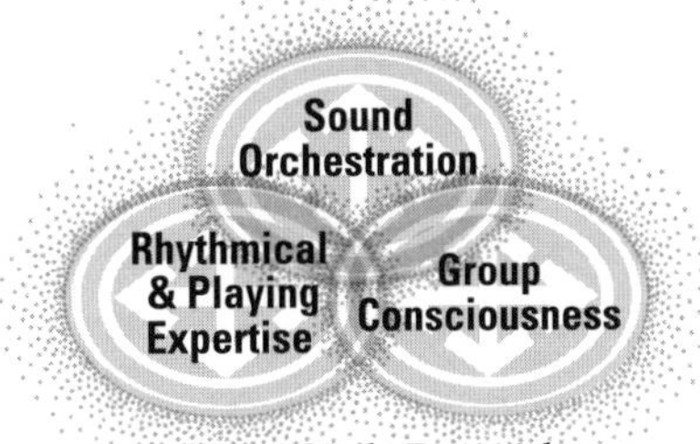

Sound Orchestration
Rhythmical & Playing Expertise
Group Consciousness

Drum Circle Potential
Triplicity

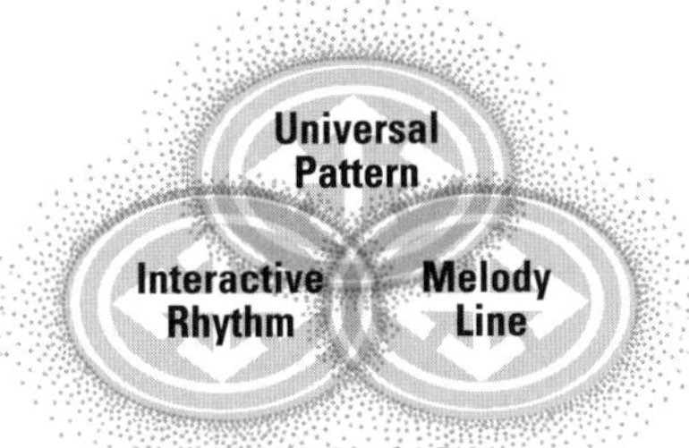

Universal Pattern
Interactive Rhythm
Melody Line

Drum Circle Song
Triplicity

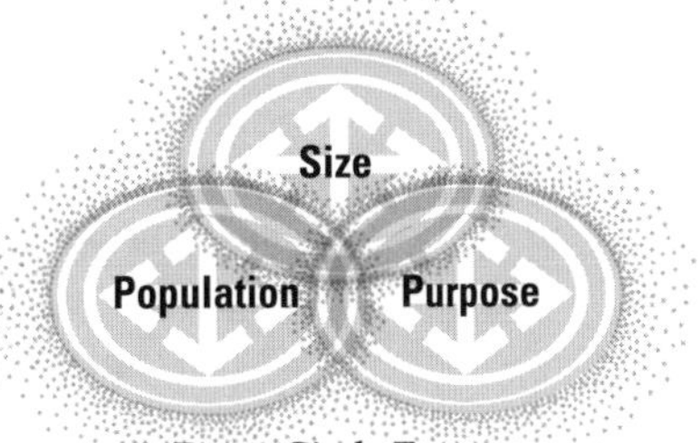

Size
Population
Purpose

Drum Circle Format
Triplicity

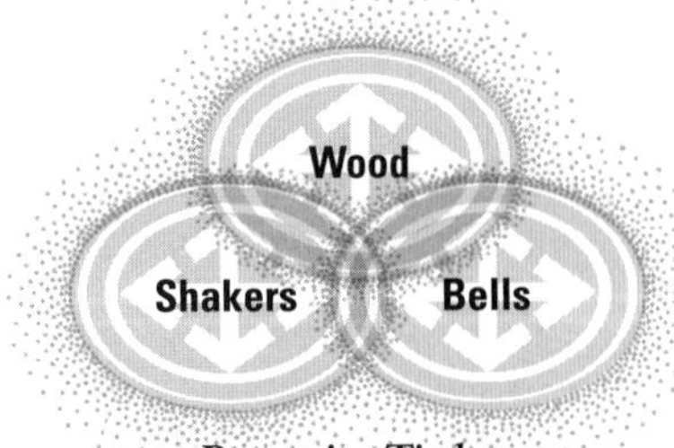

Wood
Shakers
Bells

Percussion Timbre
Triplicity

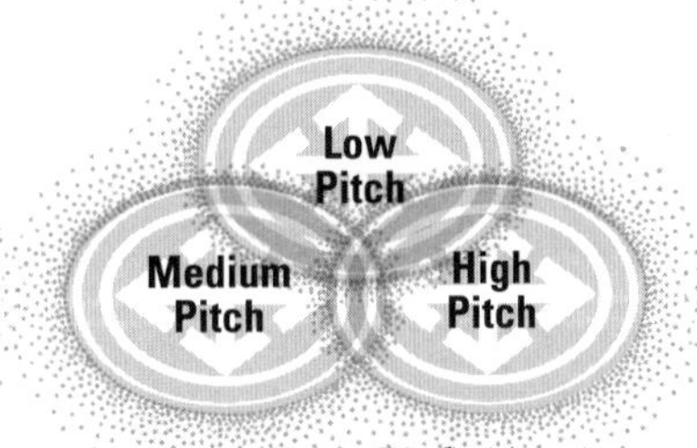

Low Pitch
Medium Pitch
High Pitch

Drum Pitch
Triplicity

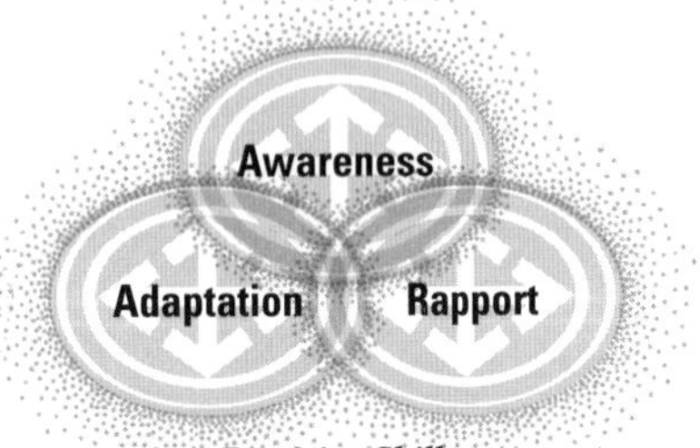

Awareness
Adaptation
Rapport

Intuitive Skills
Triplicity

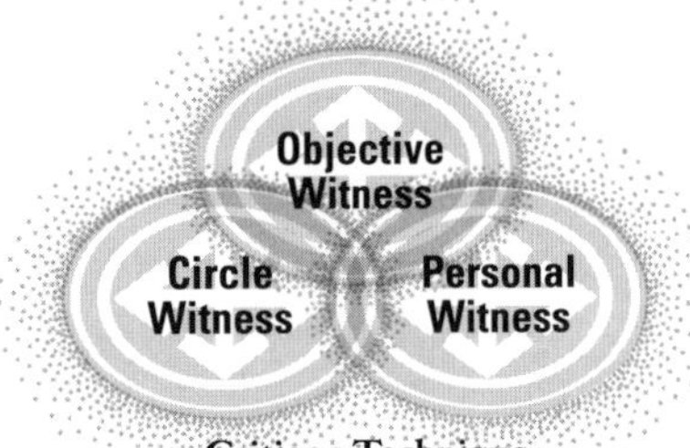

Objective Witness
Circle Witness
Personal Witness

Critique Technique
Triplicity

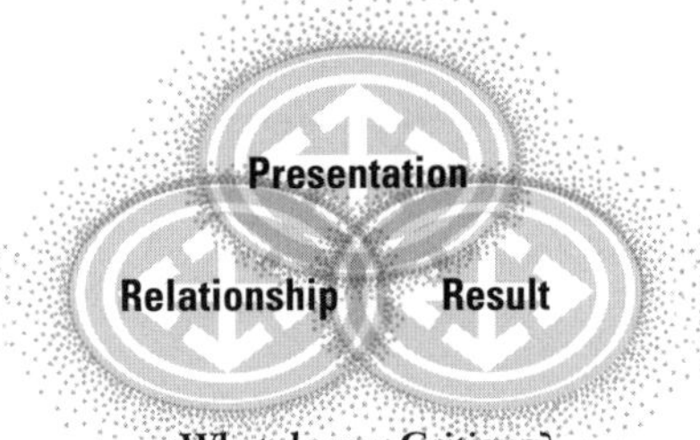

Presentation
Relationship
Result

What do you Critique?
Triplicity

Share your Rhythmical Bliss
Serve your Community
Develop Business Skills

Career Development
Triplicity

VILLAGE MUSIC CIRCLES™

Drum Circle Facilitator Tools

DVD
Drum Circle Facilitation

- Techniques for Drum Circle Facilitators
- Motivational Methods
- Community-Building Strategies
- Inspirational Stories
- Drum Circle Philosophies

BOOK
Drum Circle Spirit

- More Drum Circle Facilitator Techniques, Philosophies and Stories
- Play-along CD of Universal Drum Circle Rhythms Included

ARTHUR HULL SIGNATURE DESIGNS

REMO Facilitator Sound Shapes

- Pre-tuned lightweight portable drums
- 6 different pitches in each set
- Color coded for easy facilitation

VIC FIRTH® DCF Stick

- Drum Circle Facilitator Baton
- Drum Stick for Facilitator Bomba Bell
- Bass Drum or West African Dunun Stick

Arthurian Facilitator Shipping Box

- Light-weight durable shipping box
- Stackable with interlocking corners
- Rollable with removable wheels
- Expandable with adjustable straps

drumcircle.com

Phone: (831) 458-1946 • Fax: (831) 459-7215 • Email: outreach@drumcircle.com

DRUM CIRCLE
FACILITATORS GUILD

The Drum Circle Facilitators Guild is a professional organization for drum circle facilitators. Founded in 2001 in Washington DC, the DCFG was established by a group of professional facilitators as a 501c(3) non-profit organization. This growing organization includes members from the United States, Canada, the United Kingdom and Japan. Guild members abide by a code of ethics and are dedicated to serving communities through rhythm-based events. The Guild supports these individuals who serve unique populations using drum circles as beneficial tools for facilitating wellness, community, and creative expression.

As a professional association, DCFG supports its members through education, marketing, and accreditation. The Rhythm Makers newsletter offers articles on everything from facilitating to setting up and managing a successful DCF business. The DCFG Web site showcases and markets Guild members, outlining their experience, education, and clientele. It also acts as a resource of information for professional DCFs, providing networking and business tools. The DCFG offers an accreditation to its members who wish to demonstrate their level of professionalism.

For more information or to join please visit: **www.dcfg.net**

DRUM CIRCLE
FACILITATORS GUILD
www.dcfg.net

3438 Littlestown Pike
Westminster, MD 21158

contact@dcfg.net
(301) 648-3235

Resources

Books

Blue Hawkins, Holly. *The Heart of the Circle, A Guide to Drumming.*
The Crossing Press, 1999.
In each of the six chapters of this book, Holly opens a specific flower of intention and purpose in the drum circle facilitator's heart. Although the book's foundation is nested in the
Native American frame drumming tradition, it covers many other technical and spiritual
concepts, including some not covered in my books. I heartily recommend it as a spiritual
guide to all of us in the facilitator community.

Eduardo, Chalo, and Frank Kumor. *Drum Circle: A Guide to World Percussion.*
Alfred Publishing, 2002.
The subtitle says it all. In this book Chalo takes us on a world tour of drums and percussion instruments. His photos and descriptions are very clear and he covers tunings, playing
positions and performance techniques. He includes rhythms that are culturally specific to
each instrument, and he makes them accessible for beginning drummers.

Kalani. *Together in Rhythm, A Facilitators Guide to Drum Circle Music.*
Alfred Publishing, 2004.
Kalani's approach makes it easy to create and facilitate programs for music education,
heath & wellness, and personal and professional development, as well as recreational drum
circles.

Maberry, Dennis. *Drum Circle Grooves.*
Rhythm Spirit Percussion, 2005. (available at Lulu.com)
With clear, concise writing and a relaxed, even conversational style of instruction, Dennis
Maberry takes the pressure out of learning to drum for beginning-beginner drummers.
Maberry's practical, step-by-step guide describes the basics, such as learning the instru-
ments and tones, as well as providing beginner and intermediate rhythms. This book
encourages readers to explore and provides choices of rhythms they can use in recreational
drum circles.

MacTavish, Heather. *Songs, Science and Spirit – Musical Keys to Open Special Doors of Ability.*
Heather's "must have" book offers extensive insights to help facilitators develop sensitivities to the needs of the various cultures they serve. Her book covers a broad scope of expe-

rience. She cross-references the knowledge of the science, medicine and health & wellness fields to the actions and results of facilitators.

Stevens, Christine. *The Art and Heart of Drum Circles.*
Hal Leonard Corporation, 2003.
Christine's well-written book contributes to our knowledge of the what, the why and the how of rhythm-event facilitation. The title of this book reveals the window of perception she offers to us. She shares a fresh point of view that, as a drum circle facilitator, I can support and use.

Thomas, Kenne. *Drum Circle Cookbook, Recipes for Group Drumming Fun.*
KenZongs Music Publishing, 2001.
A fun and accessible book full of drum circle games named after foods. Dispersed throughout the book are activities you can use to get a crowd going at a drum circle, gathering or a meeting. Material about facilitation is sprinkled throughout the book as a seasoning.

Magazines

Drum! Magazine
http://www.drummagazine.com
(888) 378-6624

Making Music Magazine
http://www.makingmusicmag.com
(315) 422-4488

Internet

Village Music Circles
www.drumcircle.com

Drum circle email dialogue list: to join the list, send a BLANK email to:
drumcircles-subscribe@yahoogroups.com

Credits

Cover Design: Bonno Bernard, Mythmaker Communications, mythmaker.com

Cover Photography: Dr. Barry Bittman

Interior Book Design and Layout: Staci Sambol, slubdesign.com

Illustrations: Peter Cerny, petercerny.com

Format Consultation: Cliff Warner

Photos:

Cover Photo and Dedication, Dr. Barry Bittman / Welcome, Shmuel Thaler / Foreword: page 13, Bruce Fox; page 15, Don Davidson; page 16, Lynna Jamison / Chapter 1: page 22, Jerry Sitser; page 25, Dr. Barry Bittman, page 27, John Yost; page 32, Arturo Carrillo / Chapter 2: page 34, Bob Anzlovar; page 40 Village Music Circles (VMC); page 42, Jerry Sitser / Chapter 3: page 46– stop cut before and after, Geir Hagberg; page 47, Jerry Sitser; page 50, Arturo Carrillo / Chapter 4: page 53, Dr. Barry Bittman; page 55, Stephen Sharpe; page 57, Jerry Sitser; page 57, Michael Clark; page 58, Jerry Sitser; page 59, Kenya Masala; page 60, Kerry Shakerman Greene; page 61, Shmuel Thaler; page 63, Jerry Sitser; page 63, Dr. Barry Bittman; page 65, Heather MacTavish; page 67, Jerry Sitser; page 71, Jerry Sitser; page 75, Kim Atkinson; page 79, Sunray; page 82, Tomoko Yokota; page 83, Robin Cardell; page 84, Sha; page 85, Dr. Barry Bittman; page 87, Dean Monroe; page 88, Heather MacTavish / Chapter 5: page 95, Arturo Carrillo; page 98, Jerry Sitser; page 100, Jonathan Murray; page 100, Lynna Jamison; page 109, Jaqui MacMillan; page 113, Joni Yecalsik; page 114, Arturo Carrillo / Chapter 6: page 122, VMC; page 123, Village Music Circles; page 123, Laurie Grossman; page 125, Jonathan Murray; page 134, Augie "Doggie" Peltonen; page 138, Stu Needel / Chapter 7: page 146, Dr. Barry Bittman; page 148, VMC / Chapter 8: page 154, 156, 156, VMC; page 157, Dr. Barry Bittman; page 158,159, 160, VMC; page 160, Augie "Doggie" Peltonen; page 161, 162 VMC; page 162, Kenya and Gabriela Masala; page 163, Taylor Rockwell; page 165, Patrick Pinson; page 167, Arthur Hull; page 171, VMC; page 172, Fusako Hara / Chapter 9: page 178, Tom Lee Music; page 181, 182 VMC; page 187, Dr. Barry Bittman; page 188, Mikael Khei / Chapter 10: page 192, Jim Boneau; page 195, VMC; page 197, Mary Tolena Anderson; page 199, 201 Jerry Sitser; page 205, Toni Kellar; page 210, VMC; page 213, Susana Millman; page 214, Jerry Sitser; page 222, Dr. Barry Bittman; 229, VMC; 230, Dr. Barry Bittman / Chapter 12: page 231, Jerry Sitser; page 232, VMC; page 239, Diana Hull; page 240, Arturo Carrillo / Closing: page 244, Marcie Kraft

About the Author

Often referred to as the father of the modern facilitated drum circle, Arthur Hull is a recognized pioneer and elder in what is now called the recreational music making movement. Since 1985 he has used Village Music Circles™ metaphors to build team spirit and promote unity in communities, schools and corporations worldwide.

A gifted rhythmatist and charismatic facilitator, Arthur leads diverse groups through joyful and inspiring experiences using music and rhythm. His wit and humor motivate people beyond their cultural and personal barriers and he inspires enthusiastic participation.

Since 1990 Arthur has provided professional trainings for community drum circle facilitators, and he has trained over two thousand facilitators internationally.

Arthur also wrote the first drum circle facilitation handbook: *Drum Circle Spirit – Facilitating Human Potential Through Rhythm* in 1998, and has authored a DVD: *Drum Circle Facilitation – Building Community Through Rhythm.*

Index

Notes

Notes

Notes

Remove from the book and laminate to use as a reference at drum circle events.

Shorthand Notation
ACTIONS

+	Start of Sequence		Listening
	Call to Groove	///	Layering In
→	Group in Groove	\\\	Layering Out
G	Continue to Play	✓	Accent Downbeats
!	Attention Call		Volume Up
⊗	Stop Cut		Volume Down
∿	Rumble	↑	Speed Up Tempo
	Call and Response	↓	Slow Down Tempo
Ø	Sculpt	☆	Showcase
	1/2 Circle Sculpt	△	Pass Out Part
	1/4 Circle Sculpt		Teeter Totter
	1/3 Circle Sculpt		Switchback
	Clap	∿∿	Modulation
			Wave

Shorthand Notation
ACTIONS

+	Start of Sequence		Listening
	Call to Groove	///	Layering In
→	Group in Groove	\\\	Layering Out
G	Continue to Play	✓	Accent Downbeats
!	Attention Call		Volume Up
⊗	Stop Cut		Volume Down
∿	Rumble	↑	Speed Up Tempo
	Call and Response	↓	Slow Down Tempo
Ø	Sculpt	☆	Showcase
	1/2 Circle Sculpt	△	Pass Out Part
	1/4 Circle Sculpt		Teeter Totter
	1/3 Circle Sculpt		Switchback
	Clap	∿∿	Modulation
			Wave

Not Copyrighted. This is a Drum Circle Facilitators' Community Work in Progress

Shorthand Notation
THINGS

O	Whole Circle		Window of Communication
⊓	Platform	D	Drums
V	Vocal	L	Low Pitch
♂	Men	M	Medium Pitch
♀	Women	H	High Pitch
K	Children	A	Ashiko
ROC	Rest of the Circle	C	Conga
P	Percussion	Dn	Dunnun
B	Bell	Dj	Djembe
S	Shaker	Dk	Doumbek
W	Wood	F	Frame Drum
T	Tambourine	Ss	Sound Shape
Bw	Boomwhackers		

Shorthand Notation
THINGS

O	Whole Circle		Window of Communication
⊓	Platform	D	Drums
V	Vocal	L	Low Pitch
♂	Men	M	Medium Pitch
♀	Women	H	High Pitch
K	Children	A	Ashiko
ROC	Rest of the Circle	C	Conga
P	Percussion	Dn	Dunnun
B	Bell	Dj	Djembe
S	Shaker	Dk	Doumbek
W	Wood	F	Frame Drum
T	Tambourine	Ss	Sound Shape
Bw	Boomwhackers		

Not Copyrighted. This is a Drum Circle Facilitators' Community Work in Progress